Studies in
African Social Anthropology

Studies in

African Social Anthropology

edited by

MEYER FORTES and SHEILA PATTERSON

1975

ACADEMIC PRESS

London   New York   San Francisco

A Subsidiary of Harcourt Brace Jovanovich, Publishers

ACADEMIC PRESS INC. (LONDON) LTD.
24-28 Oval Road,
London NW1

United States Edition published by
ACADEMIC PRESS INC.
111 Fifth Avenue,
New York, New York 10003

Library of Congress Catalog Card Number: 75-10738
ISBN: 0 12 262250 2

PRINTED AND BOUND IN GREAT BRITAIN BY
HAZELL WATSON AND VINEY LTD
AYLESBURY, BUCKS

The Contributors

FORTES, MEYER *Emeritus William Wyse Professor of Social Anthropology at the University of Cambridge; Fellow of King's College*

FORTUNE, G. *Professor of African Languages, University of Rhodesia, Salisbury*

GLUCKMAN, MAX *Research Professor in Social Anthropology, University of Manchester*

HOLLEMAN J. F. *Professor of Customary Law, University of Leiden, Holland*

KRIGE, EILEEN JENSEN *Emeritus Professor of Social Anthropology in the University of Natal, South Africa*

KUPER, ADAM *Lecturer in Anthropology, University College, London*

KUPER, HILDA *Professor in the Department of Anthropology, University of California at Los Angeles*

LOUDON, J. B. *Senior Lecturer in Social Anthropology, University College of Swansea, Wales*

MAIR, LUCY *Honorary Professor of Anthropology, University of Kent, formerly Professor of Anthropology, London School of Economics*

PATTERSON, SHEILA *Honorary Research Fellow, Department of Anthropology, University College, London*

WERBNER, RICHARD *Lecturer in Social Anthropology, University of Manchester*

WILSON, MONICA *Emeritus Professor of Social Anthropology, University of Cape Town, South Africa*

Essays presented to
Professor Isaac Schapera

Professor Isaac Schapera

Preface

In bringing together this tribute to Professor Isaac Schapera the Editors were faced with some difficult choices. It was obvious from the outset that some limitation of scope would be essential if the book was not to become too unwieldy for publication. This posed a dilemma, for we knew very well that Professor Schapera has a large circle of friends and admirers, ex-colleagues and former pupils, who are active in many different branches of scholarship and research and who would all wish to be associated with this tribute.

Realistic considerations had, however, to prevail. It was therefore agreed that the contributions to this book should be regionally restricted to Africa south of the Sahara, with the major emphasis on Southern Africa, since this is the ethnological area with which Schapera is most closely identified. This meant that many of Professor Schapera's friends, former colleagues and ex-pupils, whose regional interests lie elsewhere and who would have liked to join us, could not be invited to contribute. The decision was a hard one to take and the Editors cannot but regret that it was necessary. We hope, however, that the reasons for it will be understood and that those who were thus deprived of the chance to join in this tribute to Schap will be with us in spirit.

As regards our fellow contributors, the Editors are greatly indebted to them for their co-operation and are grateful for their patience in the face of publication delays which have been due to circumstances beyond the control of either the Editors or the Publishers. We should also like to express our particular appreciation of the help and attention which we have received from the Publishers.

We are grieved to have to record that Professor Max Gluckman died while this volume was in the final stage of publication.

M. F.

S. P.

Contents

I | Isaac Schapera: An Appreciation

Meyer Fortes

This volume is a small offering of esteem and affection to Professor Isaac Schapera in celebration of his seventieth birthday. Schapera was born on June 23, 1905 in South Africa, being the third and last but one son of immigrant, East European Jewish parents. In stark contrast to their East European countries of origin, the newly established Union of South Africa was, for the immigrants who arrived in the first decade of the century, a land of unparalleled freedom and opportunity, and their children were the immediate beneficiaries. It was a period of rapidly expanding educational and professional facilities and South Africans of the generation to which Schapera and I belong were free to make the most of them.

His (and my) generation is well represented, I am happy to note, among the contributors to this volume. But what the contributors have most in common is that every one of us has strong anthropological links with him. Some of us were his students as undergraduates or while engaged in field research under his supervision; some of us were his colleagues; and some have links with him through having worked in areas or on topics where he has led the way. And all of us are indebted to him for ideas, inspiration and material bearing on our researches in social anthropology or in African studies.

But much more than professional links with Schap (as he is affectionately known to successive generations of anthropologists and Africanists, other academic colleagues, and many other varieties of men and women) has brought us together in this volume. For each of us is also attached to Schap by personal ties. In my own case this goes back to our undergraduate days at the University of Cape Town in the mid-twenties. Schap was already then acquiring a legendary reputation. To begin with there was his choice of social anthropology as his main subject of study. It was so newly established in the University that its very existence, let alone its scope and nature, was pretty well unknown to the majority of the students; and its connection with the—to the average member of the university—unorthodox, if glamorous, personality of Radcliffe-Brown made it seem even more esoteric than its novelty implied. Next, there were such things as Schap's academic virtuosity and his reputation for knowledge, his prowess as a chess player, and his penchant for collecting books. His affability and his fund of good stories were known only to his close friends.

How, in the circumstances of South Africa and in the University of Cape Town in the twenties, did Schapera discover the fascination and interest of the study of the indigenous peoples of the country that led him to social anthropology? It happened before the happy coincidence of Radcliffe-Brown's tenure of the Chair at the University with Schapera's undergraduate career there. He has told parts of the story to some of us from time to time. During his boyhood his family lived in the small town of Garies in the north-west of the Cape Province close to the border of Namaqualand. Aboriginally, before the incursion of the white man, that part of the country had been occupied by Hottentot tribes—Khoikhoi groups, in the terminology of today which Schapera helped to establish; and the mixed-blood descendants of these original inhabitants were still numerous in the area in the nineteen twenties. Schapera was at school at Cape Town but went home to Garies for the holidays. It was at one such time that he became acquainted with a local resident who as an amateur archaeologist and ethnologist had made a considerable collection of books by explorers and other writers about the interior of South Africa and its indigenous inhabitants from prehistoric times to the present century. Given the freedom of this library, Schapera steeped himself in this literature and thus embarked on the pursuit that brought him into anthropology. It is, perhaps, not unconnected with this background that his first book was his classical monograph on the Khoisan peoples of South Africa. Nor perhaps is his life-long concern with the early history of exploration, of ethnological observation and of missionary endeavour in Southern Africa unconnected with this background. His editorship and publication of archival material, unpublished journals of travel and administration and other documents relating to the exploration of Southern Africa from Van Riebeeck to David Livingstone, far from being a sideline to his ethnological and sociological research, represents a major feat of historical scholarship in its own right.

To return to chronology, an outstanding undergraduate career at Cape Town led to a postgraduate scholarship which brought Schapera to the London School of Economics in 1926. There, as he records in the Preface to *The Khoisan Peoples*, he worked with Seligman and Malinowski as one of that first close-knit group of postgraduate students which included Firth, Audrey Richards, Evans-Pritchard, Gordon Brown, Lucy Mair, and others who later became famous in setting the pattern of modern social anthropology. (Adam Kuper, gives an interesting description and assessment of the group in his book on *Anthropologists and Anthropology*, 1973.) Schapera had a short spell as Malinowski's research assistant but it is, I think, fair to say that he found the sober, scholarly and undoctrinaire temperament of Seligman more congenial.

After his doctorate, Schapera returned to South Africa to begin his field work and presently, to take a post at the University of Witwatersrand (1930) where Mrs. Hoernlé was in charge of the department. There Max Gluckman, Hilda (Beemer) Kuper, and Ellen Hellman were among his students and Eileen (Jensen) Krige was beginning her researches on the Zulu under Winifred Hoernlé's direction. From Witwatersrand he went later to a post at the University of Cape Town, where in due course (1935) he was elected to the Chair that Radcliffe-Brown had inaugurated. It is, may I add, specially gratifying to have Monica Wilson, Schapera's distinguished successor in the Cape Town Chair, among our contributors.

In the meantime he had, in 1928, begun that masterly programme of research in what was then the Bechuanaland Protectorate which has given us the most complete and comprehensive body of knowledge relating to the history, the social and political life and the contemporary situation of any single group of African peoples as yet assembled. It is a body of work that is unique in the literature of African sociology and anthropology. For it is the result, not only of superlative field work and meticulous documentary research covering every aspect of Tswana social life, but also of a significant theoretical position. Schapera from the outset took the view that the task of the social anthropologist is to confront the contemporary situation of any community he was concerned with in its totality, warts and all, we might say. The law and politics of any of the Tswana tribes he worked with could not be understood, he showed, without taking into account the Protectorate Administration within the framework of which the tribe ran its social life, the missionary influences that had at different times impinged on chiefs and councillors, the changing norms due to the experiences of labour

migration and town life in the neighbouring territory of South Africa, and
so forth. Moreover, change is implicit in every such contemporary situation; and to understand this, consideration of the relevant historical factors
is essential. Thus what might seem to be custom of immemorial antiquity
at a given time could be shown to have come about through a series of
legislative enactments by earlier chiefs (cf. Gluckman, *infra*).

Schapera's Tswana corpus is notable also in another respect. It is presented in a style and language that have made it as accessible to the Tswana
peoples themselves as to international scholarship. His works are accepted
as authoritative records of their customary laws and social history by the
Tswana leaders.

Let me return again to chronology. After revitalizing the School of
African Studies at the University of Cape Town and establishing social
anthropology as its core subject, and following a spell as Visiting Professor
at the University of Chicago, Schapera returned to the L.S.E. in 1950, to a
Chair in the Department of Anthropology. With Raymond Firth as Head
of the Department, Schapera was thus enabled to play a major part in the
post-war development of social anthropology and African studies in
Britain and the Commonwealth. He served on the Colonial Social Science
Research Council, was Chairman of the Association of Social Anthropologists from 1954 to 1958 and President of the Royal Anthropological
Institute from 1961 to 1963. When he retired from his Chair in 1969
British social anthropology which had, in the twenties and thirties, been no
more than an intellectual *movement* of the handful of young scholars who
had studied with Radcliffe-Brown and Malinowski had been transformed
into a routinized *profession*.

Retirement from his teaching activities has not, of course, meant an end
to Schapera's scholarly work. Indeed one of his most beautifully written
and absorbing ethnographical studies appeared in 1971 just when the idea
for the present volume was being mooted. I refer to *Rainmaking Rites of
the Tswana Tribes*, published in the Leiden African Social Research
Documents series of which Schapera is one of the editors.

This is not the place nor have I the qualifications to review Schapera's
enormous and wide-ranging scholarly output. There are eight substantial
books and as many book-size other publications on the bookshelf in my
own study which is set aside for Schapera; and there are some I do not
possess. His papers in learned journals (dating from his student days at
Cape Town) are too numerous to refer to here. (His main publications are
listed in the entry under his name in the 1974 Register of Members of the

Association of Social Anthropologists of the Commonwealth.) I must content myself with a reminder of the great range of the Tswana *corpus* and related works. In part it reflects some of the extra-academic tasks Schapera undertook, such as the advisory services he gave to the Bechuanaland Protectorate Administration. His famous *Handbook of Tswana Law and Custom*, still one of the basic monographs in the field of African legal and political studies, and his *Native Land Tenure in the Bechuanaland Protectorate* come to mind in this connection. But whichever topic relating to the ethnology, the social anthropology, the politics or economics or familial institutions of the Tswana peoples in the first half of this century we may wish to know about, the data are there in full in the Tswana corpus. Some now fashionable studies for which resounding rhetorical claims are being made, were, in fact, already being developed by Schapera in his researches of thirty or more years ago. This is the case, for instance, with the use and evaluation of oral traditions as sources of tribal history and, at the other end of the scale, with the current (to my mind I must confess, somewhat exaggerated) emphasis on the study of social change. I have already mentioned Schapera's contributions to the historiography of the indigenous peoples of Southern Africa. In a more specialized vein is his splendid book on *Praise Poems of Tswana Chiefs*. One cannot read this book without realizing what a mastery of the Tswana language and, moreover, what literary sensitivity and what a gift for translation lie behind it. I daresay this is connected with Schap's life-long addiction to literature. He is an omnivorous, catholic, judicious and encyclopaedically knowledgeable bibliophile and connoisseur of literature. Some day, perhaps, he will be persuaded to write that piece on kinship and the family in Jane Austen's novels or on collectors' editions of *The Diary of Samuel Pepys* or even on the evolution of the detective story from Sherlock Holmes to the present day, or of the historical novel in recent decades, for which he is so well primed.

As I have already remarked, every contributor to this volume has been indebted to Schapera's work and to Schap himself for ideas, inspiration and material. I must, however, make special mention of one of my own many debts to him. In 1940 Evans-Pritchard and I brought out *African Political Systems*—Professor Mair's paper in the present volume says all that needs to be said about it in relation to Schapera's work in political anthropology. But what is not known is that the project was originally inspired by Schapera. In the spring of 1937 I went back from Ghana (the Gold Coast as it then was), after my second field trip to the Tallensi, to Cape Town on a short visit. Looking up Schapera I found him engrossed in the proofs of

The Handbook of Tswana Law and Custom and I was delighted when he allowed me to read them. The contrast between Tswana political organization and what corresponded to it among the Tallensi was so striking that it opened a new point of view to me. I discussed this with Schapera and it was then that the idea of a wider comparative study emerged. I returned to England that summer to fulfil my obligations as a Fellow of the International African Institute and put the suggestion for the book first to Evans-Pritchard and then to Professor Diedrich Westermann, at that time one of the Consultative Directors of the International African Institute. The further history of the project is not relevant here. Suffice it to say that Evans-Pritchard consented to collaborate in it partly out of characteristic generosity, but largely because of Schapera's interest in it. For Evans-Pritchard, who admired, respected and had a deep attachment to Schapera this was enough to show it was a worthwhile undertaking.

I have said nothing about the academic and professional honours and distinctions that have accrued to Schap in the course of his fifty years of scholarly activity. They are listed in the usual works of reference; and anyhow, ours is a personal tribute, not an exercise in academic appraisal.

We congratulate Schap on his attainment of his seventieth year and add our best wishes for many more productive and convivial years.

2 | How Far Have We Got in the Study of Politics?

Lucy Mair

Schapera was one of the eight contributors to *African Political Systems*, and in the exhaustive ethnography of the Tswana chiefdoms which has occupied such a large part of his working life he has given us a full picture of their political constitution and mode of government (1938), the history of their dynastic disputes and the influence of the kinship structure on the form of these (1947, 1963), and the activity of chiefs as lawgivers ard innovators (1943, 1970). He was the first British anthropologist to offer a wider definition of "political system" than that proposed by Radcliffe-Brown, and the study in which this is found was the first to put into practice his own theory that profitable comparisons can best be drawn between neigh-bours; to this end he examined the major ethnic divisions of southern Africa—Bushmen, Hottentots and Bantu—from the point of view of what could be called their constitutional arrangements. He is an anthropologist who knows how to use history, aware that it is not necessary to know *the whole past* in order to understand any aspect of the present; aware too that traditional history is concerned predominantly with political events and that the effects of a change of ruler are limited as long as the ruler is not seeking to alter the system of production; indefatigable in pursuing the historical records that bear on his problems. If Fortes and Evans-Pritchard pointed the way to the study of acephalous societies, Schapera was the pioneer in the anthropological treatment of chiefdoms. He has been singled out by Easton as one of the "few scholars" who have "cirected their attention to strictly political phenomena".

Definitions

African Political Systems was the first attempt of British social anthropologists to isolate the political aspects of the societies they studied and present these in a form that would make comparison possible. Less than thirty years later Goody (1969: p. 11) can call for "a political sociology that does not limit itself to the party politics of the Western world", and Abner Cohen (1969: p. 213) can describe social anthropology as "essentially a branch of political science" and social change as "essentially a change in the forms, distribution and exercise of power". We have come a long way, so far that some anthropologists, particularly in America, salute the pioneers only to repudiate them: *African Political Systems* was a benchmark, but nowadays we order things better.

What that book gave us, essentially, was a key to the identification of political activity in a society where its presence had not been suspected, and a formula for the political analysis of other such societies. The people analysed in this new way were the Nuer, the formula Radcliffe-Brown's famous definition. This has been followed by some writers, rejected by many, read carefully, and in context, by a few. Among the latter W. J. M. Mackenzie is aware that Radcliffe-Brown called political organization "*that aspect of the total organisation* which is concerned with the control and regulation of the use of force" (1940: p. xxiii, my italics). Although he did not make this qualification in his initial definition, and there referred not to the regulation of the use of physical force but to the maintenance of order by the use, or possibility of the use, of it, it is clear that he never thought of force as the sole sanction for order; the whole of his introduction contradicts this interpretation. "Government and law", is Mackenzie's gloss (1967: p. 195), "are among the methods of social control; we shall do violence to common sense if we identify them with the whole of society".

Balandier, who also quotes both Radcliffe-Brown's statements, says that the identification of the legitimate use of force as the criterion of a political system gives us a signpost rather than a definition (1967: pp. 19, 35). I should prefer to say it gives a definition rather than an inventory. Just as Tylor said, in effect, "Wherever you see a belief in spiritual beings, you know that you are dealing with religion," Radcliffe-Brown says, "Wherever you see recognised means of enforcing recognised claims, you are dealing with a political system". "One cannot start", as Mackenzie says elsewhere, "without knowing what to look for" (1967: p. 336). It might have been preferable to say "You are dealing with a political *institution*", for the nub of the criticism that has been made of the pioneer anthropological studies is that they confine themselves to institutions (or constitutions) and neglect the dynamics of the struggle for power. They were in fact looking for institutions which fulfilled the functions of *government* in the absence of specialized governmental roles; and if they had not identified such institutions, the political scientists would never have heard of them.

Maquet (1970), in contrast to nearly all the writers who have found Radcliffe-Brown's definition too narrow, offers one even narrower. Political relations, according to him, are those between governor and governed, recognizable by the fact that they are sanctioned by physical force; power relations, which may, but need not, be political, are relations in which one party can exact economic benefits without making an equivalent return. Maquet rejects definitions in terms of function, on similar grounds to those for rejecting Radcliffe-Brown's reference to the maintenance of order by the (political) use of force: that social order is maintained by institutions other than those defined as political. He rejects the introduction of legitimacy or consensus into the definition: colonial regimes do not rest on consensus, but it cannot be said that they are not in political relations with their subjects. In effect Maquet accepts a definition which was intended to widen the category of societies with political systems, only to exclude from it the "tribes without rulers" for whose sake it was formulated.

Schapera's reason for rejecting Radcliffe-Brown's definition was different. There were two grounds: that the organization of co-operative activities does more to maintain social order than the exercise of force, and that a political system can be identified in societies where leadership roles do not rest on the command of force. His example is provided by the Bergdama, among whom he everywhere finds acknowledged leaders with governmental functions; he includes among these the responsibility of the Bushman chief for carrying out decisions reached collectively by the men of the band and for leadership in raids (force?), and the ritual decisions of the Bergdama chief. He does not discuss the question whether individual rights are maintained, and compensation secured by approved self-help, the type of activity which almost exhausts Nuer political institutions as described by Evans-Pritchard. One wonders uneasily whether he takes Radcliffe-Brown's adaptation of Weber to mean, not all forms of legitimate use of force, but force exercised by a legitimate *authority*. But the value of the definition is precisely that it does not require a specialized authority, an embryo state, as the criterion of a political system.

Nevertheless, Schapera's definition, which gives the organization of public affairs priority over the maintenance of order, comes nearer to that definition of the sphere of politics as "the authoritative allocation of values" which David Easton has made famous. The critics of so-called "static" analysis would take exception to the implied assumption that "decision-making" does not involve any conflict of values (sc. interests) calling for an authoritative resolution. Yet, at any rate in the field of fully-fledged governmental institutions, Schapera has much to say of secessions, rebellions and rivalries for succession; more than can be found in general-ized accounts of the recognized checks on the abuse of authority character-istic of different systems of chiefly rule.

Schapera defined a "political community"—"I use the term", he said, "for lack of something more suitable"—as "a group of people organised into a single unit managing its affairs independently of external control" (1956: pp. 8, 203). Studies covering a wider field than this would, for the political scientist, fall under the rubric of international relations, where he considers negotiation or conflict between independent authorities. If the object of study is a "total" social system in its political aspects, the bound-ary must be drawn around the largest population having common norms and its own institutions for the management of public affairs. In my judg-ment this *must* include some provision for the maintenance of order by the protection of individual rights—though studies of food-gatherers some-times imply that "peace" is valued by them so much more highly than "justice" that people are persuaded to forget their grievances rather than offered remedies for them (e.g. Turnbull, 1965). Evans-Pritchard found among the Nuer no arrangements for the management of public affairs even at the village level (if we discount the minimal activity of the "man of the cattle" in opening and closing initiation periods). He did not use the phrase "political community", but called a Nuer tribe "the largest political segment" of a "people" defined by a common language and a sense of common identity. The tribe was the largest population who not only claim a common territory but "acknowledge the right of their members to com-pensation for injury". More succinctly he says elsewhere that there is law within a tribe but not between tribes (1940a: pp. 5, 121). Law, as his account makes clear, is enforced by self-help; Radcliffe-Brown's definition is the only one in terms of which the Nuer could be said to have an internal political system.

Evans-Pritchard remarks that their (sc. total) political system "includes all the peoples with whom they come into contact" (1940: p. 5). He has little to say, however, about their dealings with their neighbours. This is done for the Karimojong by Dyson-Hudson (1966), whose book is entitled *Karimojong Politics* and whose concluding chapter, "The Political Community", has a section describing their attitude towards their neighbours and towards the Kenya government as represented by those of its agents who move among them.

Dyson-Hudson is among the anthropologists who have found useful Easton's definition of a political community in his article on "Political Anthropology" (1959). Easton does not here refer explicitly to the famous definition, but says the members of a political community "are prepared to regulate their differences by means of decisions accepted as binding because they are made in accordance with shared political norms and structures" (1959: p. 229). In the world of the political scientist this must refer to policy decisions reached after debate; in the context of the Nuer it could have no meaning, and one is driven back on the organized force behind the law as the minimum political institution. In these terms Evans-Pritchard described the feud, and Gluckman, calling in aid a study of a vengeance group in a very different society, made explicit the reasons, implicit in *The Nuer*, why feuds are compounded before they have torn society asunder. Easton considers that such studies, as well as those of Turner (1957) and Middleton (1960), are not concerned with politics as such, but with the sociology of conflict, and he is echoed by one of our latest writers, Adam Kuper (1970). Kuper claims to be concerned with "the daily stuff of modern politics" and tells us that Easton's theories are "now rapidly being absorbed into social anthropology" (1970: p. 4). The latter assertion needs more justification by the use of examples before I would accept it.

Kuper's treatment of his subject is initially described in terms of Eastonian analysis; he begins by specifying the political institutions of the village where he worked, and places this as a sub-system of the local government structure which, with the social structure of the village population, constitutes its environment. He identifies the subject of his enquiry as the policy-making process. Here he is on the same ground as Dyson-Hudson, but the latter is concerned more with policy-making *institutions*—an aspect of the system that Easton plays down—than with "the daily stuff".

Transaction Theories

Kuper's discussion of factions is in line with the studies initiated by Bailey and continued by various anthropologists whom he has influenced, all of whom would surely claim to be observing the daily stuff of politics. The importance of factions in political analysis was noted first in India, at a time when social anthropology was perhaps too much inclined to assume the universality in pre-industrial society of the Nuer rule of obligatory solidarity of structural groups. To call this "conventional structural analysis", as Firth (1957: p. 294) does, is to do less than justice to the anthropologists whose recognition of the importance of ascribed group membership never led them to ignore the field of relationships that are open to choice. To refer, as a more recent writer has done, to a "structural pose" that has now been "abandoned" (Vincent, 1971), is to misunderstand the development of the subject. Where structure was earlier thought of as a system of continuing relations between social groups with a high degree of stability (Evans-Pritchard, 1940: p. 262), it is now conceived as a body of rules (Bailey, 1969: p. 10). A political structure is a constitution, though Godfrey Wilson (1939) seems to be the only anthropologist to have used the word in the title of a publication. Just as political scientists have rejected the idea that constitutions describe real-life interactions, so anthropologists have come to look at the process of adjustment of competing interests *as well as*—not instead of—stated norms concerning authority and obligation. One of the landmarks in this advance was Barth's (1959a) study of the formation of alliances among the Swat Pathans, a population among whom a unilineal descent structure identical with that of the Nuer is combined with other "constitutional" principles so as to produce oppositions of a completely different type.

Barth, like Bailey later, is interested in strategy, a concept that has no place in Easton's depersonalized system. He has given us an analysis of segmentary opposition in Swat in terms of games theory (1959b), and Bailey has used his material in a book (1969) that uses metaphors from games but does not pretend to make mathematical calculations. He makes use of Easton's conception of a system maintaining itself in an environment subject to stresses which may sometimes be too much for it, but he does not fit his data into the input-output framework. He offers a picture of the essentials of political strategy that can be applied to the whole, not only the Third, world, but he is not interested in trying to treat his material in a way that would be appropriate for any system of whatever nature (something that Easton himself has found difficult, as his introduction of the term "withinput" shows). Bailey rejects, he says, "any analysis which does not allow man a central role as entrepreneur" (1969: p. 18).

Games must have rules, a fact that Easton recognized in his first schema for systems analysis but ignored in the second. This was throwing out the baby with the bathwater with a vengeance; to describe political norms and leave it at that would be preferable, at any rate for anthropologists, who have been professionally concerned with systems unfamiliar to their readers. Rules are central to Bailey's theory: the relation between normative and pragmatic ("how to win") rules, the possibility of changing the rules, by attrition or by direct challenge. The former method corresponds to Easton's adaptation of the system under stress; the latter, which can be described only in terms of human action, has no place in Easton's flow diagram. Bailey's vocabulary is not confined to games analysis, however, and cannot be, since he is discussing games that do not end when a whistle blows. His strategies of confrontation and encounter remind one more of what one finds in international relations studies of crisis management. Some writers use such terms as "strategic resources" for the "values" which for Easton are the object of competition and therefore need some authority to allocate them. Bailey employs the notion of resources in another way, as means to success in the competition the object of which he calls the prize; of course this *is* Easton's "value". Bailey's metaphor enables him to discuss the changes in strategy, and also in the qualifications of competitors, that result from the appearance of new resources, and he uses this idea to good purpose in his discussions both of caste-climbing and of factions in India, as well as of the "broker" who collects votes for the Indian politician. The notion of the neutral "referee" links together the various instances—Nuer, Berbers, Bedouin, Pathans—in which opponents anxious to avoid or end a state of hostility can have recourse to a ritually qualified mediator.

Though this can hardly be what Shakespeare had in mind, the aim of the stratagems is to secure the spoils. For the rank and file of a political party these are the fruits of some economic policy. For the leaders they are the fruits of office, that is to say, power. If "the struggle for power" is too crude a definition of politics, and some writers prefer circumlocutions such as "authoritative allocation" to the simple word, it is still hard to eliminate the idea of power from the subject. Indeed it would be accepted as an essential aspect of political action by most of those who reject Radcliffe-Brown's definition in terms of physical force. Balandier (1967), here borrowing from the systems analysts, says that power results from the need to combat the tendency to entropy. But he quickly adds, echoing Schapera, that every mechanism that maintains or restores internal co-operation is to be taken into account and adds that ritual is a form of political action in this sense. He insists on inequality as the basis of power, even in the most supposedly egalitarian societies.

Power

Maquet finds the common feature of three periods of African history—traditional, colonial, post-colonial—in the use by rulers of their command of force to secure economic advantages. He distinguishes between the *function of a political system* and the *tasks of government*; the latter are a matter of expectations, the former of actuality. What *does* the political system do? The subjects bring their tribute, which provides the subsistence of the rulers; this enables the rulers to exercise constraint (through the armies and police whom they maintain) and thus obtain the tribute. This system is meshed in with other systems, each dependent for its efficacy on the working of the others. Hence, and for no more lofty reason, the political system maintains social order.

Here Maquet's approach contrasts strikingly with that of British anthropologists from the time of *African Political Systems* onwards. The influence of Malinowski has been nowhere so lasting as in the defence of African institutions against the derogatory interpretations put on them by administrators and missionaries who sought to "improve" them. This attitude, which to our later successors makes us "the handmaids", not to say running dogs, "of imperialism", was nothing to be ashamed of. Ethnocentric stereotypes and misguided notions of a civilizing mission bedevil relations with the Third World as much today as they ever did, and the "translation of culture" that is still the anthropologist's task must still consist in showing why the institutions that create obstacles to "development" are valued by the peoples among whom they are found. In the context of political institutions we were concerned to show that African chiefs were not despots activated by arbitrary "whims"; and it may be worth recalling that, in most cases, their replacement by other, possibly more despotic, rulers has not been the effect of rebellion against *their* authority. We emphasized, therefore, the importance of the restraints which existed against the arbitrary exercise of power, and the dependence of rulers on tribute for the means to perform what we saw as the beneficial functions of government.

For Maquet such functions, if they exist, are of secondary importance. He sees in traditional Ruanda not even a rough reciprocity between rulers and subjects, no consensus or legitimacy, simply the consolidation of an "essentially temporary" superiority gained by force of arms. For several centuries an "equilibrium of high tension" was maintained between rulers (with their associates, the rest of the pastoral class) and subject peasants. The metaphor implies a fragile kind of stability, and Maquet refers to recorded instances of rebellion and suggests that there may have been others the memory of which has been suppressed in Ruanda's rich historical traditions. He mentions an underground "counter-tradition" of a savage and cynical character.

Maquet regards the client-lord relationship characteristic of the Interlacustrine Bantu as a peculiar form of dependence because it was institutionalized. For this reason he calls it feudal, seeing the essence of the feudal in the dyadic interpersonal contract; and because it is not imposed by force he will not call it political. It is an institution, he argues, found only in stratified societies, where it both brings material advantages to the superiors and mitigates the lot of the inferiors. It both creates and maintains the power of the dominant population. It is "a remarkable device for balancing exploitation with protection" (1970: p. 214). Possibly he does not give enough weight to the need of individuals among the conquerors to build up their own following in times which must surely have been turbulent up to the very recent past; it may have been as great as the need of individual peasants for protection. Certainly the lot of the peasants—granted the consolidation of superior power—would have been even harder without the protection system; but how was the consolidation achieved? It is only on the assumption that conflict is to be expected between the two strata and not within the dominant one that one can interpret this institution as a stabilizing factor.

Process

The earliest studies to take process into account were those focused on the changes produced by external influences. This was from the start a central interest of Malinowski's pupils who worked under the auspices of the International African Institute, and intensive work in this field was done after the war by the group attached to Makerere. Like Maquet, they followed Schapera's principle and took a geographical area—in this case also a "culture area"—and compared different Interlacustrine Bantu chiefdoms, in this case covering Uganda and Tanganyika but not Ruanda and Urundi.

(Richards ed., 1960; Fallers ed., 1964). The most detailed historical account of this kind is Beattie's (1971) of the Nyoro.

Such studies took as their starting-point a system that was supposedly self-regulating until it came under foreign domination, and in defence of such an approach it must be pointed out that historical records in Africa give very little information about internal changes in the different polities. Oral tradition remembers conquests, but very rarely their social and political implications. Where it has been possible to trace changes in traditional institutions they have been pieced out from such sources as records of succession and the manner of death of rulers, or, where the student was more fortunate, taken from documents. Thus Evans-Pritchard (1940b) traced from the remembered history of Anuak kings three stages in which the contest for the ritual emblems of kingship was conducted in different ways. Godfrey Wilson (1939) built up from oral tradition an account of the transformation of the Ngonde divine king into a secular ruler. Southwold (1961) deduced from records of the clan membership of Ganda chiefs that there were periods during which they asserted hereditary claims to office and others when the Kabaka made appointments at his pleasure. Smith (1960), one of the fortunate as regards documents, has compared two stages in the political organization of Zazzau, before and after the Fulani conquest (but has had to conjecture what the likely conflicts of interest would have been).

A new line was taken by Leach (1954) when he interpreted the history of the Kachins as one of periodic revolutions against chiefs who claimed more privileges than their subjects were willing to grant them. He made this the ground of an attack on the concept of equilibrium, that vague metaphor, hardly deserving the name of model, which is sometimes taken to mean immobility; but Gluckman (1968) commented that the Kachin system, on Leach's own showing, oscillated between two poles and did not change cumulatively in one direction. A stronger stimulus towards the study of process came from Gluckman's (1955, 1963) treatment of conflict, although this too in its earlier form emphasized the function of conflict, not in producing desired changes but in maintaining stability. Gluckman rightly distinguished between a rebellion aimed at replacing the incumbents of established offices and a revolution seeking to change the whole political structure. His followers have concentrated attention not on actual rebellion, but on the various ways of manipulating inconsistent norms in the pursuit of political power on a minimal scale, a line which has culminated in Bailey's work already referred to. This is what led Easton (1959) to say that anthropologists treat politics as a dependent variable, and do not in fact examine or even identify *political* systems as he conceives them. Kuper's treatment of the Kalahari village explicitly follows Easton's schema, and makes policy-making its main theme rather than competition for office. Yet one of the two policy decisions that he deals with in detail is a contest for the lowly office of pumpman at the borehole, and the process followed out is a matter of rivalry between factions. Kuper uses the Easton vocabulary to show how demands and support come from different directions according to the nature of the decision to be taken, and how decisions react on the system as a whole. He does not convince me that the Easton formula is more than a recipe for *describing* political systems. If the analysis applies to all systems of whatever kind, it offers no variables for comparison. Studies of entrepreneurial behaviour strike me as far more likely to be fruitful, and this seems to be the point of view of another recent writer on political anthropology, Abner Cohen (1969).

Ethnicity

The transfer of power to African governments made them and their well-wishers acutely conscious of the sources of diversity in the new states. African politicians condemned "tribalism", and political scientists, rather earlier than anthropologists, set themselves to study "problems of integration". If this is to be done at the level of the total political unit it calls for other techniques than that of intensive fieldwork—though the newest school of social anthropology in France is demanding, not that the study of politics should be constituted a unified discipline, but that anthropologists should themselves cover the whole field (Copans *et al.*, 1971). In what I may be allowed to call the British tradition, though its practitioners are to be found in many countries, studies have appeared of the differences between societies in their willingness to incorporate outsiders (Cohen and Middleton eds, 1970) and of the motives leading individuals to seek such incorporation (Barth ed., 1969). The discussions of the plural society that have continued since Furnivall introduced the term in 1944 have turned largely on definition and typology, but inevitably have had political implications. Barth makes a distinction between the economic and the political aspects of ethnicity, the term we now use in preference to tribalism. Abner Cohen (1969b) in contrast believes with Copans *et al.* that the economic and the political cannot be separated, and that where a population insists upon a common ethnic identity the motive will be found in the need to develop an informal political structure in order either to maintain a privileged economic situation or to improve an unprivileged one. His brilliant study (1969) of the Hausa trading community in Ibadan shows how, by insisting that anyone who seeks to enter the north–south trade must have certain diacritical characteristics—*not* in fact drawn from traditional Hausa culture—they are able to maintain a monopoly which the Yoruba have been trying to break for decades. This conclusion recalls Colson's (1953) demonstration that what holds the Makah Indians together in the absence of any cultural criteria is their monopoly position as land-owners and their claim to preference in local employment.

Cohen (1971) has further developed this theme by showing how membership of a ritual community can provide a group which has some kind of ethnic basis with shared symbols and occasions for interaction that take the place of formal political organization. Both the Hausa in Sabo and the Creoles in Freetown found their earlier dominant position threatened by a change in "the rules of the game", in each case a last-minute attempt by the British to democratize their colonial subjects in preparation for independence. In Nigeria the deliberate dismantling—not, as Cohen puts it, "collapse"—of the Native Authority system ended the political autonomy of the Hausa quarter, and the representation of any ethnic exclusiveness as "tribalism" cut the ground from under their earlier claim to the right to "practise their own customs". Their resort was to join the Tijanniya order of Islam, adherence to which not only differentiated them from the Moslem Yoruba but gave them a sense of superiority over more lax Moslems. This order requires its members to meet daily for prayer under the leadership of a ritual master, and these constant meetings were not only a medium of communication of political decisions but created strong bonds of solidarity between members of ritual groups; at the same time the Friday prayer in their own mosque proclaimed the separation of Hausa from Yoruba. The business leaders now derived from the Mallams the legitimacy that had earlier been conferred by the Nigerian government, and they appealed to religion instead of "custom" to justify the exclusiveness on which the Hausa monopoly of trade depended.

Cohen (1971) has described another situation which, though utterly different in externals, is closely similar in process: that of the Creoles in Freetown. They too have lost the formal political status that they had when they alone had representation in the legislature and municipal government. They too are reduced to a minority position, in this case by the introduction of universal suffrage. They have found a basis for solidarity and exclusiveness in Freemasonry with its rigid hierarchical organization that transcends the divisive effects of competition within other systems to which its members belong. They make a parade of the secrecy which binds them (if this is not a contradiction in terms). Masonhood is asserted in frequent meetings which are no less ritual because the occasion is a banquet. Here again close bonds and frequent communication are established through membership of a ritual body and used to maintain solidarity and exclusiveness and defend the privileged position of a minority.

Although both these studies are concerned with power struggles, Cohen is not content to see the political process solely in these terms. In his view (1969) the essential contribution that social anthropology can make to the study of politics is an analysis of the interaction between manipulative, or power-seeking, and symbolic behaviour, the latter including the appeal to "custom", ethnic "brotherhood" or ritual solidarity. The questions to which he turns our attention are questions of the way in which shared symbols hold groups together and can be activated when the need for group action arises, how such ideologies (in the end one cannot evade the word) are built up and manipulated, whether some symbolic forms are more politically efficacious than others, how the different processes, symbolic and political, affect each other, since neither is determinant. This is a programme for a new synthesis. We have come a long way since *African Political Systems*, but we still look a long way ahead, and not, I think in Easton's direction.

References

Bailey, F. G. (1969). *Stratagems and Spoils*. Blackwell, Oxford.
Balandier, G. (1967). *Anthropologie Politique*. Presses Universitaires de France, Paris.
Barth, F. (1959a). *Political Leadership among Swat Pathans*. Athlone Press, London.
    (1959b). "Segmentary Opposition and the Theory of Games". *J.R.A.I.* **89**, 5–21.
    (ed.), (1969). *Ethnic Groups and Boundaries*. Allen and Unwin, London.
Cohen, A. (1969a). *Custom and Politics in Urban Africa*. Routledge and Kegan Paul, London.
    (1969b). "Political anthropology: the analysis of the symbolism of power relations". *Man*, n.s. **4**, 215–235.
    (1971). "The politics of ritual secrecy". *Man*, n.s. **6**, 427–448.
Cohen, R. and Middleton, J., (eds), (1970). *From Tribe to Nation in Africa*. Chandler, Scranton.
Colson, E. M. (1953). *The Makah Indians*. The University Press, Manchester.
Copans, J., Tornay, S., Godelier, M., and Backes-Clement, C. (1971). *L'anthropologie: science des societés primitives?* Denoël, Paris.
Dyson-Hudson, N. (1966). *Karimojong Politics*. Clarendon Press, Oxford.

Easton, D. (1959). "Political Anthropology", In Siegel, B., (ed.), *Biennial Review of Anthropology*. The University Press, Stanford.

Evans-Pritchard, E. E. (1940a). *The Nuer*. Clarendon Press, Oxford.

(1940b). *The Political System of the Anuak of the Anglo-Egyptian Sudan*. Lund Humphries, London.

Fallers, L. A. (ed.) (1964). *The King's Men*. Oxford University Press, London.

Firth, R. W. (1957). Introduction to "Factions in Indian and Overseas Indian Societies". *British Journal of Sociology* **8**, 291–295.

Gluckman, M. (1955). *Custom and Conflict in Africa*. Blackwell, Oxford.

(1963). *Order and Rebellion in Tribal Africa*. Cohen and West, London.

(1968). "The Utility of the Equilibrium Model in the Study of Social Change", *American Anthropologist* **70**.

Goody, J. R. (1969). *Comparative Studies in Kinship*. Routledge and Kegan Paul, London.

Kuper, A. (1970). *Kalahari Politics*. The University Press, Cambridge.

Mackenzie, W. J. M. (1967). *Politics and Social Science*. Penguin, Harmondsworth.

Maquet, J. J. (1970). *Power and Society in Africa*. Weidenfeld and Nicolson, London.

Middleton, J. F. M. (1960). *Lugbara Religion*. Oxford University Press, London.

Radcliffe-Brown, A. R. (1940). Introduction to Fortes, M., and Evans-Pritchard, E. E., *African Political Systems*.

Richards, A. I., ed. (1960). *East African Chiefs*. Faber and Faber, London.

Schapera, I. (1943). *Tribal Legislation among the Tswana of the Bechuanaland Protectorate*. Lund Humphries, London.

(1947). *The Political Annals of a Tswana Tribe*. School of African Studies, Cape Town.

(1956). *Government and Politics in Tribal Societies*. Watts, London.

(1963). "Kinship and Politics in Tswana History". *J.R.A.I.* **93**, 159–173.

(1970). *Tribal Innovators*. Athlone Press, London.

Smith, M. G. (1960). *Government in Zazzau*. Oxford University Press, London.

Southwold, M. (?1961). *Bureaucracy and Chiefship in Buganda*. East African Institute of Social Research, Kampala.

Turnbull, C. (1965). *Wayward Servants*. Eyre and Spottiswoode, London.

Turner, V. W. (1957). *Schism and Continuity in an African Society*. The University Press, Manchester.

Vincent, J. (1971). *African Elite: the Big men of a Small Town*. Columbia University Press, New York.

Wilson, G. (1939). *The Constitution of Ngonde*. Rhodes-Livingstone Institute, Livingstone.

Anthropology and Apartheid: The Work of South African Anthropologists

3

Max Gluckman

Many younger anthropologists, and indeed some of their elders, nowadays allege that the colonial situation dominated the work and theories of social anthropologists until, in the aftermath of the Second World War, most of the dependent territories of Africa and Asia, and some in Oceania, were liberated. These allegations have not been supported by detailed analyses of the work of specific anthropologists. The Union of South Africa had, and has, the hardest-line colonialist segregation of ethnic groups, with inferiority in socio-politico-economic position enforced on the indigenous people; hence, if the above allegations were correct in their general form, one would expect all South African anthropologists to be affected more than anthropologists going out from Europe for a tour of field research in a colonial territory, and then returning to their home base. I consider that this expectation is fulfilled—but not in any simple way. The work and the theoretical approach of South African anthropologists show the full range of political approaches that developed among Whites, and even Blacks, in South Africa. Some of them indeed are deeply influenced positively by the policy of segregation which after the election of the Nationalist, dominantly Afrikaner, Government in 1948—which has held power since then— became hardened into what is called apartheid (separateness). This does not appear blankly as a theory that indigenous cultures are inferior, even if some of them argue that the people are less intelligent in terms of biogenetic endowment: their contention is that indigenous culture is excellent in its own right, not only appropriate for its bearers, but indeed something they should cling to and fight for, as Afrikaners fought for their language and culture against the might of English culture, supported as it was in South Africa by the manifestations of that culture in Britain, the other English-speaking Dominions of the Empire (to become the Commonwealth), and even the United States of America (cf. L. Kuper, 1965: Chapter 4). This theory of course accorded, as L. Kuper stresses, with the entrenched political, economic and social interests of Whites in South Africa; but I consider it would be unwise to neglect the ideological basis which sees African culture not only as appropriate and valuable for Africans, but Zulu culture as good for Zulu, Xhosa culture as good for Xhosa, Pedi culture for Pedi, and so forth. Again, the policy here may rightly be seen to be, in one aspect, as a policy of *divide et impera*. But, I repeat, the ideological basis is also important. There have been also "liberal" segregationists who, in my judgment, tended to emphasize the beauty and harmony, and even the appropriate uniqueness, of each African culture.

At the other extreme of the political spectrum were anthropologists, who either before or after they did field research, believed in the integration of Africans and Whites—and other ethnic groups—within a single social system based on equality of all men. Some of these were socialists, others what may be designated as "liberal" and against segregation, but not socialistic. The work of these anthropologists, across a wide range of politics, laid much less emphasis on the harmony, and certainly very little on the uniqueness, of the cultures; while all of them contended that the various peoples in South Africa were in their biogenetic potential very similar and all were able to participate equally in modern economic and political life.

It would take a full study to document this correlation, and again the connections would not be simple. The work of South African anthropologists was affected by theoretical developments in Europe and North America: at least ten of them worked for periods with Malinowski, aside from coming under the influence of his published work. Yet I consider that there has been a specific contribution by some South African anthropologists, and pre-eminently by Professor I. Schapera, to the development of *British* social anthropology, and through that an influence on American and Continental-European anthropology. As I have said, a full study would be needed to document this complicated situation in detail: but it is necessary to sketch this background, even in a short essay, in order to pay tribute to Schapera's superb contribution to the development of social anthropology.

I consider too that there is more than historical interest in doing so; some recent trends in social anthropology appear to me to lead their practitioners to positions not very different from those adopted by South African adherents of segregation and apartheid—a stress on the uniqueness of cultures. These are the people who may not appreciate the great historical, and continuing, contribution of Schapera, whose theoretical leads in the subject have never been adequately honoured, because he rarely writes in terms of the theoretical speculations that to some extent bedevil our subject.

Schapera's case is of especial interest also because of the allegations, to which I have referred, that anthropology has been the handmaiden of colonialism, and even of colonial administration. Virtually all his field research was done in the Bechuanaland Protectorate over a period of some twenty years. His *Handbook of Tswana Law and Custom* was a response to a complaint of Tswana chiefs that younger men were growing up ignorant of their traditional law (1938; 2nd ed., 1955: pp. vii–viii). His studies of land tenure (1934b) and migrant labour (1947) were also reports on problems which were worrying greatly both Tswana chiefs and people, and British administrators. No-one reading those reports of Schapera's could possibly conclude that they were grist to the mill of oppressive colonialism: on the contrary, they document in superb detail, validated by careful archival and field research, ecological and economic difficulties, social dislocations, and political strains, created by the establishment of "European" rule and of a modern farming and industrial complex in Southern Africa. (They presented facts which were as comforting for the colonial régime as were Booth's studies of *Life and Labour of the People of London* (1889–1891) for the régime of the rich in Britain.) Schapera was the first British anthropologist to set out to investigate fully[1] how Africans had been brought into that new complex society, how they lived within it as members of a single socio-economic system, and how their indigenous cultures were affected by that situation. He had already dealt with these problems as they had arisen for *The Khoisan Peoples of South Africa* (1930), a compilation and analysis based on everything written about the Hottentots and Bushmen. He wrote an article emphasizing their importance in the economic life of Africans in the first volume of *Africa* (Schapera, 1928), and six years later (1934) edited

---

1. Schapera (1938) acknowledges that when A. R. Radcliffe-Brown was teaching at the University of Cape Town (1921–26) he wrote articles in *The Cape Times* on this situation, and my own principal teacher, Mrs. A. W. Hoernlé, also taught it. But Schapera initiated full research into these problems.

a collection of studies on the general effect of Western civilization on African social life and culture. When he reported his field research among the Kgatla, he dealt with these changes in one aspect after another.

I cannot overstate the importance of Schapera's contribution, in stressing that anthropologists in the field should deal with the here-and-now of what they observed among the "coloured" peoples on the study of whom anthropology, out of its traditional origin, had concentrated. When I make this praising statement, I have to emphasize too that he knew far more about the history of the relationships between these people and the incoming Whites, and about their traditional history as collected from them in the field and culled from study of records written by Whites and Blacks, records in archives as well as published, than any other British anthropologist has known about the people he or she studied. Schapera has published extensively on this history in Tswana as well as English, and he has edited magnificently the records left by Livingstone and even earlier visitors to the region. He directed the compilation of a fine annotated bibliography, covering centuries of records (1941). His standing as an historian is equal to his standing in anthropology. But here I want to praise the insight which led him to say, as early as 1935, in a series of essays on culture contact in Africa in 1935–36 (see Schapera 1935: p. 317: all collected with an introduction by Malinowski [Mair, ed. 1938]): "the missionary, administrator, trader and labour recruiter must be regarded as factors in the tribal life in the same way as are the chief and the magician," and to speak of the former as integral parts of tribal social life. This may seem obvious to us today, and to have been obvious for some time. But it ran against the current theoretical approach in social and cultural anthropology. I pointed out long ago (Gluckman, 1940: pp. 173–174; 1958: pp. 51–52), that the current theoretical approach led Malinowski to misread Schapera, whose plea that these personages *be studied in the same way*, Malinowski countered by pointing out that they did very different things culturally. He changed Schapera's "integral" to "well-integrated" and criticized that. These very misunderstandings emphasize the importance of Schapera's breakthrough (cf. Gluckman's 1947 comment on Malinowskian theory here). American anthropologists at the time were worrying about the problems of "acculturation". Schapera's achievement was to bring into anthropology the view that district commissioner and chief, missionary and magician, were persons within a single social system, composed of groups of different culture, and that their relationships to one another and to others should be studied in the same way. It was this view that I learnt from Schapera and A. W. Hoernlé when I was an under-graduate at the University of the Witwatersrand; that he drove home to me when he took me as an apprentice, with Ellen Hellmann and Hilda Kuper, for a short visit to the Kgatla; that he has constantly reminded me of when-ever I have discussed my work with him through our long period of friendly colleagueship; that speaks all the time through his writings.

I have said that Schapera brought this view into anthropology. It was present in other social and behavioural sciences in South Africa. In history, it started with G. M. Theal in the nineteenth century, and was present in the work of other South African historians: I cite here W. M. Macmillan's *Bantu, Boer and Briton* (1929), a book which followed Theal in dealing with South Africa's African "tribes" as independent polities, with specific forms of economic and social organization, and involved in types of foreign policy not so different from those of Boer and Briton, each of whom had their own forms of economic and political organization. When I studied economics under S. H. Frankel (e.g. his 1938), Africans were inevitably treated as fully involved members of the South African economy. I. D. MacCrone in psychology (e.g. his 1937, and others cited Schapera, ed. 1941) taught us that our attitudes to Africans were an integral part of our psychical make-up. But historically, Schapera was the pioneer who made anthropologists aware of the problems in this situation, anthropologists outside, as well as inside, South Africa. Some South African anthro-pologists, thus, in terms of their history and of the fact that they lived in a nation composed obviously of members of groups and categories not only of different colour, but also of different culture, yet all interacting with and influencing one another, inevitably saw that they were dealing with social persons whose roles though varied were an integral part of the same system, and that these roles had to be studied in the same way. This comes out clearly in the series of essays on *Culture Contact in Africa* (ed. Mair 1938) to which I have referred above. The view of the field as a single social system is clearest in Schapera, but appears also in the essays by Fortes (1936) and Hunter (1936: now Monica Wilson—see also her 1934). Hilda Kuper (1948) and Gluckman (1940) followed in this line. Meanwhile, under the aegis of both A. W. Hoernlé and Schapera, "urban anthro-pology" was born in the work of their pupils, Hellmann (1935, published 1948; and E. J. Krige, 1938): the social-anthropological problems created by hundreds of thousands of Africans working and residing in South African cities could no more be overlooked by scholars than could the political and economic problems of their employment, their subsistence, their subjection, and their change and development. And the way people made their living, how and with whom they collaborated and struggled, how they thought about the past and the present, in both urban and rural areas, were problems for us not only as scholars, but also as citizens. Anthropologists in Europe and North America could, and can, concern themselves abstractly with differences in patterns of culture and alleged differences in mentality of people: for us it was a matter of the here-and-the-now of our own lives. It was Schapera who gave the lead by setting models of report and analysis; and it was a lead which was followed by others than South Africans, to shift the anthropological view in Britain, particularly, from the study of culture to the study of social systems of various types.[2]

The solution of the segregationist South Africans continued to be an emphasis on the cultures of African groups, as not only unique but also harmonious.[3] The integrationists also studied traditional cultures, and some of them produced excellent analyses of these, notably Schapera. But they were also concerned with the problem of how Africans fitted into the South African nation, and hence with the question whether differences in cultures were associated with human beings of a quite different type from ourselves. For us—both as scholars and as citizens, as I have said—this was an urgent question. Inevitably, perhaps, all of us saw a marked difference between the people and the traditional culture. We all knew from our nation's history and our personal experience how quickly Africans could adapt to living in a modern economy and how quickly they could, given the opportunity, learn the techniques and expertises of Europe: there was no barrier to this within themselves. We knew too that the reverse could happen, since there were Whites who became as Africans. As one example, I cite how Portuguese seamen shipwrecked in 1593 found a countryman who had been cast away among the Southern Nguni forty years earlier, and reported that he was indistinguishable from the local inhabitants, having forgotten his language and his God.

In his *Anthropologists and Anthropology: The British School 1922–1972*, A. Kuper (1973: pp. 91–92, 178–179), who is a South African a generation

2. Theoretically inspired by Radcliffe-Brown, but marked in the work of Evans-Pritchard, who started as an historian, and Firth, who started as an economist. I have already listed South Africans.

3. Marked in the work of the Ethnological Publications of the South African Department of Native (later Bantu) Affairs. But see also as an example from a very liberal anthropologist, J. D. Krige's (1939; and, with E. J. Krige, 1943: Chap. XI) account of Lovedu courts as entirely different from White courts, and my discussions of his analysis and analogies (Gluckman 1955, 1962). Cf Schapera's treatment of Tswana courts and law (Schapera 1938; 1955).

younger, has seen that some South African anthropologists made a specific contribution: "As a group . . . [Mrs. Hoernlé's students] also saw their commitment partly in political terms . . . At a time when their British [*scilicet*, United Kingdom] contemporaries tended to avert their eyes from the realities of power and deprivation in the colonial societies, they [Hoernlé's pupils] never forgot the context of the systems which they investigated." This statement, in my judgment, is too comprehensive, but its germ is true; it errs mainly in overlooking the influence of Schapera when he taught us, Mrs. Hoernlé's pupils, during the year when he had just ended his first research among the Kgatla. And in terms of publications, Schapera's influence was far more important than Mrs. Hoernlé's, who, great teacher though she was, published little.

One asks, therefore, whether the political stance of anthropologists so coloured their observations, that the facts they recorded, and the conclusions and theories they based on those facts, cannot be taken as accurate. Here too Schapera's work is crucial. He himself never *openly* took up a political stance in anything he wrote. And his fieldwork was so comprehensive, and his historical knowledge so deep and detailed, that his analyses were authoritative. I consider that the work of his pupils and followers on the whole (for I will not speak for my own work) is similarly convincing. In the now fashionable trend against positivism there is a tendency to decry the importance of "facts". My own opinion—and it was supported by Evans-Pritchard in the last conversation I had with him before he died—is that the solid corpus of Schapera's work will be studied and conned when superficially exciting analyses, inadequately grounded in "facts", become intellectual curiosities.

In these terms, I as a South African and as a professional anthropologist am seriously disturbed by recent work in anthropology which, because of the developing interest in symbolism within cultures, confuses the problems of differences and similarities in cultures, with the problems of differences and similarities among human beings. Before I show the importance of this distinction through specific examples from Schapera's and my own work, I have to draw attention to what is involved in the confusing of these radically different sets of problems. I cite an essay by E. R. Leach in a somewhat ephemeral but nonetheless influential journal, influential among outsiders to our profession and possibly within the profession—*The Times Literary Supplement*. *The Supplement* on July 6th, 1973, had a special issue on "The State of Anthropology", to which Leach contributed an essay on "Ourselves and Others". Leach is influential both inside and outside anthropology and therefore I consider that I am justified in dealing with the essay. And though the journal is ephemeral, the essay reflects views that Leach, and others, have expressed elsewhere.

Leach opens his article with an account of what he calls "false starts" in social anthropology. One of the false starts, ascribed largely to Malinowski, is that "if we are to 'understand' the culturally determined behaviour of 'the others' it is not sufficient to try to project upon their manifest actions our own prejudiced view of what constitutes rationality. To do that is to act like an experimental psychologist who explains the behaviour of his laboratory rats by saying: 'Now if I were a rat, this is how I should feel.' " (Leach, 1973: p. 772). I do not think this is how laboratory experimentalists interpret the behaviour of their rats—which are indeed members of human society. It is certainly not how Malinowski presented his analyses. Malinowski's analyses were exhibited in, and in many respects validated by, very detailed reporting of facts. Leach makes much of Malinowski's reporting in his diary of his own emotional difficulties in carrying out participant observation and trying to become like the Trobrianders: all anthropologists have those difficulties. They were likely to be greater for Malinowski: Leach, and other critics of the diary, have not seen it in adequate historical perspective. As he says (loc. cit.), Malinowski came to do that kind of field research "partly by accident" (see Gluckman, 1963: p. 245). He had not been prepared emotionally to look forward, as to the finding of a Holy Grail, to entering into the field as we, his successors, were. But Malinowski did not, as Leach alleges, project the principle of reciprocity onto the Trobriand economic system and hence on to the Trobrianders: he published a substantial body of facts which showed conclusively that the principle influenced their actions and that they were aware of it. Hence Leach's examples do not support his conclusion that "all forms of social anthropological functionalism are observer-orientated" as if they were the interpretations of a fictional experimental psychologist deducing from his own feelings how rats may feel. The truth is that Leach himself is interested in one problem only: "Our problem is to reach down into the 'grammar' of the other culture, so as to establish a translation, not just of the words but of the poetic meaning . . . The linguists have shown us that all translation is difficult, and that perfect translation is usually impossible. And yet we know that for practical purposes a tolerably satisfactory translation is always possible . . . Languages are different but not so different as all that. Looked at in this way social anthropologists are engaged in establishing a methodology for the translation of cultural language" (loc. cit.).

I would not question that this attempt to understand and interpret cultural languages, or symbolic patterns, is as important as it is difficult. But it is only one of the sets of problems with which social anthropology is concerned, not "our problem", the only one. And insistence on it as the only problem is politically dangerous, as well as restricting in scholarship. It is also a serious lapse in logic, if differences in cultural languages are taken to mean that one cannot find similarities in behaviour and in modes of thought—or in those languages. Leach (loc. cit.) writes that "we started by emphasizing how different are 'the others'—and made them not only different but remote and inferior. Sentimentally we then took the opposite tract and argued that all human beings are alike; we can understand the Trobrianders or the Barotse because their motivations are just the same as our own; but that didn't work either, 'the others' remained obstinately other." The reference to the Barotse presumably brackets me with Malinowski—which I take as high praise. But with his usual inability to see more than one facet at a time (see Schneider, 1964: p. 838f), Leach oversimplifies what Malinowski and I wrote.[4] We in fact argued that Trobrianders and Barotse respectively were alike in some respects, and unlike—different—in other respects. Both the culture and the members of those other societies remain obstinately different and obstinately alike: this latter is the fact that protagonists of apartheid, political and scholarly, are finding most obstinate. It is possible in the cloistered seclusion of King's College, Cambridge (or Merton College, Oxford—see Needham, 1973), to put the main emphasis on the obstinate differences: it was not possible for "liberal" South Africans confronted with the policy of segregation within a nation into which "the others" had been brought, and treated as different—and inferior.

II

I judge that this emphasis on difference in the work of Leach and others plays into the hands of the Government in South Africa, as did the studies of those South African anthropologists whose politics were segregationist in bias. This emphasis may also be politically dangerous as we become,

---

4. I assume that Leach refers here to my study of *The Judicial Process among the Barotse* (1955) in which I reported in detail a number of cases tried in Barotse courts and analysed them to show that there are many similarities in modes of reasoning between Barotse and Anglo-American judges. I also demonstrated that there were important differences, which I contended could be referred to differences in social organization and culture. I was able to cite one case tried shortly after White penetration into Barotseland expanded (1955, pp. 161–162), a case which supported texts I collected from Barotse, to show that even after 50 years of British protection their modes of ratiocination and argument had not changed entirely. See also Schapera 1938.

all of us of all cultural groups, part of what Wendell Wilkie called *One World*. Our problem is not only the translation of cultural languages: for it is also an assessment of the varying weight of likeness and unlikeness both in cultures and in human beings, and whether individuals of a different culture think and feel quite differently—where Evans-Pritchard's study of *Witchcraft, Oracles and Magic among the Azande* (1937) argued they did not. This clear analysis of different types of likeness and unlikeness followed on Malinowski's searching study (1925) of the differences, in Trobriand institutions and thinking, between "Magic, Science and Religion", a problem well dealt with by H. A. Junod as far back as 1913 in his *The Life of a South African Tribe*. The extent of likeness I now illustrate in this tributary essay to Schapera, by discussing, all too briefly, his findings in a field in which he has made a unique contribution. As I pointed out in a general book on *Politics, Law and Ritual in Tribal Society* (1965a, p. 169), Schapera was the only author at the time I wrote who had dealt in detail with legislation by an indigenous African polity (Schapera 1943a). And Schapera in a later book expanding that early study, *Tribal Innovators: Tswana Chiefs and Social Change 1795–1940* (1970, at p. 10), is still able to say accurately that the subject has not yet been treated adequately by anyone else, including myself.

Legislation by a people to cope with new types of problem raised by their absorption into the expanding empires of Europe, implied a conscious and deliberate attempt to perceive the problems in some form, to think about their material and social causes and effects, and to attempt, "rationally", to find solutions. Legislative activity by people in this situation therefore is a form of social and mental activity which, as Schapera says, merits much fuller treatment than it has been given by anthropologists. I begin with an example from Schapera's books cited above, of a legislative debate among the Kgatla in 1926, some 130 years after they first came into contact with Europeans. Clearly we are hearing about Kgatla who had been born and grew up when their relationships with Whites had brought them into what can be called a single economic and political system, even a single social system, and when many of them were being educated, to varying degrees, in European-style schools. We cannot therefore assume that the insight provided by this debate presents to us the "mentality" of the Kgatla before they were so greatly influenced by Western society and culture. Fortunately Schapera's deep historical knowledge of South and Central Africa enables us to assess whether quite different types of human beings, in a psychical sense, had by then been produced.

The debate took place during the reign of Chief Isang, who was literate in both Tswana and English. Indeed, as a student I heard him, in a lecture at the University of the Witwatersrand, draw on a typical English saying to say of his people: "What Western civilization has done for us is to put a square bed into a round hut." Nevertheless, I start from this relatively recent debate, because it illustrates the turning of people, still to some extent involved in traditional magico-religious patterns of belief, to a "modern" technological solution (see Schapera 1970: pp. 40–41, 75; 1943: p. 45):

In the following instance, again involving a choice between different methods of action, the final decision was made by the [full] assembly itself [of the Kgatla men]. In 1926, during a period of severe drought, the Kgatla asked Chief Isang to revive the rainmaking ceremonies, which had been abandoned by his father Chief Lentswe (p. 125). He agreed, but said also that "something better" could be done. He told them "how Europeans obtained water", and instanced the Rustenburg district of the Transvaal, well known to many of the people and still occupied by part of the tribe, where "dry places had been made habitable" by boring and damming. After lengthy discussion at several meetings, they accepted his proposal, and decided that boreholes at home and in cattlepost areas would be more useful than dams across rivers (where during the dry season there was already much overgrazing). They agreed also to finance the scheme by a levy of £6 10s. per taxpayer, "so that each man should feel he was paying for the cost of a day's work" (according to the estimate submitted by the contractors). (Information from Isang, 29.x.1932.) [£4,000 was obtained in this way.]

The witticism I have quoted from Chief Isang's lecture shows that he was deeply conscious, as indeed the rest of his lecture showed, of the considerable changes which Kgatla culture had undergone, changes many of which he regretted. Nevertheless, he decided that a reinstitution of the rainmaking ceremonies, an important duty traditionally of the chiefly power (see Schapera 1971; 1929), was not alone sufficient, and that the Kgatla should also make provision for water by adopting White technology. It is not surprising that he also allowed the reinstitution of rainmaking ceremonies, whether or not he himself believed in them: in 1926 the drought was so severe that the Prime Minister of the Union of South Africa ordered a national day of prayer and penitence. But Chief Isang did initiate a discussion between himself and his people on whether they could adopt the technology of the Whites, as they had observed it beyond the border of the Protectorate. Then they had to decide which of two technological measures they should adopt, and they decided in terms of their clear perception of the technical difficulties of grazing cattle during the long, dry winter. To provide money for the communal enterprise so that they could employ skilled contractors with machinery to bore for water, the Kgatla then turned, as they and other Tswana both as polities and as individuals had long turned, to earning money in the economy established by the Whites.

In 1942 I recorded a debate in the Barotse National Council about trying to control the price of fish and other goods. By that time, the Barotse had been under British protection for half a century, and, like many Tswana, some (but not all) of their councillors were literate in both the vernacular and English, and had been to European-style schools. Since the beginning of the War, there had been a steady rise in the price of local produce as well as goods bought at White-owned stores. In August 1942 my Research Assistant, the late Mr. Davidson Silumesii Sianga, while I was working away from the capital, recorded a case there (see Gluckman 1955: pp.69–70) when the British Provincial Commissioner sent to the Barotse Mongu District Court a youth caught selling fish at four small fish for 6d., under police escort. Many judges said that this price for fish "was just stealing the people's money", and the price of fish should be fixed at 1d. each. The head of the court said: "If the kuta [Court and Council] wishes to inform the whole country of Barotseland of the price for fish set by the kuta, I have not power at this time to summon the whole nation to the kuta because the NGAMBELA [title of prime minister] is not here. When the NGAMBELA arrives I will report this affair to him because we all know very well that reeds, grass and poles are no longer bought at the decent prices agreed to in the past; . . . If the owner of the country [the NGAM-BELA] agrees in this affair as we have spoken, it is easy for me to gather the country and tell the people the price set." Meanwhile he dismissed the youth on the grounds that he had not committed an established offence.

I cited this case before to illustrate that though Barotse judges were also legislators and administrators, they differentiated clearly between their various functions: if they wished to punish selling at excessive prices, they had to legislate and announce the new law to the people (loc. cit., where I also cited another case to this effect). I cite the case again here, because later that year (1942) there was a debate in the legislative chamber, the Barotse National Council, on the subject. The National Council was composed of all members of the senior council at the king's capital, and of representatives of each District Authority. The proposal from the local District Authority, after the case cited above, was that the price of fish be controlled. In the ensuing debate, the councillors who spoke pointed out that they were fully aware of the problems of both fishermen and consumers, since they themselves both fished and bought fish. One stressed that the supplies of fish varied with the month and the state of the flood (in the great Zambezi plain in which they lived), and that when fish were scarcer, prices obviously rose; in addition, the fish caught varied in number in different places within the kingdom, so that prices would vary. If a man carried fish from the Zambezi plain, where they were plentiful, into the adjacent areas of woodland where they were scarce, he must get more money for his "business" and his "shoulder" which carried the burden. Another argued that if the fisherman needed money badly, he would accept little money, while the buyer, if staging a feast, would be prepared to pay a lot. On the other hand, another councillor countered, fish were essential and were relatively cheap compared with other goods, so that a small rise in price would be acceptable to buyers. He was supported by a councillor who maintained that the fisherman had to make or buy his nets and work in cold waters from morning to night, and therefore he was entitled to a good price. But, said others, the fishermen must not be allowed to rob the country.

Some councillors emphasized that the rising price of White goods in White stores was the cause of the trouble: both fishermen and sellers of meal had to raise their prices to enable them to buy from traders.

The debate took place at Lealui, about 360 miles from Livingstone. The head of the council at Sesheke, 100 miles from Livingstone by river, but with quick rail transport on a logging railway relatively nearby, said that if they did decide to fix prices, these would have to vary with locality, for fish at Lealui were cheap (in terms of denominations of money) because money was scarce there, while at Sesheke fish were dear because money was more plentiful.

Other councillors dwelt on the practical difficulty of controlling prices. First, fish varied in size, and there were not enough scales in the country to fix the price by weight. Second, it would be difficult to enforce the maximum price set, because buyers would be willing to pay more in secret.

The NGAMBELA, in concluding the debate, said that they as rulers were placed there to establish laws for the good of the country as a whole, and they must see that the price they felt to be fair was enforced.

Later, local fishermen were summoned and were told that the price for fish would be 10 for one shilling, and that "detective-traps" would be used to see that it was adhered to. I do not know whether this policy was in fact successful for any period: shortly afterwards I moved to the southern capital, and later worked in Sesheke before returning in 1947 to Lealui. By then prices of everything had risen considerably.

As I write in Britain in 1973, I might be reading the speeches of Government Ministers, and the Barotse debate even had some echo of trade-union views. I am therefore justified in citing the debate in order to show that the relatively uneducated (in our British terms) Barotse councillors, faced with the kind of problem which confronts Britain now, showed a clear appreciation of certain basic economic facts, and even in concrete form an appreciation of various laws formulated by our economists: the right to a return on capital and labour; the relation between supply and demand; the principle of marginal utility; the right of the middleman to some return; the problems created by a spiral of rising prices; the need to measure commodities as exactly as money can be measured in fair fixing of prices; and the difficulty of controlling the sale of goods on private markets. Most strikingly, the chief councillor from Sesheke, who was literate in English and Barotse, up to Standard VIII in terms of formal schooling, had comprehended in a simple way, at least as set out in his statement, that money was a commodity whose supply as against supplies of other goods would affect prices, and that variations in the supply of money in different parts of the kingdom would have to be taken into account in fixing prices.[5]

I could, given more space, cite other debates from my notes on this meeting of the National Council to fill in this account of a government discussing the problems created for their nation by their coming under British protection, and thus subject to certain types of control by first the British South Africa Company and then the Northern Rhodesia Government, and by their being involved, as producers and migrating labourers as well as consumers, in world economy. The attempt to deal with the resulting disturbances in social organization and morals, as well as with the technical problems arising from increase of population and absence of males working in White areas so that it became more difficult to maintain the canals which drained their more fertile land (see Allan and Gluckman in Peters 1960), was marked by an appreciation of facts which throughout showed that one would be justified in saying that the Barotse of the 1940's thought about the world and tried to remedy their difficulties within it, in

5. As part of our South African response to the standard insistence on the differences between Whites and Blacks, and the inferiority of the latter, it is significant that I immediately sent an abstract of this debate to *The South African Journal of Economics* (1943, pp. 227–228). It was further summarized in the *Colonial Review*, 1944.

ways very similar to those of Whites in Europe. In 1946, partly under pressure from the Northern Rhodesia Government, the Barotse Government revived, in a new form, an old council, aimed to give the general populace a chance through elected representatives to bring their complaints and their views to the councillors nominated by incumbent councillors when one of their number was promoted, discharged or died (Gluckman 1951: p. 18). This new council, some of whose members were illiterate, discussed many problems, such as the effect of agricultural regulations on productivity in gardens; the campaign to innoculate their cattle against bovine pleuropneumonia; the silting up of canals since the abolition of tribute labour for the king; size of mesh for seine- and gill-nets; the necessity to build more rural dispensaries; the necessity to train women as well as men as medical orderlies to enable ailing women to be treated by their own sex; the unfairness of making the women, and the men at home, build schools without pay; and so forth. There was a long debate on the propriety of people continuing to hold land which they were not using, as they were entitled to do under Barotse law (Gluckman 1965b: Chapter III), when with the increase of population many were short of land (loc. cit. p. 105). The Barotse Government had recently agreed with the Northern Rhodesia Government to reduce the size of their councils and many councillors had been discharged; there were protests against Barotse kingship being thus destroyed without the people being consulted. As one Lunda said: "The kingship is our house. One day we will find that the Government has taken our house. When we complain, Government will truthfully answer: 'You gave it to us'." (Gluckman 1951: p. 18). There was also a short final debate on the truth or validity of witchcraft, which was initiated when a member of the new council asked me whether I believed that there were witches who had power to harm others. I replied that I thought people could be poisoned, but not that they could be killed by stabbing their footprints with a porcupine quill full of *miliyani* (medicines as it is translated) and so forth, or by a "zombie" (*silumbu*). The NGAMBELA strongly endorsed my view. For the rest, the discussion was down-to-earth (as we would say), dealing with the problems and concerns of everyday life for a people in difficult circumstances.

I have said that both Schapera and I, in reporting these legislative debates, made our observations long after the people had come under White rule and entered the White economy. Schapera's deep historical knowledge has enabled him to demonstrate in his *Tribal Innovators* (1970) that the Tswana debated similarly their problems as far back as 1795. His careful editing of the journals of Burchell and Livingstone and other records (cited in his general bibliography) enforces this lesson. In these and in his many other studies he has thus emphasized that "the others" are alike to us in many respects: he has also demonstrated that often the differences in their culture may lead them to argue and act somewhat differently. He has analysed both fundamental similarities and fundamental differences in culture and in social organization.

The importance of keeping clear whether we are dealing with the structure of ideas in a cultural pattern, or with the structure of individual thought operating with a cultural pattern, was emphasized by Durkheim. In the *Preface* to the second edition of *Les Régles de la méthode sociologique* (1895: cited from the English translation 1938: pp. li–lii), Durkheim urged that "we need to investigate, by comparison of mythical themes, popular legends, traditions, and languages, the manner in which social representations adhere to and repel one another, how they fuse or separate from one another, etc. . . . it will evidently be impossible to determine [pre-determine—M.G.] with certainty whether or not . . . [the relevant laws] parallel those of individual psychology." Durkheim considered that research would show that even if resemblances existed between the two sorts of laws, the differences would be "nonetheless marked". He stressed, with great prescience, that the peculiarity of what he called "laws of social thought" (i.e. of social representations), would explain "the apparently strange combinations and segregations of religious ideas (which certainly are collective in origin) and their transformations which produce compounds of contradictory elements widely different from the ordinary products of individual thought." It is on the former that Leach lays weight: and if there are differences between social patterns of this kind, it does not mean that the individuals living with them think, and feel, either individually or in collective debate and intercourse, entirely differently. Schapera was one of the many anthropologists to demonstrate this in detail.

But dominantly he drove home in anthropology the importance of studying what lay before our eyes and came to our ears: that the Africans in Southern Africa were, with Whites and others, integral parts of a single social system, so that all had to be studied in the same way—even though their roles might differ considerably. This theoretical approach helped reorientate British anthropology in the 1920's and 1930's. The fine fieldwork and vast scholarship which supported that approach drove and drives home the most humane of lessons: that all men are alike in some respects and unlike in others; and that all cultures are alike in some respects and unlike in others. Even Leach concedes that cultural "languages are different but not as different as all that." Schapera has filled in for us the differences and what is not-so-different, for the Tswana and other Southern and Central African peoples.

References

Allan, W. and Gluckman, M. (1960). "Introduction" to Peters, D. U., *Land Usage in Barotseland*. Communication No. 19 from the Rhodes-Livingstone Institute.

Booth, C. 1889–1891 (1902–1903). *Life and Labour of the People in London*. 17 volumes. Macmillan, London.

Durkheim, E. (1895). *Les Régles de la méthode sociologique*. Alcan, Paris. Translated as *The Rules of Sociological Method* by Solovay, S. A. and Mueller, J. H. The Free Press, Glencoe III (1938).

Evans-Pritchard, E. E. (1937). *Witchcraft, Oracles and Magic among the Azande*. Clarendon Press, Oxford.

Fortes, M. (1936). "Culture Contact as a Dynamic Process: An Investigation in the Northern Territories of the Gold Coast". In *Africa*, vol. IX, No. 1 (January), pp. 24–55.

Frankel, S. H. (1938). *Capital Investment in Africa: Its Course and Effects*. Oxford University Press, London.

Gluckman, M. (1940). "Analysis of a Social Situation in Modern Zululand". In *Bantu Studies*, Vol. XIV, No. 1 (March), pp. 1–30 and No. 2 (June), pp. 147–174. Republished as Rhodes-Livingstone Paper No. 28 (with a Preface by J. C. Mitchell), 1958.
(1943). "Views of Rhodesian natives on some economic questions" In Correspondence, *South African Journal of Economics*, vol. 11, No. 3 (September), pp. 227–228. Reprinted in summary form in *The Colonial Review*, March 1944.
(1947). "Malinowski's 'Functional' Analysis of Social Change". In *Africa*, vol. XVII, No. 2 (April 1947), pp. 103–121. Republished in *Order and Rebellion in Tribal Africa*, pp. 207–234. Cohen and West, London.
(1951). "The Lozi of Barotseland in North-Western Rhodesia". In Colson, E. and Gluckman, M. (eds), *Seven Tribes of Central Africa*. Manchester University Press for the Institute of Social Research, Zambia (new impression—first impression by Oxford University Press).
(1955). *The Judicial Process among the Barotse of Northern Rhodesia*. Manchester University Press, for the Rhodes-Livingstone Institute.
(1962). "African Jurisprudence" In *The Advancement of Science*, vol. XVIII, No. 75 (January), pp. 439–459.
(1963). "Malinowski's Contribution to Social Anthropology". In *Order and Rebellion in Tribal Africa*, pp. 235–243. Cohen and West, London.
(1965a). *Politics, Law and Ritual in Tribal Society*. Blackwells, Oxford.
(1965b). *The Ideas in Barotse Jurisprudence*. Yale University Press, New Haven.
(1967). 2nd enlarged edition of 1955, *The Judicial Process among the Barotse of Northern Rhodesia*.
(1972). 2nd impression of 1965, *The Ideas in Barotse Jurisprudence*, with a new Preface. Manchester University Press, for the Institute of Social Research, University of Zambia.

(1973). New impression of 1967, 2nd enlarged edition of *The Judicial Process among the Barotse of Northern Rhodesia* (Zambia), with a new Preface.

Hellmann, E. (1940). *Problems of Urban Bantu Youth*. Institute of Race Relations, Johannesburg, South Africa.

(1948). *Rooiyard: A Sociological Survey of an Urban Native Slum Yard* (thesis of 1935). Rhodes-Livingstone Paper No. 13.

Hunter, M. (later Wilson, M.) (1934). "Methods of Study of Culture Contact". In *Africa*, Vol. VII, No. 1 (July), pp. 335–350.

(1936). *Reaction to Conquest: Effects of Contact with Europeans on the Pondo of South Africa*. Oxford Univesity Press, for the International Institute of African Languages and Cultures.

Junod, H. A. (1913). (2nd ed. 1927). *The Life of a South African Tribe*. Macmillan, London.

Krige, E. J. (1936). "Changing Conditions in Marital Relations and Parental Duties among Urbanized Natives". In *Africa*, vol. IX, No. 1 (January), pp. 1–23.

Krige, E. J. and J. D. (1943). *The Realm of a Rain-Queen: A Study of the Pattern of Lovedu Society*. Oxford University Press, for the International Institute of African Languages and Cultures.

Krige, J. D. (1939). "Some Aspects of Lovedu Judicial Arrangements". In *Bantu Studies*, vol. XIII, No. 2 (June), pp. 113–130.

Kuper, A. (1973). *Anthropologists and Anthropology: The British School 1922–1972*. Allen Lane, London.

Kuper, H. (1947). *The Uniform of Colour: A Study of Black-White Relationships in Swaziland*. University of the Witwatersrand Press, Johannesburg.

Kuper, L. (1956). *Passive Resistance in South Africa*. Cape, London.

(1965). *An African Bourgeoisie: Race, Class and Politics in South Africa*. Yale University Press, New Haven.

Leach, E. R. (1973). "Ourselves and Others". In *The Times Literary Supplement*, The State of Anthropology, July 6th, 1973, pp. 771–772.

MacMillan, W. M. (1929). *Bantu, Boer, and Briton: the Making of the South African Native Problem*. Faber and Gwyer, London.

MacCrone, I. D. (1937). *Race Attitudes in South Africa: Historical, Experimental, and Psychological Studies*. Oxford University Press, London. (First publications from 1930.)

Mair, L. (ed.) (1938). "Methods of Study of Culture Contact in Africa". Memorandum XV of the International Institute of African Languages and Cultures. Oxford University Press, London.

Malinowski, B. (1925). "Magic, Science and Religion". In Needham, J. (ed.), *Science, Religion and Reality*, pp. 19–84. Sheldon Press, London. Reprinted in Malinowski, B., *Magic, Science and Religion*, pp. 1–71. The Free Press, Glencoe, III.

(1938). "Introduction" to Mair, L. (ed.), 1938.

(1946). *The Dynamics of Culture Change: An Inquiry into Race Relations in Africa*. Edited with an introduction by Kaberry, P. M. Yale University Press, New Haven.

Needham, R. (1973). "Prospects and Impediments". In *The Times Literary Supplement*, The State of Anthropology, July 6th, 1973, pp. 785–786.

Schapera, I. (1928). "Economic Changes in South African Native Life". In *Africa*, vol. I, No. 2 (April), pp. 170–188.

(1930). "The 'Little Rain' (Pulanana) Ceremony of the Bechuanaland Protectorate". In *Bantu Studies*, Vol. IV, pp. 211f.

(1934). *Western Civilization and the Natives of South Africa.* Routledge and Kegan Paul, London.

(1935). "Field Methods in the Study of Modern Culture Contact". In *Africa*, Vol. VIII, No. 3 (July), pp. 315–328.

(1936). " 'Tribal Politics', Rainmaking and the Levirate among the Christianised Kxatla of Bechuanaland Protectorate". In *Man*, No. 23.

(1938). *A Handbook of Tswana Law and Custom.* Oxford University Press, for the International Institute of African Languages and Cultures.

(1943a). *Tribal Legislation among the Tswana of the Bechuanaland Protectorate: A Study in the Mechanism of Cultural Change.* Monographs on Social Anthropology of the London School of Economics. No. 9 Percy Lund, Humphries, for the University of London.

(1943b). *Native Land Tenure in the Bechuanaland Protectorate.* Lovedale Press, Lovedale, South Africa.

(1947). *Migrant Labour and Tribal Life: A Study of Conditions in the Bechuanaland Protectorate.* Oxford University Press, London.

(1955). Second edition of 1938, *A Handbook of Tswana Law and Custom*, with a new Preface.

(1970). *Tribal Innovators: Tswana Chiefs and Social Change 1795–1940*, Monographs on Social Anthropology of the London School of Economics No. 43. Athlone Press for the University of London.

(1971). *Rainmaking Rites of Tswana Tribes*, African Social Research Documents, Vol. 3. African Studies Centre, Cambridge.

Schapera, I. (ed.) (1941). *Select Bibliography of South African Native Life and Problems.* Oxford University Press, London.

Schapera, I. (ed.) (1934). *Western Civilization and the Natives of South Africa: Studies in Culture Contact.* Routledge and Kegan Paul, London.

Schneider, D. M. (1962). Review of Leach, E. R., "Rethinking Anthropology". In *American Anthropologist*, vol. 64, No. 4 (August), pp. 838–843.

4 | Changing Lines of Cleavage

Monica Wilson

One of Isaac Schapera's notable contributions to social anthropology has been his documentation of political conflict. He analysed conflicts in eight Tswana chiefdoms over a period of 150 to 200 years, tracing 107 internal disputes and providing evidence on the occasions of quarrels and the lines of cleavage (Schapera, 1963: pp. 159–173). Where and why social groups split, and why and how conflict is overcome are fundamental questions of social anthropology. A scholar with the knowledge of how to prevent fragmentation, how to maintain cohesion, might command political leadership in one world. This essay is concerned with the first question only: *where* splits occur. What are the consistencies and differences in lines of cleavage in a range of societies through time?

In pre-literate, cattle-owning and/or cultivating societies in southern Africa, the common lines of cleavage were between kin. In patrilineal systems the descendants of one man divided according to "houses", i.e. according to their mothers. In matrilineal systems the cleavage was between sisters, the daughters of one woman. These divisions were reflected in space in the placing of houses (huts) in a homestead, or the houses of one lineage segment in a village, or in scattering the houses of groups of wives in a number of homesteads or villages in various parts of a chiefdom (Hunter, 1936: pp. 15–18, 380–381, 401.). Among Nguni and Sotho speakers and a number of other peoples, houses were ranked, each wife having a recognized position. Among the Nguni, the Nyakyusa of Tanzania, and many others, there were two main divisions headed by two senior wives. Among the southern Nguni they were known as "the great house" and the "right-hand house", the great house being that of the mother of the heir to the chiefdom, the right-hand house that of the first wife married whose son was likely to be older in age than his senior half-brother. Among the Nyakyusa the two senior wives were married simultaneously, at the "coming-out" or coronation ritual.

Cleavages in south Nguni and Nyakyusa chiefdoms usually followed the division of senior wives. David Hammond-Tooke has analysed eighteen cases of cleavage among the Xhosa, Thembu, Mpondomise, and Bhaca, and to these three further cases among the Mpondo may be added, giving 21 cases of splitting or attempted splitting of a southern Nguni chiefdom (Hammond-Tooke, 1963: pp. 143–167). Eighteen of these splits were between the great house and the right-hand house; three further splits were secessions of minor houses. Among the Nyakyusa 30 cases of splitting of a chiefdom in 10 generations are recorded in one lineage, and 17 cases of splitting in 7 generations are recorded in another lineage. In 7 of the 30 cases, and 6 of the 17 cases, the chiefdom subdivided between more than two brothers (Wilson, 1959: pp. 3–5, 26–27 (genealogies), 88–97.) Clyde Mitchell, Victor Turner, and Max Marwick have analysed the cleavages among matrilineal peoples of Central Africa, and demonstrated the lines of division between sisters (Mitchell, 1956a; Turner, 1957; Marwick, 1965.).

Evidence now exists for a wide range of societies in southern and central Africa, showing what kinship ties were held important, and precisely where the lines of cleavage came. Details vary, but the principle of division according to "houses", the descendants of co-wives, or division according to "wombs", the descendants of sisters, remains constant. Where the split was of a chiefdom or village it was the line of cleavage of kin of the chief or village headman that was important, not the "houses" or "wombs" of junior lineages.

Not only is the kinship basis of division among all the people cited indisputable; there is also a tendency for territorial and kinship divisions to coincide. But they did not coincide exactly. Sometimes they are spoken of as if they did, or it may be suggested that once-upon-a-time they coincided, but the evidence indicates that everywhere a man had *some* choice as to where he would live. The measure of his choice varied with the people, the period, the wealth and status of the individual. Among the Nguni in the nineteenth century a man was expected to live in his father's homestead until some years after his marriage. Before his father's death he might receive permission to build his own homestead but it was expected that he would build in the same neighbourhood. Only a poor man who had no hope of obtaining marriage cattle from his own father was likely to attach himself to someone else, and live as a client, serving a rich man not related to him, or only distantly related, in the expectation of gaining cattle with which to marry and establish a herd. In Xhosa idiom areas were referred to by the name of the leading lineage living there *as if* that lineage alone occupied the area, though it has been shown that in a conservative part of Pondoland in 1931, of 22 homesteads on one ridge the men of five were of one lineage, the men of 10 homesteads were of four other lineages, and the men of four homesteads were not related to any other on the ridge. One of these was the homestead of the teacher appointed to the local school and come to live near the school. One homestead was of an old dependent (*induna*) of the dominant lineage, and two homesteads were of women (a widow and a divorcée) living independently with their children and practising as doctors. Within each homestead headed by a man, all the men were of one lineage and all the women wives or daughters of the lineage, with two exceptions. There were two adult dependants, one a man dependent on his sister's wealthy husband, and one a woman visiting a married sister since she herself had been deserted by her husband, and her son was working on the mines. There were also three boys herding for homesteads other than their own (Hunter, 1936: pp. 61–64).

In 1949 in Bhaca country, of 117 homesteads in one area only eight were not related to any other in the area, but the remaining 109 were divided among 16 lineages (Hammond–Tooke, 1962: pp. 55–57).

An Nguni woman's choice was very limited: married or widowed she should live at her husband's homestead; single or divorced she should live with her father or her brother. Visiting a married sister could only be a temporary expedient; and for a woman to establish her own homestead depended upon her having some source of income, such as a practice as diviner or herbalist.

Schapera has shown that kinsmen lived together in the large Tswana villages, and if a man moved away his place could be taken only by someone of the same ward (Schapera, 1943: p. 102), nevertheless members of one *seboko* are found scattered through many chiefdoms and all totems are represented in all chiefdoms, proving that dispersion of lineages in fact occurred (Schapera, 1952, passim).

The measure of coincidence between any particular kinship ties and local group appears to have been still less among Yao, Bemba, Ndembu, and Chewa than among Nguni or Tswana. Mitchell and Marwick have shown how the leader of a sorority group recruited followers who had a choice as to which kinsman they would support and live near. Turner has shown how men and women had a wide choice as to which kinship links they would assert in deciding where to live: "structural rigidity . . . is never found in the mobile Ndembu society" (Turner, 1957: p. 62). When a territorial split occurred in a village or a chiefdom one party to the dispute moved, (or usually it moved); all those living in the segment of the leader who moved might go with him but it seems that commonly there was some reshuffling. Here again an element of choice entered.

Choice of where to live diminished with scarcity of land, and the importance of lineage ties which determine inheritance became correspondingly greater. This is most evident among Xhosa and Mfengu of the Ciskei, and the Nyakyusa of Tanzania (Wilson, 1963: pp. 374–388), peoples among whom pressure of population is acute, but it is widespread.

Since kinship and territorial groups did not coincide at all precisely, kinship loyalties and territorial loyalties were sometimes in opposition. Among the southern Nguni, when the right-hand son of a chief moved away from his senior half-brother to form an independent chiefdom, followers might be recruited from different parts of his father's chiefdom. But the army was based primarily on territorial grouping and local loyalties were strong. Boys and young men from adjoining villages or neighbourhoods continually challenged one another to stick-fighting contests and the divisions and rivalries between *local* groups were clear at any feast (Hunter, 1936: pp. 217–218, 365, 370, 410–411). It happened repeatedly that ties of locality dominated ties of kinship and an *area* ruled by a subordinate chief sought independence. This happened in the case of the Khonjwayo in Pondoland. The original Khonjwayo was right-hand son of the paramount chief eight generations back in 1931. Three generations back in 1931 the Khonjwayo had fought to gain independence as a chiefdom (Hunter, 1936: pp. 399, 411), but according to oral tradition (collected in the Khonjwayo district in 1931) they had failed to gain it.

Local cleavages continue to be evident (1973) in stick-fighting contests between boys of neighbouring villages (locations) (Mayer, 1970: pp. 164–174), and in what are called by the government "faction fights" in the Transkei, Ciskei, Natal, and Zululand. In these fights a number of men are killed each year: they recur repeatedly, particularly during the Christmas holiday and at harvest time, when beer drinks are numerous. The lines of cleavage are territorial and apparently constant, but the root causes of conflict are much more obscure. Competition for grazing between adjoining districts is probably one factor, and possibly also competition for fields. As will be shown, local rural cleavages reappear among migrant labourers in towns, but the effective lines of division do not necessarily coincide with those in the country. Men coming from neighbouring villages may be in opposition in fighting in the country but members of the same home-boys[1] rugby team in town, in opposition to men from more distant villages.

A third principle of solidarity and cleavage, distinct from lineage and locality, is that of age. Men of one generation may support a contemporary in opposition to other generations, whether fathers or sons. Among both Xhosa—and Sotho—speaking peoples those circumcised with the son of a chief were expected to become his closest followers, and if he sought to establish an independent chiefdom to move with him (Dugmore, 1866: p. 155). In Zulu, Swazi, Pedi, and Tswana kingdoms or chiefdoms age-regiments created bonds cutting across lineage and territorial ties, and conflict between regiments was liable to erupt (Kuper, 1947: pp. 120–121, 203, 224). The groups which moved out of Zululand under military leaders in the early nineteenth century were men of one regiment together with their dependants. Age-mates lived together during the period of initiation among southern Nguni and Sotho generally, and members of Zulu and Swazi regiments lived together for periods. Young men and boys occupied Tswana cattle posts. But in all these cases the coincidence between territorial and age groups was for a term only. In Ndembu villages it lasted longer; there grandparents and grandchildren occupied one half of a village and the parents the other. Among the Nyakyusa the principle of territorial separation of age-mates was pushed still further: fathers and sons were required to build separately and continued to live in separate villages throughout their lives with the proviso that a son who inherited from his father (or father's younger brother) might move to his homestead and join his generation, taking his father's name and legal position. The system of age villages depended upon redistribution of land each generation, something which disappeared when long-term crops were planted and substantial houses built, and the separation of fathers and sons became more and more difficult as density of population increased. By 1955 it had greatly diminished and by 1969 it had disappeared in large parts of the Nyakyusa country.

A fourth principle, sometimes explicitly formulated as a ground of cleavage, was difference in language and custom. The legal rights of Sarwa hunters were subordinate to those of Tswana in the various Tswana

1. "Home-boys" is used as a translation of the Xhosa *amakhaya*.

chiefdoms, and marriage of Tswana with Sarwa was disapproved by Tswana. Similarly the Nyakyusa, up to 1938, rejected marriage with neighbouring Kinga or Safwa, whom they thought dirty. In Zambia another cleavage was visible between those who spoke Bemba or languages related to Bemba, and Lozi speakers. In South Africa there has tended to be a division on the line of language difference between Nguni and Sotho, particularly since their rules of marriage differed radically, Sotho speakers preferring cousin marriage, and Nguni speakers insisting on clan exogamy, and usually extending the prohibition to mother's and perhaps grand-mothers' clans, as well as to father's clan.

But the cleavage on language and custom was not constant. Tswana, even chiefs, intermarried with cattle-owning Khoikhoi. Sotho and Xhosa married San hunters as well as Khoikhoi herders (Wilson and Thompson, 1969: I, pp. 97, 102–106, 165–167), and along the escarpment of the Drakensberg where Nguni and Sotho interacted, they married each other in some places, notably in Swaziland and Lesotho.

There is good reason to think that cleavage between Khoikhoi and San in South Africa was cultural not racial, and there is evidence to suggest that the cleavage between San hunters and Nguni or Sotho herdsmen was also largely cultural in the eighteenth century; certainly intermarriage occurred until the late nineteenth century (Wilson and Thompson, 1969: I. pp. 63–64, 106). But from the time of the first Dutch settlement at the Cape awareness of racial differences began to increase, and legal differen-tiation based on race developed to the point that, in 1973, legal discrimina-tion overshadows everyday relationships in South Africa. It impinges more and more as interaction in the economic field increases. Only occa-sionally, in churches and clubs and in personal friendships, is it partially overcome.

A sixth cleavage, widespread in Africa but differing in degree in different areas, was that between conservative and radical, pagan and Christian, the people who seized the opportunity presented by schools and those who rejected school education. The cleavage was sharpest on the eastern Cape frontier, where there was war between black and white for a hundred years, and "school people" identified, or were felt to identify, with white conquerors in opposition to the Xhosa resistance (Wilson and Thompson, 1969: pp. I, 265–266, II, 74–76). As elsewhere, but for longer and more consistently, the parties were distinguished by their clothing, the school people, men and women, wearing some form of western dress, and the con-servative pagans (except for men at work) wearing blankets or sheeting stained with ochre, hence the colloquial South African appellation of "reds" meaning pagan conservatives. The cleavage was minimal among the Ngwato whose chief Khama himself became a Christian, while retaining his independence, and he carried many of his people with him, but even there the cleavage existed.

Sometimes this cleavage was reflected in territorial separation, the Christians being established in separate villages, but this did not occur everywhere and was early rejected by the leading Xhosa convert, Tiyo Soga. It was a cleavage most evident in the early stages of mission history and diminished as awareness of the advantages of school education in gaining employment became evident. African national leaders in the south have deliberately sought to diminish the cleavage and in some districts where, 40 years ago, it was obvious, it has now (1973) virtually disappeared (Wilson, 1951: pp. 40–43).

Professor Mayer has shown how strongly the school-red cleavage persisted in East London in the 1950's (Mayer, 1961: *passim*), that being the centre of employment nearest conservative Xhosa areas, and one which had many Xhosa speakers among whites: at the same period it scarcely existed in Cape Town, 600 miles away, for Cape Town was the preferred centre of work among the more sophisticated school people (Wilson and Mafeje, 1963; pp. 17–18). Jobs in Cape Town commanded higher wages but usually required some knowledge of English or Afrikaans.

In the work centres in South Africa the most widespread groups have been home-boy groups based on locality. In Cape Town these did not take account of the school-red cleavage, though in East London they did. The size of the home base on which home-boys divided depended upon two factors: firstly, the number of people from a given area at the centre of employment and secondly, the activity. In Cape Town Sotho speakers were relatively few and in 1961–2 they formed only one or two groups; Xhosa speakers were many and they divided by territorial base. Therefore the divisions did not match exactly the cleavages of rural localities discussed above (p. 45). As already indicated, those who came from neighbouring villages (or "locations") might be in opposition in the country but members of the same home-boy group in town, in opposition to those from more distant villages or from outside the reserve. In 1961–2 all the Mpondo in Cape Town were acting for one purpose as a group though fighting between men of neighbouring districts repeatedly occurs in Pondoland.

Moreover, in Cape Town, the cleavage between those coming from reserves and those coming from European-owned farms or from country towns overshadowed divisions between those from reserves. The "squatters and vagrants" from farms were looked down upon by landowners from reserves, and those from farms retorted with remarks about "unteachable sheep" from remote reserves. They formed separate home-boy groups. Those from European farms made common cause with those from country towns—dorps—which have close links with the farms of their surrounding neighbourhoods (Wilson and Mafeje, 1963: pp. 47–73, 116–117, 153–161).

Home-boy ties were expressed in living quarters and messes, men from one local area living and eating together in the barracks provided for migrant labourers who came to work without their wives and families. The same ties were expressed in sports clubs and choirs, most of which were based on the country locality from which men came. Furthermore, if numbers increased, clubs divided on the basis of home locality.

The town-born had no home-boys and there was a greater cleavage between town clubs and country clubs than between the various country clubs. A case was recorded of an incipient split in a country rugby club being contained so that it might defeat a town club. Countrymen who had long lived in town and aspired to be townsmen might also join a town club, but not all who so aspired were admitted. The townsmens' clubs were beginning, in the 1960's, to subdivide on the basis of class, as defined in terms of education, wealth, and manners. It became possible to predict along what lines any particular club, whether of countrymen or townsmen, would split (Wilson and Mafeje 1963: pp. 114–131).

Not only did the town-born align themselves in new ways: cases were found in Langa in which countrymen joined clubs because they had been at the same boarding school as other members, not because they came from the same village, so the old boy network impinged on the home-boy network. But the most significant fact visible in Langa was the occasional choice of clubs for their excellence in the skill they fostered, whether music, rugby, soccer, football, cricket, or some other game. A few cases were recorded in which a countryman left his home-boys, or a townsman his African fellows in the city, to join some other club because of the quality of the music or the skill in a game (Wilson and Mafeje, 1963: pp. 120–122, 129–130).

Soweto, the African town adjoining Johannesburg, has a population of about one million, and many different home languages are spoken in it. Those speaking an Nguni language (Xhosa or Zulu, or Swazi, or a dialect of one of these) are generally mutually intelligible, and for some decades a major cleavage between Nguni and Sotho speakers was reported. At the

Bantu Men's Social Centre in Johannesburg, for example, separate enter-
tainments were organized for Nguni and Sotho in the 1920's because of
repeated clashes between them (Philips, 1938), and more recently the
administration has sought to separate "ethnic" groups by compelling
Xhosa, Zulu, Sotho, and Venda to live in different quarters. But research
on African churches in Soweto, 1969–1971, by Martin West, has shown
that all the churches studied included Sotho and Nguni speakers among
their members, and interpretation from one language to the other was
commonly made at church services. Most of the churches had a country
membership, often larger in one reserve than in another, but in town the
cleavage was not on language or home-boy lines. People selected churches
primarily on account of the activity—the worship and healing they found
there; the personality of the healer or other leader directing the activity;
or personal friendship with a member (West, 1972). In 1973 the activity
centred association, not the home-boy group, is characteristic of sophisticated African townsmen in South Africa.

The Kalela dance bands of the Copperbelt, so well analysed by Clyde
Mitchell in his pioneering study, were home-boy groups as defined here
(Mitchell, 1956: pp. 2–4, 18–22). The use of the term "tribal", however,
obscures the fact that groups based on rural locality are formed, even
though the majority of the population in an urban centre speak the same
language, follow the same customs, and acknowledge the same chief or
chiefs.

In Cape Town, and apparently also on the Copperbelt, divisions depend
not solely on cultural diversity or political affiliation but upon the numbers
from any rural area at the work centre (Wilson, 1964: pp. 1–20). Furthermore, the degree of subdivision depends upon the purpose of the group.
In Cape Town messes are smaller than rugby teams, and rugby teams
smaller than some groups of men co-operating for a major undertaking at
home: but in each case the line of cleavage is rural locality. Already, in
1956 Kalela bands on the Copperbelt, like home-boy teams and choirs in
Cape Town in 1960, could include individuals other than home-boys who
joined on account of personal interest or friendship (Mitchell 1956: p. 4
note 1), and therefore these bands had begun to partake of the characteristics of the activity-centred association. It would be interesting to know how
far this process has gone during the last sixteen years.

In Central and East Africa the home-boy base had a further elaboration
in work centres: languages and chiefdoms were many and links between
men of certain language groups were recognized, though they did not

occupy contiguous areas. Notably those who regarded each other as worthy enemies in war recognized mutual obligations. They were referred to in KiNyakyusa as *abatani* (cross-cousins) and had the quality of "sparring partners". They had fought each other in the past, but at a labour centre a man expected an *untani* to come to his aid in emergency if none of his own people were there; thus Nyakyusa would call on Ngoni, or Ngoni on Nyakyusa. This was a phenomenon of an early period of extension of travel, and movement to town of migrant labourers (Moreau, 1944: pp. 386–400; Mitchell, 1956: pp. 35–42; Wilson, 1957).

Lines of cleavage may therefore be summed up as occurring among kinsmen between "houses" or "wombs"; between territorial groups whose divisions coincided more or less closely with kinship groups; between age-groups; between language groups; between race groups; between conservative and radical; in towns between groups of home-boys; between classes (defined in terms of education, wealth, and manners); and between those concerned with the pursuit of different specialized activities.

Whatever the nature of a quarrel, it is likely to be expressed (at least in part) in terms of the major lines of cleavage of the society in which it occurs. Even domestic conflicts between spouses or siblings, or parents and children may be linked to cleavages of race, class, lineage, language, or religion where these are dominant. Quarrels tend to be expressed in terms of the familiar cleavages, as when in the late nineteenth century, the conflict between radical and traditionalist among the Ngwato was attached to a conflict between kinsmen, rival claimants for the chiefship, and in the 1960's the conflict in Thembuland between those prepared to work within a system of segregated Bantu Authorities and those who rejected such a system was linked to a cleavage a hundred years old between the great house and the right-hand house. Chief Sabata represented the great house, Matanzima (who became Chief Minister of the Bantu Authority in the Transkei) the right-hand house, and formal recognition of his status as an independent chief was part of his reward from the South African government. In the Ciskei in the 1930's domestic conflict was sometimes expressed in terms of a hundred-year old opposition between Xhosa and Mfengu (Hunter, 1969: p. 459). In the same way much of the drama of the 1950's in England turned on the linking of conflicts between husband and wife to class conflict.

Dominant cleavages are *both* the form of expression and a source of exacerbation of conflict. The particular quarrel is magnified by being attached to some far-reaching issue, or differences themselves create friction. The danger of exacerbation was consistently recognized by tribal elders who opposed marriage with those living at a distance even if familiar in language and custom; by the Scottish Presbyterian aunt who warned her nieces (me among them) of the dangers of marrying across national boundaries—"even Americans"—or (much worse) with Catholics; and by sophisticated marriage-guidance councillors who recommend a measure of similarity in background as contributing to a lasting marriage. But though the principle of marriage within a familiar and homogeneous group remains constant, the definition of the group changes. Such change was visible among the Nyakyusa people between 1935 and 1955 as communication developed and the acceptable range of marriage expanded fast; it was visible in Scotland where the aunt in question had no objection to marriage between English and Scottish, though her forbears certainly had; and is apparent in some societies outside Ireland, Spain, and Italy in which a Protestant-Catholic difference may now be felt unimportant, as a barrier to marriage.

Anthropologists have long recognized that cross-cutting ties make for social solidarity, and the coincidence of cleavages for fragmentation. Where age-regiments cut across local and kinship groups central authority was strengthened, as among Zulu and Swazi in the nineteenth century; where churches, or scientific and artistic associations cross national, language, or racial barriers the sharpness of the cleavage on these lines is somewhat diminished, as it was in Europe during two wars, 1914–18 and 1939–45.

Repeatedly—perhaps indeed in every society—men have made forays into history searching for moving symbols with which to rally support for themselves or for some cause, or to maintain a distinction. This is reflected in the creation and celebration of "national" days by various groups in South Africa: "Dingaan's Day" which became the "Day of the Covenant" among the Afrikaners, celebrating an Afrikaner defeat of the Zulu: "Settler's Day" recently established for celebration by English-speaking South Africans; "Fingo Day" celebrated by descendants of Mfengu refugees at Peddie and in schools of the Eastern Cape since 1908; "Ntsi-kana Day" established in 1913 by the Xhosa attending the same schools and distinguishing themselves from Mfengu; "Moshweshwe Day" celebrated by Sotho at these schools; and, in due course, by the celebration of all five days in South African towns (Hunter, 1961: p. 459; Wilson and Mafeje, 1963: pp. 35–37). In each case the suspicion is that the annual observances are organized by political leaders to rally support or maintain old rivalries, rather than a spontaneous celebration. Politicians, seeking support or to maintain separation, dig up old bones, sometimes quite literally. Bones of some Afrikaners who died in the concentration camps of the Afrikaner-British war of 1899–1902 were dug up in 1972, and reburied on the "Day of the Covenant", the ritual being organized by a politician rallying Afrikaner support. Shortly afterwards, during the campaign preceding elections for the Ciskeian Territorial Authority, the cleavage between Xhosa and Mfengu was also revived for party purposes, and the son of a Xhosa candidate expelled from an Mfengu initiation school in Alice district. This happened in January, 1973.

There is a myth that old cleavages never die. It is true that some are deliberately resuscitated over centuries and become virulent, after being dormant for forty years, as in Ireland; it is equally true that cleavages seemingly once equally bitter remain as a matter of display and poetry, rather than of bombs and knifing. The cleavages between Scots and English on their border; between highland and lowland within Scotland; between church and chapel in England may still be discernible but are not a matter of war or persecution, nor do they coincide at all precisely with lines of division between political parties. In Africa since independence one of the surprises has been the maintenance of boundaries of the old colonial territories. These had repeatedly split chiefdoms and language groups, leaving kinsmen who maintained their ties in different states. On the boundaries with which I am most familiar, those between Malawi, Tanzania, and Zambia, Nyakyusa-Ngonde people were split in this way; also Nyamanga, Iwa, Mambwe, Lambya: and on other boundaries there were similar divisions of peoples speaking one language. But in 1955 Nyakyusa men who went to work in Zambia were consciously identifying themselves as "BaTanganyika" in distinction to men from Malawi who spoke their language. It is apparent also that, as men travel, the importance of very local distinctions diminishes and one name or another is extended to include people who previously would neither have used the name themselves nor been accorded it by neighbours. This is plain in the history of England where the Kingdoms of Mercia and Northumbria were no part of the Kingdom of the Angles of Kent, but later were included in "England". It happened also among Nyakyusa, Xhosa, Zulu, and many other peoples. In everyday usage these names are now more inclusive than they were a hundred years ago, *Nyakyusa* being used outside the local area of Rungwe district to include Kukwe, Penja, Saku, Lugulu, and even Ndali and others speaking dialects of the Nyakyusa language; Xhosa being applied outside the Transkei to Thembu, Mpondo, Mpondomise, Bomvana, Bhaca, Xesibe, even Mfengu and others speaking Xhosa in one dialect or another. Thus old cleavages can and do diminish and even disappear: others are repeatedly resuscitated as a rallying cry, and hooked onto some new cause. The anthropologists' job is to analyse this process; to understand why some cleavages disappear and others persist. The first step is to define the major social cleavages at successive periods in time and trace what happens to them.

References

Dugmore, H. H. (1866). In Col. J. Maclean, *Compendium of Kaffir Law and Custom*. Cape Town.

Hammond-Tooke, W. D. (1962). *Bhaca Society*. Oxford University Press, Cape Town.

Hammond-Tooke, D. (1963). "Segmentation and Fission in Cape Nguni Political Units", *Africa*, *35*, 1, see p. 42 above.

Hunter, Monica (1961). *Reaction to Conquest*. Oxford University Press for the International African Institute, London.

Kuper, H. (1947). *An African Aristocracy*. Oxford University Press for the International African Institute, London.

Marwick, M. G. (1965). *Sorcery in Its Social Setting*. Manchester University Press, Manchester.

Mayer, P. (1961). *Townsmen or Tribesmen*. Xhosa in Town series, Oxford University Press, Cape Town.

Mayer, P. and I. (1970). "Socialization by Peers", In Mayer, P. (ed.), *Socialization: the Approach from Social Anthropology*, A S A, pp. 164–174.

Mitchell, J. C. (1956a). *The Yao Village*. Manchester University Press, Manchester. (1956b). *The Kalela Dance*. Rhodes-Livingstone Papers, *27*, pp. 2–4, 18–22.

Moreau, R. E. (1944). "Joking Relationships in Tanganyika", *Africa*, xiv, 7, pp. 386–400.

Philips, R. E. (1938). *The Bantu in the City*. Lovedale Press, Lovedale (South Africa).

Schapera, I. (1943). *Native Land Tenure in the Bechuanaland Protectorate*. Lovedale Press, Lovedale (South Africa).
(1952). *The Ethnic Composition of Tswana Tribes*. L.S.E. Monographs in Social Anthropology, London.
(1963). "Kinship and Politics in Tribal Society", *Journal of the Royal Anthropological Institute*, *93*, 2 pp. 159–173.

Turner, V. W. (1957). *Schism and Continuity in an African Society: Study of Ndembu Village Life*. Manchester University Press, Manchester.

West, M. (1972). *African Independent Churches in Soweto*. Unpublished Ph.D. thesis, University of Cape Town.

Wilson, M. (1951). *Good Company*. Oxford University Press for the International African Institute, London.
(1957). "Joking Relationships in Central Africa. *Man*, LVII, pp. 111.
(1959). *Communal Rituals of the Nyakyusa*. Oxford University Press for the International African Institute, London.

(1963). "Effects on Xhosa and Nyakyusa of Scarcity of Land". In Biebuyk, D. (ed.). *African Agrarian Systems*, pp. 374–388. Oxford University Press for the International African Institute.

Wilson, H. and Mafeje, A. (1963). *Langa*. Oxford University Press, Cape Town.

Wilson, M. (1964). "The Coherence of Groups", In Holleman, J. F. (ed.), *Problems of Transition*, Bailey Bros, London.

Wilson, M. and Thompson, L. (eds), (1969). *Oxford History of South Africa* Vol. I. Clarendon Press, Oxford.

5 | Divine Kingship, Change and Development

Eileen Jensen Krige

This essay is dedicated to Isaac Schapera in admiration of his great contribution to the social anthropology of the peoples of South Africa. Much of his work has been in the field of government and politics. In appreciation of this I attempt here to take a particular example of divine kingship, that of the Lovedu with whom I have had life-long contacts,[1] and to examine it as an on-going process, as it grew and developed in response to the historical challenges of the nineteenth century.

Until 1959, when Modjadji III died a natural death, the political system of the Lovedu met the requirements of Seligman's definition. He limited the term divine king to rulers who, "being held responsible for the right ordering and especially the fertility of the earth and domestic animals, end their lives by being killed or killing themselves . . . often at a fixed period . . ." (Seligman, 1934, pp. 5–6). Lovedu political organization is relatively simple, lacking the elaborate hierarchy of officials and centralized system found in parts of West Africa, as also the carefully regulated series of daily rituals often found in association with the institution. On the other hand, divine kingship among the Lovedu has developed certain characteristics that merit attention and which pose problems, the elucidation of which shows the institution in a perspective that has not been emphasized before.

Let us enumerate briefly some of these special features and the nature of the problems arising from them:

1. I hereby gratefully acknowledge a research fellowship of the International African Institute (1936–8) and grants from the Human Sciences Research Council of South Africa for research during the years 1964–70.

Note: 'v' (as in Lovedu and Varozwi) stands for the bilabial fricative, *passim*.

(1) In contrast to other examples of divine kingship the Lovedu are ruled by a woman and it is important that she should have no husband. This may or may not be significant. But what is arresting is the fact that the first rulers for a long period were males, that in *c*. 1800 a woman succeeded to the throne and that ever since then there have been only female rulers and an expressed preference for queens, Modjadji III having succeeded in preference to her elder uterine brother. (See Fig. 1.) How is this change to be explained? And how could a decision taken in *c*. 1800 have shaped policy over the next century and a half?

(2) A question relating to the succession of women arises out of the state of affairs in Southern Africa during the nineteenth century. This was a period of great political upheaval. The conquests of Shaka the Zulu set into motion wave after wave of marauders: Umzilikazi raided extensively in the Transvaal before coming to rest in Rhodesia, where he established the Matabele kingdom; Sotshangana laid waste Mozambique and drove a continuous stream of refugees into the Eastern Transvaal from 1840 on; Zwangendaba and his Ngoni came to rest as far north as the Great Lakes. The Lovedu were inferior to their neighbours in military strength; they were ruled by a woman. How is it that not only did they survive when neighbouring peoples were broken up and displaced, but that during this period they rose from being an insignificant people to a position of some fame and importance, able to absorb large numbers of refugees into their political system?

(3) There is strong emphasis on the seclusion of the queen; and royal incest is regarded as essential to maintain the purity of blood and powers of the ruler. But the Lovedu also have a remarkable institution whereby the queen marries wives, whom she uses for a variety of political purposes and who play an important part in the integration of the kingdom. This system could not have operated in the same way under male rulers and represents a nineteenth century development of some importance. How did it come to be?

Obviously historical perspective is essential in the examination of the above problems. But how can this be achieved? There is documented history for the nineteenth century and much valuable work has been done by specialists in African history and by archaeologists on the Rhodesian Iron Age and the Kingdom of Monomotapa. But in addition we shall have to rely on oral traditions of the Lovedu and surrounding peoples.[2] Archaeological research in the North-eastern Transvaal has been limited but what evidence there is must be brought into relation with oral tradition. Geographical and climatic factors must be taken into account. All this, however, would be inadequate without the light that analysis of the present-day social and political structure of the Lovedu, of their system of kinship and marriage, of factors making for political integration, can throw on these questions. We shall have to draw on all these sources.

2. In 1937 J. D. Krige and I visited 26 tribes in the Northern Transvaal to obtain information on their traditional history.

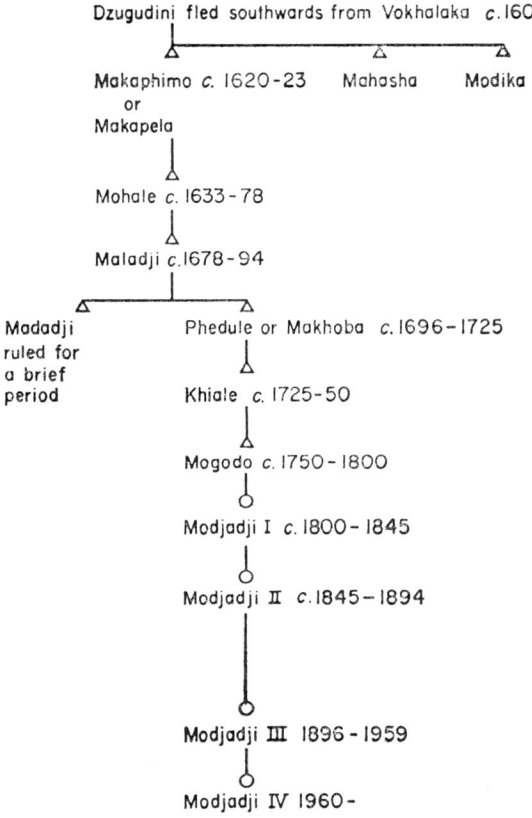

FIG. 1. List of Lovedu chiefs.

There can be no doubt that the ideology underlying Lovedu divine kingship stems from Rhodesia. One of the praises of the royal group, viz. *Varozwi vya Rrantheme*, links them with the Varozwi. According to oral tradition the Lovedu once lived at a place called Maulwe (Maungwe?) which formed part of a kingdom called Monomotapa, ruled by a mambo. The daughter of the mambo, it is said, bore a child by her brother. Forced to flee before the wrath of her father, she left with her infant son and a following, taking with her the rain charms and *ditugula* (sacred amulets). They went south and after many vicissitudes, including the hiving off of a section, the Mamabolo (who do not have a sacred kingship), eventually arrived in the area they occupy today, ousting the aboriginal inhabitants (the Khioka) whom they depict as inferior, with no knowledge of fire. Archaeological evidence in the form of extensive contour terracing in stone, walled ruins reminiscent of those in Rhodesia and ancient beads in present-day religious use resembling those found by Caton-Thompson at Zimbabwe corroborate a Rhodesian origin for the Lovedu.

The Lovedu multiplied, joined by Sotho accretions, but also at times losing sections such as Mamaila and Sekhopo. By the reign of Mogodo, the last male ruler (c. 1750–1800), the Lovedu held loosely the territory between the Great and Little Letaba Rivers. Mogodo is depicted as a ruler of some standing in close diplomatic contact with the Venda, his chief source of iron. He had a number of wives and a bunch of unruly sons who sought to oust their father. Mogodo's kingdom seems to have held together loosely under a system of overrule without adequate mechanisms (other than reliance on the ruler for rain) for political integration. The Lovedu do not appear to have had the practice of placing royal sons in charge of portions of the kingdom, a device used extensively by other South Bantu peoples. Towards the end of Mogodo's reign his kingdom began to disintegrate, probably through lack of integrating machinery. Civil war between two of his headmen was ended only with Venda aid and when, shortly after this Mogodo died, the country was torn in bitter civil strife between Malegudu, his eldest son by his first wife, and Modjadji, who had been given the rain charms and became the next ruler. There is no evidence in oral tradition that male chiefs were ever secluded, nor is there any reference to their ritual death; but power to make rain again and again validated accession to chieftainship in the fierce struggles for succession that took place before the succession of a line of women rulers.

The Change to Female Rulers

The myth that was sometimes recounted in 1936 in explanation of the change to female rulers is to the effect that, deciding his sons were unfit to rule, Mogodo gave the rain-charms to his daughter Modjadji and committed incest with her to ensure the purity of blood of her successor. This may be interesting for its emphasis on the control exercised by a reigning sovereign over the succession by virtue of the rain-charms and for the importance attached to purity of blood of the ruler, but it is an unlikely story because it makes Modjadji II past childbearing age at the time of her succession in the mid-nineteenth century and renders ridiculous the serious attempts to cure her barrenness during the early decades of her reign.

The royal family itself, always very secretive about the biological parentage of its rulers (the father of a queen is not known, says the proverb) considers A, half-brother of Modjadji I, to have been the father of Modjadji II and quotes in support the proverb A *ke kheolo khe gwa nthwa*—A is the antheap whence comes the ant (referring to the queen). The royal genealogy is given in Fig. 3 p. 70.

A more adequate explanation than that attributing the change in succession to the arbitrary decision of one person can be found in present-day social structure and everyday rules of succession. There is in Lovedu society a close link and complementarity between uterine brother and sister, especially where the brother has used his sister's bridewealth for his own marriage. In the case of a district headman or kraal head the eldest son of the chief wife will succeed his father as political head, while his sister is ritual head responsible for sacrifice and offering and exercising some control over the brother's household (Krige, E. J., 1964: pp. 177, 192). If there is no son in the chief house of a district head the daughter succeeds as headman in preference to any son of another house and will rule in her own right until her death. But, and this is where the situation differs from the case of the queen, her children cannot succeed to the position. She must raise an heir by marrying a woman with the property of her mother's "house" and appointing a genitor. Just as a male ruler relies on his sister in ritual matters, so a woman ruler requires the help of a male relative for trying court-cases and other duties and activities that cannot be carried out by a woman. He acts in a rather menial capacity as her *modzeta* or assistant. Where a woman of royal blood or a *motanoni* (wife) of the queen is made head of a new district she is always given a husband as well. In this case a different principle of succession comes into operation and her own children (who belong to her husband's family) usually succeed her as rulers.

That a female should have ascended the throne, then, is not strange or revolutionary in a Lovedu context. That a preference should have developed for female rulers needs explanation. Among the Khaha who told us in 1934 that their first woman ruler in *c.* 1829 succeeded because of the success of Modjadji I, there have been both male and female rulers since that time (Jaques, A. A., 1934: p. 372).

The rules of succession to chieftainship among the Lovedu have always been uncertain. During the time of male chiefs, sons succeeded fathers but there was no stated principle in favour of any one "house" nor any means of publicly identifying the chief or tribal wife, as among Tswana, by a tribal levy for her bridewealth. The general rule among the Lovedu is that a man's chief wife is his mother's uterine brother's daughter or, failing her, the wife first married with cattle belonging to the father. For succession to chieftainship three important criteria came to be used, viz., knowledge and possession of the rainmaking charms (this gave the reigning chief some control over the succession); purity of blood (which gave the chief's counsellors or royal advisors some say over who should succeed) and, lastly, divine ratification by the yielding of the door of a special hut, in which the previous ruler had died, to the rightful heir (here, too, the counsellors controlled the situation). What this amounted to in practice is that in all except one case, that of Modjadji III, the daughter of the queen by a half-brother has succeeded (see Fig. 3). But this has been kept a closely-guarded secret, and was unknown to anyone but a few of the queen's closest relatives. The Lovedu have never had any public installation ceremonies in connection with the rulers, such as have been reported for divine kings in other parts of Africa. Possession of the rain-charms which contain bodily remains taken from previous chiefs, purity of blood and divine ratification by the opening of the door are sufficient to ensure that the successor has all the qualities necessary in the divine king.

Some clue to the preference that developed for female rulers may be obtained by examining the next problem that has been posed. At the end of Mogodo's reign the Lovedu kingdom was falling to pieces. With a woman as its ruler and in the absence of a strong army or military prowess, how did the Lovedu escape the fate of their uprooted and defeated neighbours?

There is no doubt that geographical factors played an important part, by making the Lovedu area less attractive to cattle-keeping marauders than many other parts of the country. The Lovedu occupied a mountainous, thickly-wooded area, ridden with malaria and other diseases, liable to become a morass in the rainy season. Lovedu military strategy, successfully employed even against Whites on a number of occasions, lay in luring the enemy deep into their country, hiding in the dense forests and waiting for the rains, disease and horse-sickness to do the rest (Dicke, B. H., 1936).

But there were other important operating factors. Modjadji's weakness as a woman seems to have become a source of strength in the turbulent conditions of the nineteenth century. "A woman does not fight", the Lovedu maintained, and set out to rely on diplomacy and strategy. But if Modjadji did not fight with ordinary weapons she certainly did so with ritual weapons. Her reputed power to withhold rain from her enemies made her a dangerous foe. She was believed to control also locusts and to be able to kill foreign emissaries by her medicines. It also came to be thought she was immortal, since all rulers went by the name Modjadji.

If these ritual weapons added to her power, the mystery that began to surround her intensified their effects. In the reign of Modjadji we hear for the first time of the seclusion of the ruler. Perhaps Lovedu rulers had been secluded before; but there is no doubt that intensified precautions in guarding their rain-making queens became necessary in the nineteenth century. Soon everything surrounding the queen became enshrouded in secrecy. Secrecy seems to have been a valuable political device enabling a small group like the Lovedu to control a large, heterogeneous population. It was also used later as a weapon of defence against administrative interference by the European. How the aura of mystery surrounding Modjadji appeared to her contemporary enemies can be gauged from Bryant's description of her in his *Olden Times in Zululand and Natal.* "She was reputed . . . queen of the locusts . . . one of her most dreaded forms of retaliation was the launching of a plague on the crops of her victims. This dramatic penalty . . . she would vary with deluge and drought. She had four breasts wherefore among the Zulu she was generally known as *Mabelemane*, Queen Four-Breasts . . . She was the most extraordinary, most powerful, most mysterious female of her time—if indeed, as was asserted, she was not eternal in all South Africa". (Bryant, 1965, p. 210).

A mysterious female ruler certainly paid dividends in the circumstances of nineteenth century South Africa and we see here perhaps one of the most important answers to the question why there developed such a marked preference for queens. The weapons Modjadji was reputed to use held great terrors for people lacking the scientific outlook of a technological age. Queens were an undoubted success.

Modjadji I must have been a remarkable woman to make the impact she did. She came to the throne in *c.* 1800, yet by 1819 she had already become a legend, and was reputed to have caused the death of Zwide, chief of the Ndwandwe, after he had conquered the Pedi (Bryant 1965, p. 211). Part of her praises refer to her lack of a husband. She is depicted as "sleeping on the road (like a prostitute), a widow with no one to look after her". Now it may well be that, like Elizabeth I of England, she remained without a husband by choice. But there was a precedent among the Rozwi of Quiteve for a celibate female ruler (Alpers, E. A., 1970: p. 211). This was so obviously of advantage to the body of royal male relatives who, with a woman on the throne, were responsible for the running of the courts and for administrative matters that it is easy to see how it could become a tradition to be perpetuated, if indeed it was not initiated by them in the first place. There grew up, in fact, a neat balance of power between the queen and her *vakololo* (royal counsellors) and policy-making became a delicate interplay between the queen, her chief counsellor (usually a brother or mother's brother or his son) and the other *vakololo* who jockeyed with each other for influence and position. Here was a field of advancement open to any royal relative at the capital with ability and ambition. There was no formal council; there were no formal meetings. The queen consulted informally with her chief counsellor and those of the *vakololo* whom she found useful and wise. In theory the queen was all-powerful; in practice most of the everyday decisions were made by her counsellors in consultation with the queen and with each other. The queen was never blamed for anything. She could do no wrong. When mistakes were made they were always attributed to the counsellors and this is true even today. Yet the queen was no figure-head. All matters were reported to her, no action was taken without her consent. She controlled all matters affecting her "wives" and her relatives. She dealt with her headmen through their representatives at court. Modjadji I and II are reputed to have put to death chief counsellors who fell out of favour and there is evidence that they exercised a good deal more power than later queens. But there grew up during the reigns of the queens, especially that of Modjadji III who succeeded in 1896, a remarkable degree of co-operation between the queen and her counsellors. As Modjadji III grew older her young and educated male relatives took over more and more responsibility for matters connected with European administration. In a system like this there could be no room for a husband who might seize power into his own hands.

Development of Integrating Machinery

Mogodo's kingdom had fallen to pieces through lack of integrating machinery. What enabled Modjadji to build up a strong kingdom? By what mechanism was the kingdom able to absorb the large numbers of foreigners that sought refuge in her country?

The change-over to women rulers had some far-reaching effects. Certain institutions became modified or developed a twist to make them more compatible with the changed circumstances. One of these was connected with the wives of the ruler. It is a widespread custom among many South Bantu people for important or influential subjects to send a daughter to the chief. The Zulu king had a large harem and placed many of his wives in the charge of female relatives who presided over military kraals. It was also a widespread practice during the nineteenth century for foreign chiefs to present girls, generally those captured in war, as tribute to a more powerful neighbour. A harem does not carry the same prestige and signi-ficance for a woman ruler as for a man and Modjadji I began to use her wives in a manner different from that of her predecessors. She capitalized upon the system, turning it into a continuing source of economic benefit to the monarchy and developed a technique whereby such women could become part of the political machinery. How does this function?

Vatanoni, as wives of the queen are designated, are expected to remain chaste until given permission to have a child, whereupon they are given their own hut, a genitor is appointed (usually a royal relative) and they bear children to the queen. These children call the queen father and are con-sidered to be brothers and sisters of the queen's own biological children. Such children are *vakololo*—royal family. No girl of Shangana-Tsonga origin could be a *motanoni*. *Vatanoni* are no expense to the queen. They produce food (from fields allocated to them) for their children and for their "husband", the queen (a plate of food from every meal cooked is sent to the queen as to a husband). All their other needs in the way of clothes, the building of huts, medical expenses, etc. are provided for by their own families or obtained from lovers.

Wives of the queen who are seduced (and these are by far the majority) are, after having been sent home to bear the first child as are all *vatanoni*, brought back by their father with pardon-beer and the offer of a replace-ment in the form of a sister or brother's daughter, sometimes as yet unborn. The seduced *motanoni* is then immediately given to a royal rela-tive or to some client or favourite of the queen. No bridewealth passes but it is expected that a daughter of the *motanoni* will be sent back to the queen to replace her mother. An interesting development was the fact that, following the pattern of cross-cousin marriage, it became obligatory also for the brother's daughter of every *motanoni* to follow her *rakhadi* (father's sister) in marriage to the queen. Thus, in Fig. 2, B follows A, E follows B, D follows C. In this way the queen and her successors are assured of a continuing stream of wives down the generations, each one being followed by her brother's daughter and, if married to a client of the queen, also by her own daughter and son's daughter, as in the diagram (p. 64) where A is followed by B, C and D.

Girls sent from foreign tribes were never followed by others in the manner described above except in a few cases of neighbouring peoples who have close links with the Lovedu.

It is impossible to over-estimate the value of the *vatanoni* system for the development of the Lovedu kingdom. Here was an integrating principle

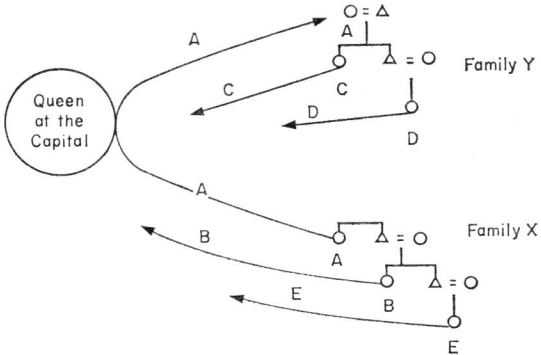

FIG. 2. Reallocation and succession of the queen's *vatanoni*.

that had been lacking in Mogodo's time when the kingdom seemed to be breaking up. *Vatanoni* are the means of establishing kinship links, not only between the queen and the family of the *motanoni* but also between that of the latter and the family of the husband to whom she is given. In this way the whole kingdom becomes criss-crossed with affinal links. Kinship links with the queen afforded opportunities to non-royals to gain prestige surpassing that of many members of the royal group itself. Social mobility was greatly increased by the use made of *vatanoni* which has modified the strongly endogamous tendencies of the royal group. The Lovedu royal group thus never became a closed group characterized by prestige and superior wealth as did the Tutsi in Ruanda.

In addition to creating kinship links, the gift of a *motanoni* sets up a strong patron-client relationship between the queen and those of her non-royal subjects that are given wives, which is particularly important in the case of headmen of districts. The *vatanoni* system also enables the queen to reinforce her blood ties with her own kin by affinal links: by giving a *motanoni* to a close relative the queen can create a supportive relationship that would make him a ready ally in family quarrels over appointments and policies. This is especially important today when the queen's relationships with her kin are not what they ought to be.

There are many other uses to which *vatanoni* are put. The queen relies on *vatanoni* for providing wives for those of her sons-by-*vatanoni* who lack sisters, whose bridewealth they can use for their own marriage. The *vatanoni* system enables the queen to reward those who serve her. Modjadji II was particularly liberal in giving to royal doctors and servants of various kinds a *motanoni* and a small area to rule.

The daughter sent by a headman must always come from the chief house. She will thus hold the position of *khadi* or priestess of the family, responsible for guiding its affairs and, more especially, for deciding (in consultation with others) on the successor to any vacancy. She is therefore an important channel of communication, able to keep the queen informed on all matters of importance to her family and the area it controls. The queen is also able through her to manipulate matters on occasion, so that the family may decide on the candidate whom she favours. Though succession to headmanship is hereditary, the queen usually merely ratifying the decision come to by the family, there is room for a good deal of manipulation, especially in cases of disputed succession.

It must not be thought that the *vatanoni* system was by any means the only mechanism for integration or the only channel of communication by means of which the interests and desires of subjects could be brought to the rulers. Every district traditionally has one of the royal relatives who lives in or near the capital as its representative or mother-at-court, through whom its cases are brought on appeal and through whom representations can be made or complaints lodged. Since the position is hereditary and the mother-at-court also has to house and feed litigants, the institution works on a highly personal level. Serving as messengers (*maharola*) both to mothers-at-court and to the queen is a host of young royals living in and around the capital who are paid "for their feet", i.e. for each journey undertaken, by the people to whom they convey messages. They are in close communication with the areas they serve, they get to know conditions there and come into touch with the common people. They are sometimes called upon to give evidence in court, e.g. about the extent of damage to crops in a particular case; they are in constant attendance at court and receive a training in legal procedure. They are the men who later on will play a responsible role in deciding cases at the capital and perhaps also in conducting affairs of state. Through the system of mothers-at-court and royal messengers many members of the royal lineage have a source of income from outside areas. Thus it is that they, as well as the queen, are maintained to some extent by the people they serve and rule. Mothers-at-court are known in other South Bantu societies but the system among the Lovedu appears to have been elaborated, developed and extended as the kingdom expanded and foreign elements had to be absorbed.

Lovedu government is not highly centralized. Headmen are left to exercise a great deal of freedom in conducting the affairs of their areas. The ordinary man has access to the central government through his right of appeal to the queen's court. But the central government never had any machinery for enforcing its judgments.

The *motanoni* system has clearly been put to a variety of uses. The very presence of the queen's *vatanoni* adds to the interest of life at the capital and acts as an incentive to her male relatives to remain there to protect and assist her. The institution is adaptable, ever being modified to meet changing conditions. In the arrangements made for an heir to Modjadji II who was barren it was the *vatanoni* system that was resorted to. Kesetwane, daughter of Leakhale, who was a sister of Modjadji II by virtue of being the daughter of a *motanoni* of Modjadji I, was chosen as successor (see Fig. 3). Modjadji II had many brothers and sisters by *vatanoni* of her mother. But Leakhale was the one whose daughter was reckoned to be biologically of the purest royal descent. (For a discussion of Lovedu succession see Appendix.)

The Modern Situation

Many of the features of the divine kingship of the Lovedu have remained unchanged. The rainmaking of the queen goes on as of old and has even been intensified by the drought that marked the first decade of the new queen's reign (1960–70). The seclusion of the queen, though not as strict as before, nevertheless makes it impossible for her to serve in person on the Tribal and Territorial Authorities[3] that have been established. She even sits, hidden from view, in a roughly constructed temporary enclosure surrounded by female attendants and visited only by those privileged to enter, when she goes to cider parties at the two or three kraals which the ruler is by tradition allowed to visit.

The accession of Modjadji IV has brought to the fore a grave problem of a type that was successfully handled in the past but is difficult to solve under a White administration, viz. the threat to the position of the royal family of the queen's paramour. The trouble began in the 1930's when the young heir, refusing to cohabit with the royal seedraiser chosen for her, ran away with a commoner and lived with him just outside the tribal boundaries. On the death of Modjadji III the heir was asked to come and rule, which she agreed to do on condition that she could choose her own chief counsellor, and that her paramour be allowed to visit her at the capital. This was agreed to on condition that he did not interfere in political matters. From the outset the new queen, mistrusting her own relatives, ruled with the advice, not so much of her counsellors but of her paramour. A fierce

3. In 1973 the Territorial Authority became Lebowe Legislative Assembly.

struggle for power, the implications of which are too complex to be discussed here has developed between, on the one hand the queen, her paramour and children and, on the other, the *vakololo*, her closest royal relatives. But the latter are not completely united because of the queen's undefined prerogatives in regard to appointments to office and her use of both these powers and the *vatanoni* system in creating "patron-client" relationships with members of the royal family as well as with commoners. The question of succession complicates the issue as the queen's children are not of pure royal blood.

Salient Aspects of the Divine Kingship of the Lovedu

This brief analysis of political change in the nineteenth century among the Lovedu shows divine kingship to have been a flexible system, modified by circumstances as social and political conditions dictated. In a period of just over a hundred years new political machinery developed out of existing institutions in response to the challenge of historical events and in a concatenation of circumstances in which the accession of a woman to the throne seems to have played a not unimportant part.

If one hunts for "traits" it is possible to trace sporadic occurrences in Monomotapa of a number of what later became the most characteristic features of the divine kingship of the Lovedu. In addition to the evidence of ritual suicide in Monomotapa it is said, "The Teve customarily allowed female chiefs to rule so long as they remained celibate" (Alpers, E. A., 1970: p. 211). Again, "at least twice a mambo was chosen on the basis of a purification test. Mwene Mutapa II Matope Nyanyehwe, is remembered in tradition as having secured the throne for himself over his numerous elder brothers by performing ritual intercourse with his sister . . ." (Ibid, p. 207). But these never appear to have developed into anything like the consistent and integrated pattern found among the Lovedu. There are also many features of the Lovedu system not found in Monomotapa. Succession to the throne in Monomotapa was collateral, eventually reverting to the son of the eldest brother, not lineal as among Lovedu; military power was important in Monomotapa and there seems to have been nothing there to correspond to the use made of royal *vatanoni* by the Lovedu.

The close relationship between the political system and the social structure is a very remarkable feature of Lovedu organization. The relation of the queen to her *vakololo* or counsellors is of much the same pattern as that between uterine sister and brother in everyday life, the sister having ritual functions as priestess of the family, together with some control over

her brother's household, while the brother is head of the family, responsible, if he is a headman, for holding court and dealing with political
matters. The use of the *vatanoni* system in choosing a successor to Modjadji II was patterned on the manner of raising a male heir when a woman
rules a district in her own right because there is no male. The *motanoni*
system also operates on the lines of ordinary cross-cousin marriage. And
there are many other parallels. A remarkable aspect of the *motanoni*
system is the short period of time in which it developed.

Basic to the divine kingship of the Lovedu, forming a matrix in which it
has grown and developed, is an ideology or *weltanschauung* in which it is
believed that control over nature can come to reside in a particular person,
who is able to manipulate his powers of control for the benefit of all. This
is true for divine kingship in general. A ruler with such powers proved to
be a protection against their enemies for the Lovedu in the nineteenth
century, but it was a protection only against enemies with the same outlook
and ideology. It did not operate with success when the European came on
the scene. That such an ideology may be so firmly held that the divine king
himself is able to accept, and identify himself with, the necessity for his
own ritual suicide after a certain fixed period is suggested by the fact that,
about 1936 Bethuel P., a close relative and confidant of Modjadji III, a
man who was a pillar of the Lutheran church and had cut himself off from
tribal politics, came to Rev. Krause at Medingen Mission Station, saying
the queen felt it was time for her to "disappear".[4] He wanted advice on what
he could say to her. Rev. Krause told Bethuel, "You, on your own, can say
the time for such things has passed and besides the Gospel does not agree
with" this kind of action. Later Bethuel returned to tell Rev. Krause that
the queen had given up the thought. (W. T. Krause, 1962). Evans-Pritchard
has a different view on this topic (1948: pp. 20; 33–38).

For security, for rain, for fertility of crops and animals, men are prepared
to submit to control and willingly give their loyalty. A ritual leader makes
for integration even in acephalous societies and a divine king or a ruling
priesthood can be a powerful instrument for political domination. Divine
kingship has been used again and again in Africa by a numerically small
but culturally superior group for gaining control over people far exceeding
them in number, e.g. Tutsi of Ruanda, Nyakyusa. Divine kingship may be
combined with military strength and economic wealth, but sometimes
domination can be achieved without them, as in the case of the Lovedu.
That the Lovedu royal group has never been able to become a strong

---

4. By ritual suicide in the form of a poisonous draught.

aristocracy with wealth, prestige, power and recognition for all its members is due largely to the absence of strong corporate lineages, the emphasis on, and importance of, bilateral kinship in everyday life, as well as other factors, such as social mobility, that have already been discussed.

In summary it may be said that a felicitous change to female rulers around whose ritual powers an atmosphere of awe and mystery developed, which evoked fear in their more strongly patrilineal enemies, enabled the Lovedu to survive the troublous nineteenth century and to attract foreign accretions whose absorption was made possible by new mechanisms for political integration that grew out of existing institutions. A neat balance of power developed between the queen, responsible for the control of nature for the welfare of her people but wielding a good deal of political power as well, and, on the other hand, her secular arm, the *vakololo*, responsible for the day-to-day activities of law and government. There was close co-operation, consultation and identity of interests between them. A certain degree of social mobility provided opportunities for non-royals to gain prestige and the absence of strong corporate lineages and the operation of the *motanoni* system in the placement of headmen prevented the development of localized dynasties over which the ruler had no control. New mechanisms for succession, evolved after the accession of women rulers, kept the Lovedu people free from succession disputes for a period of over 150 years. (Contrast Tswana dynastic disputes, Schapera, 1963: p. 161.)

These developments indicate the rapidity with which fundamental changes can take place and new institutions come into being even in traditionally-orientated societies. There is an indication that some of these changes worked towards, rather than away from, what are called the "traits" of divine kingship. The seclusion and secrecy surrounding the queen if they did not develop anew, were at any rate greatly enhanced by the prevailing conditions of the nineteenth century. It is impossible to gauge to what extent ritual suicide could have survived in the unsettled conditions of a major migration of a small and weak group or why it is not found among later arrivals from Rhodesia such as the Venda whose concepts of chieftainship and whose social arrangements show similarities to those of the Lovedu. Perhaps there are features latent in the ideology underlying divine kingship which require a certain concatenation of circumstances to bring them into operation.

Appendix: Succession to Divine Kingship among the Lovedu

When the rulers of the Lovedu were men, succession was from father to

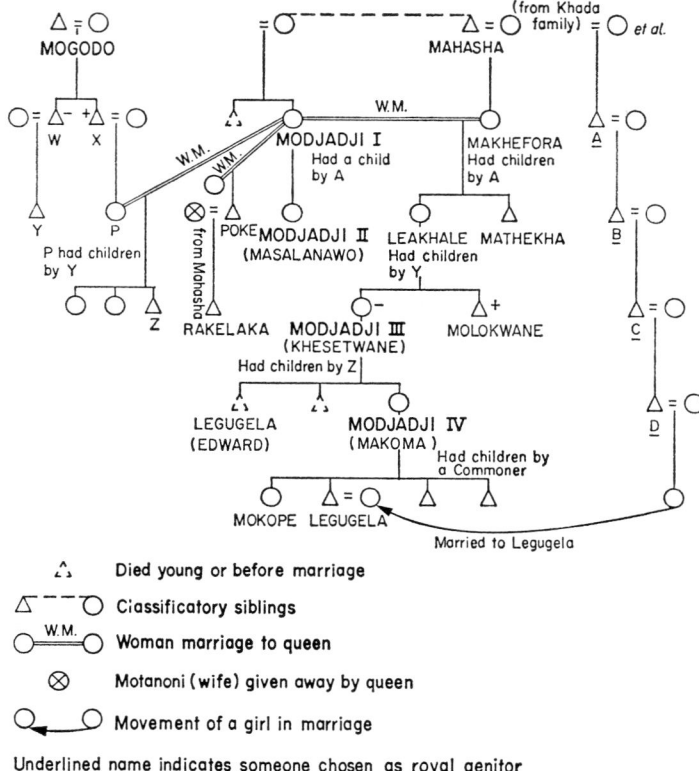

FIG. 3. Genealogy of Lovedu queens and their genitors.[5]

son; but if a king was unable to make rain he was liable to be ousted by a rival. In the case of queens there came to be great emphasis on purity of blood, which is curious in view of the extent to which biological parentage is ignored in everyday life, where an heir can be raised by woman-marriage and the child of an unmarried woman is not only considered as the child of the man who gives bride-price for her, but succeeds its sociological father to a position of headmanship if its mother is chief wife. The biological parentage of the Lovedu queens and of the children of *vatanoni* of the queen was always a closely-guarded secret. Anyone divulging the parentage of the queen or her children was liable to be put to death. Even today it is

5. Since the names of genitors of members of the royal family are regarded as royal secrets I have refrained from using them here. The relationships indicated in the genealogy in this Figure are, however, correct and illustrate the principles and facts of the succession.

virtually impossible to get the true facts because most people do not know them and the few that still do know do not wish to give the correct information.

The genealogy given in Fig. 3 indicates that in all but one case (that of Modjadji III), the daughter of the queen has succeeded to the throne. The genitor in each of these cases was a half-brother of the queen (both sociologically and biologically): Modjadji II was begotten by A, half-brother of Modjadji I; Modjadji IV was fathered by Z, son of *motanoni* P, daughter of Y. Z is said to have been the personal choice of Modjadji III. C had been chosen as genitor but the queen went her own way and, with Whites in control, could not be forced to conform. Z, as son of a *motanoni*, was a brother (sociological) to Modjadji III. What she probably did not know was that he was also her biological half-brother, both Z and Modjadji III having been fathered by Y, son of W, brother of X. When Makoma, daughter of Modjadji III came of age in *c.* 1932 the chief counsellors, looking to the house of A, chose D as genitor; but Makoma refused to fall into line with traditional requirements.

Different plans had to be made for succession in the case of Modjadji II, who was barren. Here the choice of an heir fell upon Khesetwane, daughter of Leakhale, a sister of Modjadji II by virtue of the fact that Leakhale's mother, Makhefora, had been a *motanoni* of Modjadji I. Makhefora was a mother's classificatory brother's daughter of Modjadji I and came from the Mahasha branch of the royal group. (When Modjadji I died, Leakhale, following her mother, became a *motanoni* of her sister Modjadji II.) Leakhale and Modjadji II, besides being sociological sisters, were also biological sisters, both having been fathered by A (see Fig. 3). Both were also of Mahasha descent, Leakhale through her mother's father, Modjadji II through her mother's mother. Khesetwane had an elder uterine brother, Molokwane, but he is said to have been passed over because of a physical defect—weak ankles. He became in due course chief counsellor to his sister and died in *c.* 1932.

Modjadji II had many sisters and brothers besides Leakhale by *vatanoni* of her mother. One of them was Poke, her chief counsellor, son of a *motanoni* who is said by some to have been of Khaha royal descent (see Fig. 3). Who Poke's biological father was no one has ever been able to tell me, but he must have been a close relative of the queen's for Poke to have been her chief counsellor. Poke's son, Rakelaka, was a claimant to the throne of Modjadji II. His mother was a *motanoni* (of Modjadji II) of Mahasha descent who had been given to Poke, his father. But the door did not yield to Rakelaka, whether because of his sex or because his blood was not quite as pure as that of Modjadji III or because of lack of support among the chief counsellors, or for other reasons, is difficult to say. (His father, Poke, had died shortly before Modjadji II.) Rakelaka took refuge in the Christian village near the capital but died shortly after, probably from unnatural causes, it is said.

When speaking of the succession of Modjadji III the Lovedu always stress the fact that her mother, Leakhale, was a sister of the queen, not that Leakhale's mother, Makhefora, was a *motanoni* of the queen, nor that Leakhale herself was also a *motanoni* and her daughter an heir on that account. It is as if Modjadji III's distinctness from the children of other *vatanoni* of Modjadji II (who were not also her sisters at the same time) needed to be stressed. Modjadji I and II had a number of wives (*vatanoni*) from the Mahasha family.

A royal genealogy of the Khaha, where women could also succeed to the throne, indicates a situation somewhat different from that of the Lovedu, though Khaha chiefs were said to "receive from Modjadji investiture and the magical power attached to the position he or she occupies" (Jaques, A. A., 1934: p. 377). Here both men and women have succeeded in recent times to the throne and though it is said that the successor to a woman ruler should be her daughter (as among the Lovedu), this is not what has happened in practice. The successor to the first woman ruler, according to Jaques, was the son born to her chief wife (her mother's brother's daughter) by a genitor distantly related to the queen. It is not clear whether the queen was barren or not but this seems likely. The second woman to rule in her own right (there had been a woman regent) was already married when her brother died and the position became vacant. To avoid having to produce her successor by a chosen genitor, she preferred to act as regent to her younger uterine brother.

There are clearly two possibilities in choosing a successor to a woman ruler among the Khaha—her own child, male or female, if she has one by a suitable genitor or, failing her own child, the eldest child by a suitable genitor of the chief wife of the queen. There is not among the Khaha the same emphasis on royal incest and close inbreeding for the purity of the blood of the successor to the throne as among Lovedu, nor the Lovedu preference for female rulers.

References

Abraham, D. P. (1961). "Maramuca: An exercise in the combined use of Portuguese records and oral tradition." *Journal of African History* Vol. II, No. 2, 211–214.

(1964). "Ethno-history of the empire of Mutapa." In (eds), Vansina, J., Mauny, R. and Thomas, L. V. *The Historian in Tropical Africa*. Oxford.

Alpers, E. A. (1970). Dynasties of the Mutapa-Rozwi Complex. *Journal of African History* Vol. II, 203–219.

Beattie, J. H. M. (1959). "Rituals of Nyoro kingship." *Africa*, 29, 134–135.

(1959). "Checks on the abuse of power in some African states." *Sociologicus*, 2, 97–115.

(1960). *Bunyoro, an African Kingdom*. Holt, Rinehart and Winston, New York.

Bradbury, R. E. (1967). "The kingdom of Benin." In Forde, Daryl and Kaberry (eds), *West African Kingdoms in the Nineteenth Century*. P. M. Oxford University Press, London.

Bryant, A. T. (1965). *Olden Times in Zululand and Natal*. Struik, Cape Town. First published Longmans Green and Co., London, 1929.

Dicke, B. H. (1936). *The Bush Speaks*. Shuter and Shooter, Pietermaritzburg.

Evans-Pritchard, E. E. (1948). *The Divine Kingship of Shilluk of the Nilotic Sudan*. The Frazer Lecture 1948. Cambridge University Press, London.

Fagan, B. M. (1965). *Southern Africa during the Iron Age*. Thames and Hudson, London.

Jaques, A. A. (1934). "Genealogy of Male and Female chiefs of a Sotho Tribe." *Bantu Studies*, Vol. VIII, No. 4, 377–382.

Krause, W. T. (1962). Written communication regarding Queen Modjadji III.

Krige, E. J. (1964). Property, cross-cousin marriage and the family cycle among the Lovedu. In Gray, R. F. and Gulliver, P. H. (eds) *The Family Estate in Africa*. Routledge and Kegan Paul, London.

(1974) "Woman-marriage with special reference to the Lovedu—its significance for the definition of marriage". *Africa*, 44, 11–37.

Krige, J. D. (1937). Traditional origins and Tribal Relationships of the Sotho of the Northern Transvaal. *Bantu Studies*, Vol. XI, 321–356.

Krige, E. J. and Krige, J. D. (1945). *The Realm of a Rain Queen*. Oxford University Press, London.

(1954). The Lovedu of the Transvaal. In Forde, Daryll, (ed.), *African Worlds*. Oxford University Press, London.

Lienhardt, G. (1951). "The Shilluk of the Upper Nile." In Forde, Daryll, (eds.) *African Worlds*. Oxford University Press, London.

Lloyd, P. C. (1954). The traditional political system of the Yoruba. *Southwestern Journal of Anthropology*, 10, 366–384.

(1960). Sacred Kingship and Government among the Yoruba. *Africa*, 30, 221–234.

(1965). The political structure of African kingdoms: an explanatory model. In Banton, M. (ed.), *Political Systems and the Distribution of Power*. A. S. A. monographs. Tavistock, London.

Meek, C. K. (1931). *A Sudanese Kingdom*. Kegan Paul, London. Trench, Trübner.

Morton-Williams, P. (1967). "The Yoruba kingdom in Oyo." In Forde, Daryll and Kaberry, P. (eds) *West African Kingdoms in the Nineteenth Century*. Oxford University Press, London.

Richards, A. I. (1940). "The political system of the Bemba tribe." In Fortes, M. and Evans-Pritchard, E. E. (eds). Oxford University Press, London.

(1960). "Social mechanisms for the transfer of political rights in some African tribes." *J. R. Anthrop. Inst.* 90, 175–190.

(1961). "African kings and their royal relatives." *J. R. Anthrop. Inst.* 91, 135–150.

(1968). "Keeping the king divine." *Proceedings of the Royal Anthropological Institute of Great Britain and Ireland.*

Roscoe, J. (1911). *The Baganda.* London.

(1923a). *The Bakitara or Banyoro.* Cambridge University Press, London.

(1923b). *The Banyankole.* Cambridge University Press, London.

Schapera, I. (1956). *Government and Politics in Tribal Societies.* Watts, London.

(1963). Kinship and Politics in Tswana History. *Journal of the Royal Anthropological Institute,* 93, 159–173.

Seligman, C. G. (1934). *Egypt and Negro Africa: A Study in Divine Kingship.* Routledge and Kegan Paul, London.

Summers, R. (1961). The Southern Rhodesian Iron Age. *Journal of African History,* II, 1–14.

Theal, G. M. (1907–10). *History and Ethnography of Africa before 1795.* 3 Vols. London.

Vansina, J. (1962). "A Comparison of African Kingdoms." *Africa,* 32, 324–335.

Wilson, G. (1939). *The Constitution of the Ngonde. (Rhodes-Livingstone Paper 3).* Rhodes-Livingstone Institute, Livingstone.

Wilson, M. (1959). *Divine Kings and the Breath of Men.* Cambridge University Press, London.

Young, M. W. (1966). "The divine kingship of the Jukun: a re-evaluation of some theories." *Africa,* Vol. 36, 135–152.

6 | Some Problems of Evidence in Shona Tribal Law

J. F. Holleman

By Way of Introduction

This essay is a tribute to thirty years of close association with Isaac Schapera, first as his student and later as his colleague and friend. My paper lies in the field of African customary law. It is not a topic on which Schapera himself has written extensively, though into the little space he devotes to it specifically in his classic *Handbook of Tswana Law and Custom* (1938, pp. 288–289) he packs, as usual, an impressive amount of information. Unlike him I shall not "resist the temptation to deal with what may be termed the 'spirit' as opposed to the 'letter' of the law" (ibid, p. xi)—which will not surprise him. But I do keep in mind some of his remarks dropped in the course of our conversations: for example—on omissions in much anthropological writings: "Even in some of the best-known studies, tribal life is described as if there had been no Europeans about the place, missionaries, government officials, traders, who for years and years must have influenced the people . . ."—on the use of tokens and other visible means of "evidence" in tribal practice: "If you suggest that the Tswana may actually be using these things as often as your Shona do. . . . They don't, at least I don't think so."

I shall therefore be writing about some aspects of evidence in the practice of Shona law. I shall be more concerned with the "spirit" than with the "letter" of the law, in that I am more interested in the actual assessment of the probative weight of certain kinds of evidence than in trying to present anything like a systematic treatise purporting to reflect the Shona "law of evidence". And I hope to show how a few customary means of juridical proof, carrying exceptional weight in traditional practice, have either lost or are losing their probative value as the result of "European influence" generally, and the operation of European courts of law in particular.

"Admissibility" and "Relevancy"

After their extensive examination of the great amount of writing on African customary law, Cotran and Rubin (1970: I, p. 83) observe that "Evidence is, in general, one of those topics . . . which has not been studied in very great detail or very systematically." Several reasons account for this. Much information lies scattered in descriptions and analyses of topics which did receive systematic treatment (marriage, land law, various wrongs, specific transactions, and so on). Moreover, because the importance of evidence becomes most obvious in situations of dispute and adjudication, it is understandable that the topic receives more specific attention as an integral aspect of judicial procedure, for "it would be extremely difficult—if not impossible—to follow the description of a trial unless some indication of the way in which evidence is led was included" (ibid, p. 47). But here also lies probably the main obstacle to any attempt to abstract from African judicial practice (however well organized its procedural aspects may be) anything like the systematically organized body of carefully defined *and compelling* rules which govern the use of evidence in most Western courts of law. There is of course nothing derogatory in this, for it is the logical consequence of some well-testified characteristics of African practice. As regards *causa*, for instance —the central issue in any judicial proceedings anywhere—African courts are on the whole guided by much broader and more flexible conceptions than our prescribed and pre-selective use of (written) pleadings would permit. This is directly related to another frequently observed tendency: a disposition to reconcile litigants. Now Gluckman has rightly argued (1955: pp. 77–78) that reconciliation (which had impressed so many observers) is neither the monopoly nor the in-variable practice of African courts, and from my own experience I agree with his qualified statement that "Reconciliation of the parties becomes one of the main aims of the judges when the parties are in a *relationship which it is valuable to preserve*" (my italics). But when most of social life and legal traffic (including disputes) takes place in rather small communities of interrelated neighbours and other fairly close acquaintances, the chances are that in many cases some such valuable relationship is indeed felt to be threatened. Furthermore, it is especially at this level also that the recog-nized judicial functionaries, being themselves actively involved in the social network, have a personal interest in preserving unity and harmonious relations in the community. Their own powers of enforcing their decisions usually being limited, the *effectiveness* of their jurisdiction (no mean element of their social prestige) therefore largely depends upon their skill of applying their knowledge of local values, people and circumstances in order to reconcile conflicting views, interests and loyalties. Their disposition to broaden the enquiry beyond the immediate cause of litigation is therefore also dictated by a keen sense of social realism. This tendency leaves, of course, little room for any preoccupation with rules *excluding* evidence on the grounds of "inadmissibility" or lack of "relevancy", which constitute such an important part of the English law of evidence.

Gluckman (1955: p. 82) reports from the judicially highly organized Lozi that they "distinguish different kinds of evidence as hearsay, circumstantial, and direct, and attach different degrees of cogency to these . . .", and he cites (p. 93) Lozi judges: "What you hear with your ears, what you saw with your eyes, describe to us. Hearing and seeing the quarrel and fight are good, hearing about them is not." Later, after discussing Lozi terms for relevant, cogent, credible and corroborative evidence, he states that "these types of evidence *are tested as* direct, circumstantial, or hearsay" (my italics). However, some of his most extensive case reports show, I think, that the last-mentioned distinctions are used not so much as strict tests for the admission or rejection of evidence at a hearing, but rather to indicate their comparative probative value. Or in Allott's words (1970: p. 84): "All those factors which would go to the *exclusion* of certain evidence in English law (e.g. with 'hearsay' evidence) go rather to the *weight* to be attached to the evidence in African law".

A few other factors may be considered. Most (not all) tribal African societies have recognized judges and other judicial functionaries, but these are not professionals. They may be especially experienced and skilled in the art of adjudication, but to a large extent their knowledge of the law, of what constitutes normative or deviant behaviour under particular circumstances (local conditions, relationships), is widely shared by common folk. Moreover, given the frequency of face-to-face encounters and the free flow of communication at collective activities and other neighbourly meetings, there is little of actual or potential social consequence that remains hidden, and a mass of often detailed information about anyone's conduct is commonly shared. This is of particular importance if we consider a common characteristic of many (most?) judicial tribunals and proceedings in Africa (and not only there). Especially at the lower and intermediate levels of the judicial hierarchy (e.g. village and tribal ward) the official adjudicators preside at moot-like gatherings of mostly social acquaintances, people mutually related by ties of kinship and neighbourhood. These people do not constitute a passive and silent audience, as spectators in our Western courts of law are expected to be. In fact, many writers have stressed the basic right of any man present to contribute to the enquiry; and in some tribal proceedings there is even a definite stage at which the audience is actively encouraged to participate. "The matter is [now] given to the dogs to bark at" (Schapera, 1938: p. 289; Holleman, 1952b: p. 32).

Where public participation is not only permitted and institutionalized but, as among the Shona, of crucial importance to the outcome of the trial, it would be wrong not to extend the meaning of "court" so as to include leading functionaries as well as the attending public. In a situation like this, judicial responsibility is widely shared, and there is ready access to, and free use of, a large and common fund of local knowledge: of facts, circumstances, contesting parties and their relationships, as well as of the rules and forms of normative behaviour. But this also means that the fields of "judicial notice" (to use our technical vocabulary), "presumptions" as to fact or law, of "admissibility" and"relevancy", are wide open, and certainly not treated as the preserves of the official judges alone.

All sorts of witnesses (*zwapupu*) may be summoned to testify in a Shona trial. But Allott's statement (1970: p. 84) that, "since African society is a society of unequal statuses, it is to be expected that a senior and respected male member of the tribe may get a more attentive hearing than a female or a young boy", needs further qualification. All other things being equal, social status does play a role, and so do personal reputations as to general trustworthiness. But the "best evidence" principle—to which also the Shona seek to adhere although they may apply different criteria from ours —aims at finding the kind of testimony considered most credible under the circumstances and with regard to the particular issue(s) in dispute. Hence among the Shona, as among the Tswana, "in cases of adultery or seduction great weight is generally attached to the word of the woman involved, just as in cases involving cattle the evidence of herdboys is given special attention" (Schapera, 1938: p. 289). Yet it often seemed to me that the preponderance of "evidence" derived not so much from these *zwapupu*, but from participating members of the public and court officials who volunteered statements in which first-hand knowledge, hearsay information and personal opinion (if not speculation) were freely mixed. Though the Shona do appreciate the superior merits (all other things being equal) of what we call direct, as against hearsay or circumstantial, evidence, they do not strictly apply such distinctions because these are not developed technical constructs for the testing of evidence. To seek to classify and evaluate the instruments of proof in Shona tribal processes in categories like these, therefore, seems to be rather meaningless. In considering evidence they appeared to be primarily concerned with its inherent perceptive qualities and probative impact.

"Production" and "Reception" of Evidence

Allott's statement, quoted above, that "those factors which would go to the *exclusion* of certain evidence in English law . . . go rather to the *weight* to be attached to the evidence in African law", reveals two radically different ways of looking at evidence, which should be clearly distinguished before we attempt any comparison. The first we may call the angle of *production*, largely focused upon the source and kind of evidence and the means by which it is (to be) produced in court. The other is the angle of *reception* or cognition, from which evidence is viewed by those who are to judge upon it in order to assess its probative quality. The first view shows, in Western jurisprudence and judicial practice, defined and refined rules and exceptions as regards "admissibility" and "relevancy"—a highly elaborate juridical screening device aimed to a large extent at *barring* information not considered "judicable" in relation to the issues as formally defined and presented to the court. For reasons I have mentioned, Shona (and most other African customary) law[1] has developed nothing remotely like it. Viewed from this angle, therefore, there is little that is really comparable in the two law systems as regards the selection or rejection of evidence.

Viewed from the opposite angle (reception) the emphasis is not on the (in)admissibility but on the *weight of credibility* to be attached to any evidence at the court's disposal. In this respect tribal courts and Western courts face essentially the same primary problem of assessing the comparative impact of different kinds of evidence as a matter of their own perception, for we cannot mentally evaluate evidence without first having perceived it through one or more of our senses (seeing, hearing, feeling, etc.). These, and not abstract classifications of evidence, are the first (but not, of course, sole) determinants when it comes to the crucial business of assessing priorities of "credibility" on some cognitive scale of probative values. In comparing the manner in which certain evidence is tested and given priority in Shona and (say) British courts, I would suggest that the former

1. For a brief but very useful general survey of this subject, see Allott, (1970, p. 83 ff.).

are on the whole more conscious of and explicit about their primary senses (especially "seeing" and "hearing"), while the latter may by training and habit be more inclined to think and express themselves in terms of "classification". Admittedly also in English judicial practice the classification of evidence is of only relative value in assessing its probative weight. While acknowledging the general "superiority" of direct as against indirect (presumptive) evidence, a leading authority like Phipson (1963: p. 3) warns from the outset that "Little is to be gained from a comparison of their weight, since, save in the case of actual production of a given thing or fact, both forms admit of every degree of cogency from the lowest to the highest". But I make this comparison because I observed in many tribal proceedings that some oral (audible) testimony which would have sufficed in our courts of law still needed to be transformed into "something that can be seen" in order to be convincing.

"Evidence" in Shona Usage

The most common word for "evidence" in Shona is *cioneso* (*cioniso*)—lit. "that which causes to see". Etymologically it therefore has a similar derivation to "evidence" in English. As in English its connotations in common usage are wide,[2] but these rarely lose the meaning of being perceptive by sight. The equivalent of the English "I see (comprehend) what you mean", would in Shona more likely be rendered by using *kuviza* (to know) or *ku(n)zwa* (primarily, "to hear", but extending to "understand"). In legal usage *cioneso* extends to "proof",[3] that which provides a sufficient degree of "clarity" (*cena*) to enable judges to see "truth" (*cedi, cokwadi*). In this respect *cioneso* appears to carry a higher and more specific cognitive value than *ciziviso* ("that which causes to know"), which is used in a more generally "indicative" sense.[4] *Cioneso* as "proof" therefore implies especially *visible* proof, the perceptive superiority of which to oral testimony may, as I have said, be emphatically stressed.

In some earlier papers (Holleman, 1951; 1952b) I gave numerous examples of this outspoken preference for visible and tangible proof. A defendant should not, especially if he had first denied the charges brought against him, admit his guilt merely verbally. His statement should be accompanied by his handing over a small personal possession as a concrete

2. Hannan's *Standard Shona Dictionary* gives under *chioneso* (*chioniso*): "Sign. Anything which indicates."

3. cf. Gluckman, 1955, p. 316, in connexion with the Lozi term *bupaki*.

4. Hannan's Dictionary (under *chiziviso*) gives: "Announcement. Sign. Sense (any of the five) "

token of his admission of guilt (*rutenda mhoswa*). In one case I discussed, the defendant was an elderly man of no mean social status. He had readily (if defiantly) admitted all charges, though he had tried to justify his wrongful behaviour because of his embittered feelings towards his son (the complainant). In spite of his emphatic and repeated verbal admissions the public at the session was not satisfied. "We must *see* it, too. We must see that you have admitted your guilt!" (1952b: p. 33). He had to give a visible token (in this case, a sixpence) to make his words sufficiently credible. Though both father and son subsequently clearly said that they were prepared to resume normal relations, the adjudicators were not yet satisfied. "Just saying with words that everything is well again, is not enough. They should take snuff together!" (ibid, p. 35). Here a recognized and *visible act* of reconciliation had to supplement oral statements to remove lingering doubt.

I observed an even more striking illustration a few months later in another Shona-speaking community. A young man, Mudakwa, had stubbornly denied being the natural father of a pre-marital child, in spite of convincing customary proof of his paternity (the mother had confessed during child-birth; his family had made the ritual payments to her parents, and had duly paid damages). He refused to marry the mother but, many years later when the child (a girl) had grown up and become marriageable, he abducted her. At the ensuing court session his paternal rights were not disputed by the child's maternal kin, but they claimed compensation for maintenance costs, legitimization, insulting behaviour, and so on, far in excess of the normally accepted rates. Mudakwa was duly contrite and agreed to pay everything. He was then confronted with his original denial of his paternity, so he emphatically recanted and solemnly declared that he was the father of the child. Even this was not "clear" enough, for "How could the child know that this man was really her father? For she has heard only that he has first denied but now agrees". He finally produced a half-crown piece from his pocket. Holding it up for all to see he declared: "This is my *ruoneso*. I give this so that no one will doubt that she is truly my child." The coin was passed from hand to hand and ultimately given to the girl herself by the senior court official. "Do you understand what this is? This is given to you by Mudakwa to state that he is your true father. Have you seen it? Keep it so that you may know the truth."

The Shona made copious use of such "symbolic" evidence also outside the judicial arena. In fact, any important verbal communication (a declaration of love, acknowledgement of a debt, a request, promise, instruction, agreement, and so on) may thus be turned into a material thing to preserve it. They stress that its probative superiority derives from its visible and tangible quality. "Words, even if heard by other people, may later be denied or forgotten. But this stays, and can even much later be shown as the truth (*cedi*)." But it should also be something that belonged to the communicator himself, or at least was handled by him personally. This physical identification is important. One of my assistants had ordered a few clay-pots from a local woman. When she delivered them he was short of money but promised to pay next week. She asked to "see" his promise. I wanted to give her a sixpence, but she refused. "He does not know this thing and he may later refuse (deny)." So I gave the coin to my assistant, who looked at it and then gave it to the woman while repeating his promise. "*Cokwadi* (this is the truth)" she said, and went away satisfied.

A verbal communication thus becomes a material and imperishable thing, a *cibato* (from *kubata*, to catch or hold) to be kept by the recipient as something capable of being produced by him at any time as a concrete and visible testimony of the original communication (Holleman, 1952b: p. 41). It carried great conviction. The Shona are, of course, far from unique in this practice (cf. earnest and wed in Anglo-Saxon law!), but they may—it is an impression gained from literature—have made more prolific use of such token evidence than many other African peoples.[5] It will be seen, however, that the changing values of modern times tend to reduce the importance attached to it.

Supernatural and Emotive Means of Proof

In traditional Shona proceedings no form of oath is taken by parties or witnesses, and I found no evidence that ordeals and other supernatural means of proof were ever used as part of the judicial process itself. Some people would, on occasion, seek to stress the veracity of their testimony by invoking some self-curse ("May such or such happen to me if I have not spoken the truth."), or by voluntarily swearing some form of oath (including "God's truth!"—in English). But I did not get the impression that this carried much extra weight.[6] On the contrary, such undue emphasis often raised a snigger.

The Shona do, of course, often resort to consultations with diviners (*ngangga*), and the outcome of such extra-judicial enquiries is sometimes

5. For the great importance attached to visible tokens in Indonesian *adat* law, see Van Vollenhoven, 1931, p. 289 ff.; Ter Haar, 1948, p. 140 ff.
6. Gluckman (1955, p. 101) makes a similar observation for the Lozi.

mentioned at court sessions. Yet I seldom found that court officials made explicit use of such testimony. They rather seemed inclined to skirt such information (fear of the *Witchcraft Suppression Act?*), though it may well have exerted its influence in some unobtrusive way. As one official confided to me: "These are things we all know about but do not like to discuss among many people."

There are, however, some kinds of "emotive" evidence which are not devoid of an element of mysticism, and which carried (and often still carry) very great presumptive weight in traditional procedure. The first is any evidence revealing an element of *daka* ("grudge", "hatred") on the part of an opponent. Also in our courts (if admitted as relevant) this would tend to render his testimony suspect. In Shona practice, however, its effect may be more devastating, in that—unless a party himself candidly volunteers such information—it readily raises the presumption that his must be a trumped-up charge, an abuse of a public judicial forum not in order to find redress for a legitimate grievance but to damage another's reputation for the purpose of satisfying a privately harboured feeling of enmity. Under such circumstances the court is little inclined to pursue its inquiry into the factual merits of the complaint, and is apt to react with indignation and, sometimes, even with signs of considerable unease. For, "A man with *daka* is like a *muroyi* (sorcerer) wanting to kill a person."

In a case (1951) among the Budya tribe (north-eastern Rhodesia) a generally respected elderly ward headman had written a note to a young schoolteacher (living in a neighbouring ward) forbidding him to visit his area, because, he maintained, the young man had insulted and publicly slandered him. When senior judges convened to thrash out the matter, public opinion was clearly in favour of the old headman (defendant), until evidence was led proving that the note had been written in *red* ink. The court (officials as well as attending public), which so far had skirted this detail, now turned against the headman, because the question of *cishava* (redness) unavoidably invoked the presumption of a mystical threat of "blood" (*ropa*), "hatred" and "killing".

This presumption, once raised, is still so effective that I found it to be one of the most common defensive tactics in Shona litigious practice to try to prove that your opponent harbours *daka* against you, and "therefore" lacks legitimate grounds for a formal action.

I wish to deal with two other, and more specific, forms of presumptive evidence—both containing emotive and mystical elements—because these were considered to be virtually conclusive in traditional Shona law. They pertain to what is probably the most common cause of litigation in tribal courts: illicit sexual intercourse. In cases of seduction or adultery, direct evidence by third parties is usually difficult to obtain. Much depends upon circumstantial evidence and, especially, the woman's own testimony. Her very detailed description under which circumstances and exactly where intercourse took place, preferably supported by the production of the love token or other payment he might have given to her, often sufficed to make her lover admit it. But if no other presumptive evidence was available and he stubbornly denied his complicity, she could, in traditional procedure, resort to *kupuma neshashiko*. Ripping off her (leather) front-skirt and slapping him with it, she would challenge him to "deny that you know this thing" (Holleman, 1952a: pp. 85, 224). It was not merely the dramatic impact of her desperate and self-humiliating act before a largely male public which carried conclusive weight. It was also the (mystical) conviction that no man being thus physically confronted with the very garment which had covered her private parts, could persist in denying that his hands and body had been in intimate contact with it before.

By the 1940's, however, women's fashion had largely changed. Cotton dresses and underwear had become common, and only older women could still be seen wearing leather loin coverings. I myself witnessed only one instance of *kupuma neshashiko*, in a remote part of the Sabi valley early in 1946. It still carried conviction, but the audience was visibly embarrassed and there was some muttering about *hure* (whore) among attending women. In the more developed areas (Wedza and Narira in 1947; Chibi and Mtoko in 1950–52) this form of evidence no longer occurred. ("In the past it was a good thing; now there is so much *cirunggu*—European influence—that it is not done any longer.") Already in 1938 the Southern Rhodesia Native Appeal Court had rejected this form of evidence. Its President, Mr. Charles Bullock, an acknowledged expert on Shona custom, held that, though he himself had earlier written that the spontaneous *shashiko* raised an "irrebuttable presumption of the man's guilt" in Shona customary law (Bullock, 1928: p. 322), this could no longer be accepted. This particular action had taken place in the Native Commissioner's court room and had not been spontaneous. It was held, moreover, that "in modern circumstances . . . many Natives are sufficiently sophisticated to take advantage of such customs . . ."[7]. This last view found strong support at a session of the Govera tribal chief's court in the Chibi area in 1950. A well-dressed and carefully made-up young woman (plaintiff) threatened to

7. *Makonzekenyi v. Paradzanyi, 1938 N.A.C., p. 42.*

slap her alleged lover's face with her panties. An indignant remark by a court official stopped her: "Now we can see that you are really a *fambi* (loose woman), for you have no shame (*manyadzi*)!"

While *kupma neshashiko* had gone out of fashion as a powerful means of proving illicit intercourse, evidence of *confessions made at childbirth* had not. Here, too, it concerns the testimony of a woman in an emotionally critical situation within a mystical conceptual context. It is based on the widespread belief that unconfessed illicit premarital or extra-marital intercourse will obstruct childbirth and endanger the life of the mother and (especially) the child. Hence the presumption, when confinement is difficult, that the woman must have had an illicit lover whose name she had not previously revealed to her husband or family. It is the responsibility of her attending midwives (*vasamukta, vanyamuta*) to obtain such a confession, if necessary by torture, in order to ward off this mystical threat.[8] If she then confesses (*kureva*) the name of her lover, this constitutes evidence of the highest probative value, for "The inference is that no woman under such dire circumstances will risk uttering an untrue statement falsely implicating the defendant" (Holleman, 1952a: p. 224). The expression *mukadzi ingangga*, a woman is a diviner, indicates the belief in the supernatural sanction of her evidence.[9]

Likewise, a woman whose young child falls dangerously ill is expected to confess the name of her lover if she has one, and the same weight of credibility is attached to her statement. Hence the saying *Kunyamwa ndiyo ngangga huru*—suckling is indeed a great diviner.

I found that it was often sufficient for the husband (or woman's father) to tell the court that such a confession had been reported to him by the midwives, but if the defendant contested this testimony the midwives, or others in whose presence the confession was made, might be called to verify his statement.

This form of evidence normally still carried great weight among the tribal judges whose sessions I attended, but sometimes they experienced difficulties. One trouble was that in some confessions several names of

8. Even such torture, e.g. the application of a torqued string around her head, is still looked upon as an act of mercy, for its explicit purpose is to save mother and child (Holleman, 1958, p. 98–100).

9. Some wives, fearing the consequence of their infidelity, try to have their confinement at a maternity clinic operated by Mission or Government, where any confession they might feel impelled to make is not likely to be reported to her husband or family. This was believed to be the reason for the large attendance at a clinic in the Chibi area, where young women were said to be of notoriously easy virtue owing to the proximity of the Mashaba asbestos mine with its pecunious migrant workers.

lovers had been mentioned. In theory it is the last-named lover who is the genitor of the child ("because after his name was mentioned the child came out—*kubuda*"), and his would therefore be the greater "guilt". In practice, however, a multiple confession, if believed *in toto*, would cast a bad reflection on her moral behaviour, and inevitably weaken her husband's or family's case because they had evidently permitted the woman a much greater freedom than she should have enjoyed. Responsible Shona judges (not all of them were) quickly pointed out that, at a time of growing moral laxity, husbands and fathers should make greater efforts to "control" (*kutongga*) their womenfolk instead of expecting the courts to help them "to be enriched by other men".

But even the evidence of a single name confession, believed by the official judges and the great majority of the attending public, was being increasingly contested by defendants (especially younger men). And not seldom without success, for even if a tribal court would find against a defendant and award compensation (*muripo*) to the woman's "owner", it had in practice little effective power to enforce its own decisions against an unwilling judgment debtor without the assistance of the European district authorities. But exactly here lay also a possible avenue of escape, of which many an adulterer or seducer found guilty by a tribal court would seek to avail himself. I shall return to this point shortly.

Proof of Adultery in a Conflict of Laws

I stated that illicit sexual intercourse is probably the most common cause of litigation among the Shona. I have no reason to believe that this was a recent development. No particular value was attached to pre-marital chastity (only among one small group in the extreme north-east—Mukota area—was I told that girls were periodically examined as to their virginity). Elopements were (and apparently had always been) pretty common, and in fact constituted the prelude to marriage in a large percentage of cases (Holleman, 1952a: p. 113n). A lover was expected to marry the girl he had impregnated, and if he complied the damages (mostly ritual payments) were slight. If he did not marry her, he (his family) had to pay several head of cattle as compensation for the delict—and an additional few head if he wanted to obtain paternal rights to the child. But even a girl made pregnant by one man could be married off to another without loss of her normal bridewealth value, provided the husband could claim the child. *Ngombe ya vuya nouswa pa muromo*—the cow comes with grass in her mouth—is an old saying expressing satisfaction because the bride arrived with convincing proof of her fertility (ibid, pp. 245, 250). A wife was expected to be faithful, but if she had committed adultery this was seldom a reason for divorcing her if she promised to mend her ways. She herself was not judicially punished, but she could expect a sound hiding from her husband.

There was a general consensus that morals had become increasingly lax among both sexes. Africans were apt to blame *cirunggu* in general, and European (mission)-operated schools in particular. In a general sense they were right, but the causes were complex and hard to combat. The Colonial Administration had weakened the judicial powers of tribal authorities—which were probably never very strong in this feebly centralized society. Perhaps worse was the influence of the European labour market. From the early 1920's, periodic migrant labour sorties had, on an ever larger scale, become an institutionalized part of tribal existence, resulting not only in the absence of many husbands for considerable lengths of time, but also in a serious and almost permanent local imbalance between the sexes generally. Moreover, young men, having tasted considerable freedom during their labour sojourns, and being aware of their strengthened social position as independent wage-earners, had become more self-centred, headstrong, and less inclined to "listen" to their family elders or submit meekly to traditional sanctions.

Both European and tribal authorities were thinking in terms of more severe legal sanctions to counter increasing licentiousness. Already in 1916 an Ordinance (later the *African Adultery Act—Cap.* 81) was passed making adultery a criminal offence for both men *and* women. But although it may be inferred from sub-section 6(2)(b) of the *African Law and Courts Act* (33/1937; *Cap.* 104)[10] that recognized tribal courts could also treat adultery as a punishable offence, they did not, in my experience, ever do so. They continued to treat the matter as a customary wrong for which the man upon conviction had to pay a stiff compensation (two to four head of cattle) while they left it to the woman's husband or guardian to discipline her.

Successful tribal legal action against illicit sexual intercourse therefore very largely depended upon proving the man's guilt *and* enforcing the court's sanction. In this respect tribal courts faced two closely related and increasingly difficult problems. The one I have mentioned: more and more defendants persisted in denying their guilt in spite of traditionally convincing proof—especially the woman's testimony. If they held out, the tribal judges had little choice but to hope that the District Commissioner's court would back them up. This court was the highest local judicial

10. Since replaced by the *African Law and Tribal Courts Act* (24/1969).

authority. It had powers of revision in terms of section 9 of the *African Law and Courts Act*, and at the application of a dissatisfied party could re-hear and re-try the case, in which event its judgment could render the decision of the tribal court "of no effect" (section 10). Here lay the source of the second problem which tribal courts often faced, and of which many defendants knew how to take advantage.

Section 7 of the same *Act* specifically laid down that ". . . the practice and procedure *and the law of evidence* in African courts shall . . . be regulated by African law and custom" (my italics). But no such specific directions applied to District Commissioner's courts or the Court of Appeal for African (civil) cases established under section 10 of the *African Affairs Act (14/1927)*. Though this gave D.C.'s, trying to do justice "in accordance with African law and custom", considerable latitude in their handling of evidence, they could not but heed the decisions of the Court of Appeal. Now this Court had, in a series of judgments over the years, taken an increasingly critical view of the customary means of proof in cases of seduction and adultery, especially with regard to the very kinds of circumstantial and presumptive evidence on which tribal justice in the absence of direct proof would rely most heavily.

In *Nyamina v. Samson* (1938 N.A.C.: p. 18), though its President (Bullock, see above) still maintained that the woman's confession—in this case not made at childbirth—was the "major factor" which, together with some presumptive and circumstantial evidence (including the gift of a pair of shoes) constituted sufficient proof, the majority of the Court disagreed and insisted on stronger corroborative evidence. In July 1940, though still conceding that a woman's confession *made at childbirth* had "great weight" in African law, even Bullock considered that it was not irrebuttable and when contested needed corroborative evidence (*Makayengayise v. Davidson, 1940, N.A.C.: p. 95*). Three months later the same Court (under another president), went so far as to rule that a confession made at (first) childbirth to the woman's mother was *inadmissible*.[11] The Court was, moreover, not impressed that the woman had even (though not spontaneously) resorted to the *shashiko* challenge (above), and that the defendant had admitted to having felt "love-lorn"; it reversed the lower court's judgment on the ground of insufficient corroboration.

In *Dune v. Nyamaru (1945, N.A.C.: p. 66)* the Court considered that in cases of adultery the evidence of the woman was "naturally suspect", but nevertheless upheld the lower court's judgment against the defendant

11. *Joshua v. Fani, 1940 N.A.C., p. 114.*

because there was very strong evidence *aliunde*. In several other cases (e.g. *Tanyanyiwa v. Yakobe, 1946, N.A.C.: p. 131*) the Court stressed the need for substantial corroboration of the women's evidence; and it invoked the common law rule against hearsay evidence when a lower court had admitted it and been influenced by it (*Idi v. Mabala, 1946, N.A.C.: p. 143*).

Did the Court of Appeal develop a general criterion for the burden of proof to be discharged by an African plaintiff in such cases? In 1938, in Nyamina's case (above), it was still considered "not necessary . . . that the plaintiff should prove his allegation beyond all reasonable doubt". But in 1944 one of the Appeal judges held that African adultery cases should be proved "beyond reasonable doubt" (*Ginger v. Kamjgariwa, 1944, N.A.C.: p. 28*), and two years later, in Idi's case (above), the Court confirmed that the corroborative evidence should be sufficient so as to "leave no room for doubt".

Thus the stage had been reached when D.C.'s knew that their immediate Court of Appeal and principal watchdog for their task of securing civil justice, "in accordance with African law and custom" (*s. 3(1), African Law and Courts Act*), was demanding a standard of proof normally applied only to *criminal* cases. This is somewhat surprising because, though African adultery did constitute an offence under statute law (above), this Court was a civil court and in all the above mentioned cases adultery was therefore treated as a civil wrong. The superior courts undoubtedly considered that, in view of the increased moral laxity among African women, the traditional means of evidence could result in convictions based on false accusations— but this was a danger to which also tribal courts were fully alive. Tribal judges had little illusion about the fidelity of women; but even less about many a guilty man's preparedness to submit to traditional sanctions if he thought he could escape through the channels of European justice. They still felt, and not without reason, that by drawing upon their own shrewd knowledge of their people, and by being guided by a public opinion based on a neighbourhood's intimate knowledge of its members, their relationships, conduct and personal reputations, they could fairly judge the probabilities of truth or deception in these notoriously difficult to prove cases.

To tribal courts, the knowledge that the superior courts applied stricter and more abstract criteria of corroborative means of evidentiary proof was less than helpful. Even if the official judges themselves had been trained to appreciate such sophisticated rules of evidence, they would have difficulty in enforcing them in judicial proceedings in which the public was accustomed to the right to volunteer information and speak its mind. They could, of course, try to curtail this right and conduct trials in European fashion. I saw one Mbire chieftain in a comparatively advanced rural area trying to do just this, but his people vociferously rebelled at being told to keep "Silence in the court!" When he persisted, he lost public support—and the obvious means of mobilizing public sentiment, the very source of extra-judicial social pressure which still compelled many a recalcitrant judgment debtor to comply with a tribal court's judgment.

And so Shona tribal courts went on operating between success and failure. Some became indifferent (except to the matter of court fees), and were quick to tell a party that he was wasting the chief's time and should go to the D.C. instead. But the reverse also happened, for on several occasions an exasperated party would bitterly complain that the chief had "forgotten how to listen" to grievances, and that he would complain to the "office" about this.

But other courts carried on to the best of their ability and in traditional fashion, trying to sort out truth and deception in the light of their knowledge of old and new values. One of the more successful ones was the court at Careva (Budya tribe in the north-eastern part of Mashonaland). It was, perhaps, the best and most conscientious court whose sessions I attended (1951–52). It was, by all standards, a conservative court, but it enjoyed a high reputation and very considerable authority. Part of this was undoubtedly due to the fact that, though it operated as a secular court, its old presiding officer and several of its regular judicial functionaries were also closely connected with a powerful *Mhondoro* (Tribal Spirit) cult. The court usually met close to the cult's centre and derived its name from it. It was proud of its work and of a tradition in which very few of its cases went "on appeal" to the district office at Mtoko, and that in fewer still its judgment had not been upheld. But shortly after my arrival it had suffered one or two setbacks (coinciding with a change of top personnel at district headquarters), and it had reacted sensitively to what it regarded as a sign of distrust in their work and wisdom. At its next session the senior assessor scathingly spoke of "some people [who] seem to prefer whiteman's law because they refuse to pay for the wrongs which we know they have committed". But it had learnt a lesson which it applied in the next two cases (appearing within two weeks of each other in October, 1951) in which a defendant stubbornly denied an allegation of adultery. As usual there was no independent direct evidence in either case.

The defendant in the first case had eighteen months earlier been found guilty of adultery with the same woman, and had duly paid two head of cattle to the plaintiff, in whose village he then resided. (To avoid further trouble the Careva authorities had arranged his transfer to another, neighbouring village.) The plaintiff now alleged that, one late evening after attending a beer party in the neighbourhood at which he had seen his wife and defendant talking and dancing with each other, he had returned home with his wife and gone to sleep in separate huts. During the night he had wanted to smoke, and going out had seen the defendant at his wife's hut. He had raised alarm, but the intruder had escaped into the dark. He had not pursued him, because when he asked his wife she had admitted that she knew that it had been her "friend". So he had waited until next midday, when he had taken her to the defendant's village to confront him with the evidence. When the defendant bluntly denied it, the husband had left the woman at her alleged lover's place (a drastic but not uncommon measure which the Budya call *kukawa*, and which aims at forcing an opponent's hand). The woman confirmed her husband's testimony, adding that she and the defendant had recently resumed their relations by making love near a *tsime* (well), as "proof" (*cioneso*) of which she produced a wrapped-up two-shilling piece which, she said, he had given her on that occasion.

It should be mentioned that the defendant had ignored the first summons of the Careva court, had then been taken to the D.C. at Mtoko who, after rebuking him for having disobeyed his tribal authorities, had referred the case back to Careva "because there were too few witnesses". At the Careva trial the defendant persisted in his denial, and said that he would rather be "arrested" (*kusunggwa*) and taken to Mtoko again. He inferred *daka* (above) on the part of the plaintiff, because the latter had not immediately informed him of the accusation but had "waited a long time and then *kawa*'d his wife". He denied having made love to the woman at the well, and ridiculed the evidence of the two-shilling piece which, he said, "cannot show that it belonged to me because all money looks the same".

During the prolonged and lively public debate which followed the pleadings and hearing of principal witnesses, the majority seemed to think that "it would have been better" if, instead of relying on his wife's admission and his own eyes (and the well-known reputation of the defendant as a womaniser), the plaintiff had raised his neighbours and immediately pursued the intruder, if necessary into his own village, in order to "catch" (*kubata*) him. Moreover, the woman herself was derided, because "if she had really loved her husband she should have helped him catch the *gomba* (lover) in her hut, or she could have kept his hat or coat" as tangible proof of his presence.

The judgment of the Careva court was a remarkable one. The plaintiff was told: "Your case has failed and your money (court fees) will be eaten because you failed closely to pursue Karidza (i.e. the defendant). *Even the Whiteman at Mtoko will ask why you did not catch him* when you saw him so near. Also, your wife must still be loving him for she did not help you to catch him. *Of course we all know that he used her,* for there was the other case of *upombghe* (adultery) in which Karidza paid two cattle, and there is the *cioneso* of the money he gave her at the well." Turning to the defendant and refunding his court fees, the court told him: "Katsande (plaintiff) has failed his case, but you should not *pemberera* (rejoice). For you are a man who cannot leave alone a woman you have once used. This is now a matter for Careva, and we shall go to Mtoko and tell the office that you must *tama* (i.e. move outside the boundaries of the tribal ward) for you are causing too much trouble."

In other words, the Careva authorities, knowing that the defendant would almost certainly have appealed against a verdict of guilty, and suspecting that the D.C.'s court would consider the evidence to be insufficient to sustain conviction, had given a *judicial* verdict of "not proven". Yet they believed him to be guilty. So they resorted to an *administrative* decision ("This is now a matter for Careva", i.e. no longer a dispute between individual litigants) to punish the culprit by arranging his removal from the area where he had been disturbing the peace.

In the second case the evidence was strongly convincing from a traditionalist point of view. The woman had made a confession (naming the defendant only) at childbirth, after first having unsuccessfully tried to have her confinement at a maternity clinic near Mtoko. She herself candidly admitted: "I was much afraid of having to confess the name, and at the hospital no one would have told my husband." There was corroborative evidence: the gift of ten shillings and two bars of soap which the woman said she had received from her lover on several occasions of lovemaking (she described places and circumstances in detail); the plaintiff's father testified that one morning, when the husband had been absent in town, he had recognized the defendant's footprints running to and from the woman's hut (confirmed by the plaintiff's mother).

The defendant (plaintiff's younger paternal cousin, living in the same village) denied all allegations and threatened to go to Mtoko to appeal. The court of Careva made a final but unsuccessful appeal to the defendant's own father "to pay something so that there may be peace again in your *mhuri* (family)", but had no hesitation in finding the young man guilty.

The matter was taken to the D.C. at Mtoko, who considered that there was insufficient evidence corroborating the woman's testimony. The next session of the Careva court opened with a stern public statemeny by its senior official: "There are certain people whom we know to be guilty but refuse to listen to us. They prefer *cirunggu* (European ways) and they go to the 'office' where the whiteman does not know when they are telling lies. All right, but when these people next come to ask us to hear their troubles, we shall also refuse to listen to them."

The Careva statement was meant for local consumption but has, of course, much wider application. In any system of law evidence serves to communicate legally meaningful information. As with all other forms of communication its effectiveness depends on the measure in which its cognitive value is commonly shared. In this respect the admissibility, relevancy and credibility of evidence are as much a product of the total complex of a society's cultural values as are its rules of substantive law. Both are the means of recognizing normative or deviant behaviour, and cannot be divorced from each other. In situations of legal dichotomy— common also in countries no longer under colonial rule—the application of "rules of evidence" pertaining to one juxtaposed or superimposed system of law, to another, is therefore apt to cause confusion[12] because many symbols and criteria of juridical proof are not commonly shared. Truth may then become even more elusive, and justice itself uncertain.[13] As one English poet said, some two hundred years ago:

> *And diff'ring judgements serve but to declare*
> *That truth lies somewhere, if we knew but where.*
>
> (Cowper, *Hope*)

---

12. See also Allott, 1970, p. 89.
13. The new Rhodesian *African Law and Tribal Courts Act* of 1969 tries to meet this problem in cases of civil justice by: (*a*) leaving the choice of judicial forum largely to the litigants themselves; (*b*) restricting the powers of D.C.'s who exercise supervision over tribal courts as a matter of *administrative* action; (*c*) the creation of a new *tribal* Court of Appeal composed of three Chiefs (presidents of tribal courts)—after which there remains only the Rhodesian High Court's power of review. Traditional procedure and evidence are explicitly recognized in all tribal courts, including the new Appeal Court which itself may hear evidence. Since the latter court is intended to be a full court of record it will be of the utmost interest to see how it will guide the evolution of these and other aspects of customary law in modern times.

References

Allott, A. N. (1970). "Evidence in African Customary Law", reprinted In *Readings in African Law* (ed. Cotran and Rubin), Vol. I, pp. 83–90, Cass, London.

Bullock, C. (1928). *The Mashona*, Juta, Cape Town.

Cotran, E., and Rubin, N. N. (1970). *Readings in African Law*, Cass, London.

Gluckman, M. (1955). *The Judicial Process among the Barotse of Northern Rhodesia*, 2nd ed. Manchester University Press, Manchester.

Hannan, M. (1968). *Standard Shona Dictionary*, MacMillan, London.

Holleman, J. F. (1951). "An Anthropological Approach to Bantu Law", *Rhodes-Livingstone Journal* X, pp. 51–64.

(1952a). *Shona Customary Law*, Oxford University Press, Cape Town.

(1952b). "Hera Court Procedure", *NADA* (S. R. Native Affairs Department Annual) Vol. 29, pp. 26–42, Salisbury.

(1958). *African Interlude*, Nasionale Boekhandel Bpk, Cape Town.

Phipson, S. L. (1963). *Phipson on Evidence*, 10th ed. by M. V. Argyle *et al.* Sweet and Maxwell, London.

Schapera, I. (1938). *A Handbook of Tswana Law and Custom*, 2nd ed. 1955, Oxford University Press for the International African Institute, London.

Ter Haar, B. (1948). *Adat Law in Indonesia*, (translated from the Dutch *Beginselen en Stelsel van het Adatrecht, 1939*, Wolters, Groningen), ed. and introd. Hoebel, E. A. and Schiller, A. A. Institute of Pacific Relations, New York.

Van Vollenhoven, C. (1931). *Het Adatrecht van Nederlandsch-Indië*, Vol. II, Brill, Leiden.

Government of (Southern) Rhodesia, Salisbury:

> *African Adultery Act (Ord. No. 3/1916)—Cap. 81.*
> *African Affairs Act (14/1927)—Cap. 92.*
> *African Law and Courts Act (33/1937)—Cap. 104.*
> *African Law and Tribal Courts Act (24/1969).*

Reported Decisions, Native Appeal Court:

> *Dune v. Nyamaru, 1945 N.A.C. 66.*
> *Ginger v. Kamjgariwa, 1944 N.A.C. 28.*
> *Idi v. Mabala, 1946 N.A.C. 143.*
> *Joshua v. Fani, 1940 N.A.C. 114.*
> *Makayengayise v. Davidson, 1940 N.A.C. 95.*
> *Makonzekenyi v. Paradzanyi, 1938 N.A.C. 42.*
> *Nyamina v. Samson, 1938 N.A.C. 18.*
> *Tanyanyiwa v. Yakobe, 1946 N.A.C. 131.*

7 | Land, Movement, and Status among Kalanga of Botswana[1]

Richard P. Werbner

Land is not merely another form of durable property. The values land has even in a single society are often highly diverse and rarely free of fluctuation. Moreover, the various ways that people conceive of and order areas of social space and locality directly affect what land represents as real estate. This relation varies, because some socio-spatial conceptions change in meaning more readily than others, when there is change in the density and distribution of population, or change in the organization of settlement and production. People may disagree among themselves about their conceptions, often without being fully aware that they do so, since few, if any, of their socio-spatial conceptions are free of ambiguity. Even more, it may be essential, given certain ecological constraints, that they negotiate adjustments in land use while not seeming to themselves to revise certain rules of land tenure. The set of jural rules which people take to be primary and axiomatic forms a seemingly fixed explanatory scheme or rudimentary paradigm. However, the meaning they give to such a scheme and the use they make of it depends, crucially, on various moral premises and current

1. I wish to thank Professor E. L. Peters for reading this article in manuscript and suggesting improvements in it. I am grateful to the Social Science Research Council and to the University of Manchester for supporting my research in Botswana among the Western Kalanga during a fifteen month period in 1964–1965 and a three month period in the summer of 1969. I mention the Eastern Kalanga of Southern Rhodesia, among whom I worked while I was a Fulbright Scholar in 1960–1961, but apart from this mention, my reference is to Western Kalanga in the high-veld area of the Tati Reserve of Botswana. I do not discuss Tswapong of the low-veld in Botswana, since this essay was substantially completed before my recent fieldwork in their small villages.

understandings of public and personal interests—all of which may be the subject of much disagreement.

Problems in the study of land tenure raise broader theoretical issues about change, regularities of choice, and cultural conceptions of value.[2] In the context of this *Festschrift* dedicated to Professor I. Schapera it is especially fitting to consider some of these problems and issues in the light of evidence from nucleated villages and dispersed hamlets in Botswana, since Professor Schapera has made a pioneering contribution to the study of land tenure through his richly documented works on Tswana settlements. My own evidence is from fieldwork among Kalanga, whose unevenly dispersed hamlets occupy a distinct and densely populated niche in the high-veld of Botswana. Thus, building from a comparison with nucleated villages in the middle veld, I concentrate my argument on processes in dispersed settlements. The comparison substantiates the proposition that there is a systematic fit between legal and moral relations about land and modes of organization of production. Following the comparison, I consider micro-adjustments in land use which neighbours negotiate in relation to scarcity of land and density of population. I demonstrate how rights and claims to productive resources are effectively associated with personal and political status and with membership in a set of neighbours. Basically, the processes I discuss centre on moves that are made not to increase agricultural differentiation but to allow for soil impoverishment. My argument takes account of strategic notions that people in hamlets have which make sense of neighbours' movements in terms of a game of spatial tactics. I do not resort to an "ideal"/"real" dichotomy or dismiss the jural scheme which people use to formulate certain aspects of land tenure. Instead, my analysis regards ideals as one component in behaviour and explains why the people themselves who categorize bits of their behaviour as exceptions from their jural scheme rationalize these morally and legally in terms of a history of contingencies and personal deviations.

The high-veld region, where Kalanga live in scattered settlements of hamlets and homesteads, is virtually a chain of miniature landscapes. Its river valleys are narrow and numerous. They run within a gently rolling, hilly terrain that rises from about 4,000 feet to 4,500 feet along the watershed which forms the international boundary between Botswana and Southern

2. I am aware that there is an extensive literature on land tenure, and another essay would be needed to consider this literature for Africa alone. For a general review of legal and economic aspects, see Allan (1965), Biebuyck (1963), Bohannan (1960), Colson (1971), Gluckman (1965), and Gluckman (1969), White (1958), and for studies of specific cases see Lloyd (1962), Mayer (1966), Richards (1939), White (1963), Wilson (1963).

Rhodesia. No large deposits of alluvial soil are left in the valleys by the many streams and brooks, known as sand rivers, which bear surface water very briefly or in flash floods after the rains. The region lacks extensive tracts of prized, differentiated land like those in the adjacent middle-veld, where Tswana live along with Kalanga in centralized villages and hamlets. The high-veld is also more fragmented, more regularly varied in topography than the adjacent region with its rugged hills and extensive plains.

In the high-veld, cultivation is intensive, great reserves of land are lacking, and the population is densely, if unevenly, distributed. Clusters of home sites alongside gardens and pastures cover each narrow river valley. Roughly two to three miles is the usual extreme between a man's hamlet and his fields or well, and his herds usually graze not much further away, and rarely beyond about seven to ten miles, except in periods of extreme drought. Thus, in the high-veld hamlets, the usual scale of economic management is petty, the distances ordinarily covered by production from a single home site tend to be small, and there is little compartmentalization of production.

This does not imply a closed, self-sufficient economy within the valleys. In the most lush and green years, usually even the richest Kalanga keep most of their cattle nearby or elsewhere in the high-veld. However, there are long dry seasons, winters in years of severe drought, when Kalanga must drive their cattle to posts remote from their hamlets, beyond their home valleys. Uninhabited areas are essential for the richest Kalanga to maintain very large herds, well over seventy-five head of cattle. Sometimes when they find the winter pasture at home inadequate for all their stock, they drive their herds from their parts of the high-veld to areas on the periphery of Kalanga settlement or beyond it, to pasture within ranches in the middle-veld, or to other land not under tribal rulers such as the State Lands (formerly "Crown Lands"). A few owners of very large herds now keep cattle regularly and for long periods away from the high-veld; an even smaller number now maintain permanent outside cattle posts. Most Kalanga, however, do not gain access to pasture elsewhere the way they do in a home valley. They gain it elsewhere on an *ad hoc* and temporary basis, from those in control of it. Outside pasture is not needed every year, or even occasionally, for a run of years. Thus it may be hired from a rancher for cash, or grazed surreptitiously, without payment, or, for a particular year, herding arrangements may be made with those nearest the pasture outside the home valley. Elsewhere I have discussed such developments in land tenure that affect the high-veld and its environs, especially land formerly rented from the Tati Company (Werbner, 1971a); and I shall[3] not pursue this theme here.

Local variability requires a multitude of micro-adjustments in land use within each narrow valley and between it and others nearby. These are micro-adjustments which have to be made irrespective of current territorial boundaries between political divisions. The periods of fertility on the high-veld's granite sands are brief, even if the soils are manured or covered by the refuse of a hamlet's ruins. Areas of land must be converted continuously from one service to another by turns, fallow, pasture, residence and cultivation. The duration of one type of service must also be comparatively short. Moreover, there is no standard safe period for cultivation. Cultivation may be interrupted, on a particular plot, in years of severe drought or poor rainfall; when oxen are weak or reduced in numbers after an earlier drought or poor rainfall; when labour is scarce, sometimes due to men having irregular periods of leave from their work in towns. Commonly, Kalanga anticipate about ten to fifteen years of somewhat intermittent cultivation and then a period of fallow at least that long and usually longer. In the sections which I surveyed, roughly twenty-five years is the longest a man has kept alternating plots and maintaining cultivation in some parts of a field—an achievement which is extremely rare. Kalanga estimate a field's decline and its regeneration largely by vegetation indicators. They consider that it is in decline when it is rank with witch-weed and that it is in regeneration when it is rich in "thatching grass" (various species of *Hyparrhenia*). Planning for a field's decline in productivity and preparing to own and work an alternative is vital for residents of hamlets in the high-veld.

From one major river valley to the next the combination of natural resources does differ somewhat, but each is basically complete for many of the people's needs. Usually, a major valley supports a strikingly flexible use of land along most of its extent, except in some eastern parts of the high-veld where soil erosion is most severe. Most of a valley sustains much variation in the growth of many small and unstable groups of kin and in their demands on natural resources. Each valley is so linked with others that there is a constant and gradual interchange of population; sometimes individual families and more rarely larger groups migrate. Only a minority are able to keep their homes first in one hamlet then another within the same major river valley throughout most of their lives until elderhood. They are,

3. Since 1970, Government has issued permits to members of a chieftaincy, *en bloc*, to enable them to graze their herds on pasture bought from the Tati Company.

all the same, a conspicuous minority, great in influence and prestige; They stake claims to fallow land, sometimes assert a title to be "owners of the country" (*beni be shango*) and are proud to deny that they are "immigrants" (*bazhi*). "I never jumped over the river" was the provocative boast I heard one such elder hurl at immigrants in a dispute.

Facts of local mobility are shown in detail in Tables I and II. This documents the marked extent to which most adults of middle-age or older have themselves immigrated or had parents who immigrated within the past fifty years. I note that Kalanga chieftaincies are small (the larges. having an area of about 88 square miles and a population of roughly 4,500t and they are divided into sections with between 300 to about 650 persons) and further divided into wards having between 50 to 350 persons, I recorded the census data of the tables in 1964/65, and my census covers the whole of a section which I refer to later as North Section (two wards) and also the two wards resident on the territory of North Section but

TABLE I. Local mobility of adults over fifty years of age

| | In Census Sections | | | | Elsewhere* | | | | Total | |
	Men	%	Women	%	Men	%	Women	%	Men	Women
Born	9	19·1	13	18·3	38	80·9	58	81·7	47	71
Reared	15	31·9	25	35·2	32	68·9	44	62·0	47	71
First Marital Residence	26	55·3	27	38·0	21	44·7	44	62·0	47	71
Residence at any marriage	32	60·4	28	38·4	21	39·6	45	61·6	53†	73†

* Elsewhere refers to outside the chieftaincy except for two women reared elsewhere in the chieftaincy, and one man born, reared, and married elsewhere in the chieftaincy.

† Six men and one woman, who were non-resident at a first marriage, later became residents and then married other residents. In addition one woman, who had been a resident at her first marriage, later married an alien in town.

TABLE II. Time of arrival of parents of adults over fifty years of age

	Arrival at least 50 years ago		Less than 50 years ago		Never arrived		Total
		%		%		%	
Parents of Men	14	29·8	6	12·8	27*	57·4	47
Women	23	32·4	4	5·6	44	62·0	71

* Two men and two women had parents who came to another part of the chieftaincy over fifty years ago, but never to these sections.

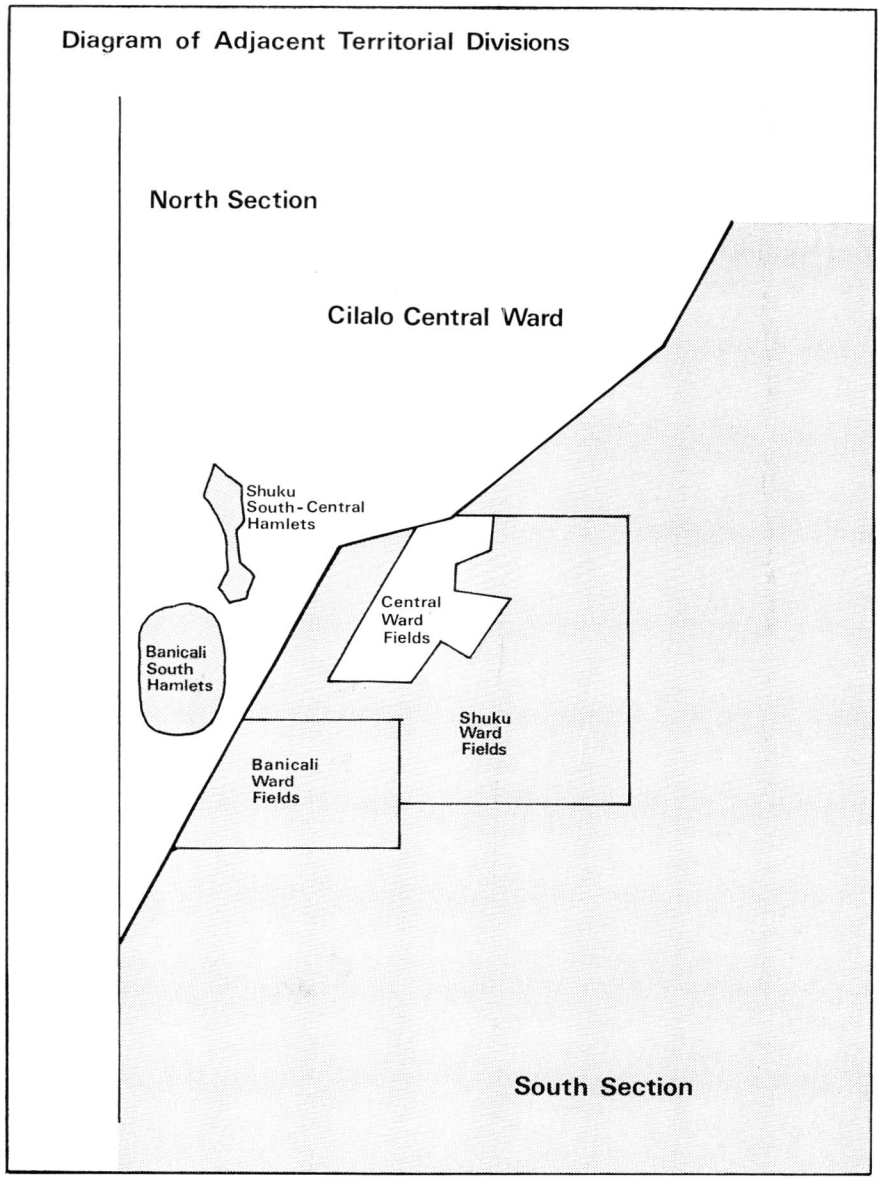

Diagram of Adjacent Territorial Divisions

North Section

Cilalo Central Ward

Shuku South-Central Hamlets

Central Ward Fields

Banicali South Hamlets

Shuku Ward Fields

Banicali Ward Fields

South Section

politically domiciled in the adjacent South Section (this has another five wards not in the census).

So far I have presented an initial discussion of conditions in the high-veld which Kalanga meet through local mobility and micro-adjustments in the productive use of land. I will return to this later and discuss the patterning of movement and competition between neighbours. First I must draw a comparison with nucleated settlements in the middle-veld in order to highlight how land tenure is associated with personal and political status in the dispersed high-veld settlements.

Compartmentalization of production is far more important in nucleated Tswana villages than it is in Kalanga hamlets. Over fairly long periods of time distinct tracts of land, at least several square miles in extent (Schapera 1943: p. 128) and often greater than most high-veld valleys, may be kept for special use as belts of cultivation. There are other, larger belts for pasture in separate areas, and usually, vast stretches of a large village's land are also held in reserve, uninhabited and unworked. In the largest villages the separation of productive belts is such that villagers may come to have their fields as much as thirty-five miles or more from their homes at the village's centre, and their pastures even further away. Cultivation on the more fertile soils of the middle-veld tends to be semi-permanent, though not constant in yield due to the erratic rainfall.

The village agriculture of the middle-veld tends to be less intensive, and its animal husbandry more extensive and a proportionately greater source of income than in the high-veld settlements. In the more temperate high-veld, the staples[4] are more reliable, and there is more likely to be an occasional bumper crop with surpluses for sale or barter. Furthermore, the grass cover is less sensitive to pressure from heavy grazing in the high-veld's open tree savanna. Each region has its prevailing and most critical hazards to subsistence production. Arrangements most suitable to insure for high productivity of either cattle or crops in one region are inadequate, even costly and harmful in the other. In particular, the large-scale, compartmentalized organization of agriculture which is basic for a large nucleated village has not proved viable in the high-veld, so that, while some hamlets now thrive as satellites or outpost communities within the middle-veld, large nucleated villages have been blocked from developing in the high-veld.[5] Despite this, there are tendencies towards somewhat more

4. Both in the middle-veld and high-veld, indeed throughout most of eastern Botswana, the main staples are sorghum and bulrush millet. These are grown along with subsidiary crops: maize, sweet cane, ground nuts, beans, pulses, potatoes, and in the high-veld, even some finger millet and in swampy patches, rice. The main staples begin to thrive, however, where rainfall is annually close to sixteen inches and, even more crucially, well distributed over the growing season.

5. There are important differences in the availability of water in the middle and high-veld, but it would be misleading to imply that the supply of water alone determined

centralized settlements, which rural development projects seem likely to favour.

Both in villages and hamlets the laws of land tenure recognize a fundamental association between status and basic resources. Yet the legal interests of residents are distinct and form different patterns, according to the different kinds of settlement. The association between status and basic resources holds in terms of domicile and also residence. By "domicile" I refer to placement for political purposes, and by "residence" I refer to domestic location. I wish to stress this usage because it is important for my discussion that follows. Thus both in hamlets and villages, domicile in a territorial group implies rights to a share in its land. In both moreover, residence in a local community provides legal grounds for production within its area. Nevertheless, there is a systematic contrast in the fit of the various legal relations and in the fit of the communities of residence and domicile. The legal aspect can be put thus: invariably, residence is subsumed under domicile in a village, but these vary independently for a hamlet, since one is not entailed in the other. To understand this sociologically, further aspects of the comparison must be considered.

At the founding of a village, each division of virgin territory is allocated, initially, among the members of a component unit of administration and residence, a ward (Schapera 1943a: p. 45–46). Once allocated, however, the land is subject to personal transactions between this and other wards' members. The land need not—in a sense, cannot—remain reserved for the founding ward, and use of the land is not necessarily restricted among the residents of any single residential part of the village. A ward may persist as an administrative and residential unit, though some of its members may come to live elsewhere in the village. Usually, it manages an estate in arable land of its own, but not one held to the exclusion of non-residents. The reach of a resident's land tenure depends on domicile in the inclusive political unit. Thus domicile in the village gives any ward's resident the right to work land in any part of the village, land which he may inherit, or be granted as a kinsman, as an affine, an unrelated friend, or as a man's

---

whether settlement has been nucleated, or not. Critical limits define the distribution of settlement from one region to the other. Since I cannot discuss this fully here, I note that the limits are: (a) in temperature, an annual mean of sixty-five degrees Fahrenheit; (b) in rainfall, an annual mean of twenty inches, along with normal variability, of less than forty per cent; (c) in altitude, a height of close to 4,000 feet; (d) in extent of acreage under cultivation or under recent fallow, thirty per cent of the area occupied (Bawden and Stobbs 1963, p. 72 f. appendix II). Great villages stop and only hamlets continue, where these limits are exceeded by a decrease in temperature along with an increase in altitude, rainfall, and extent of land under cultivation or recent fallow.

client (Schapera 1943a: p. 151). Widely separated localities are within the legal reach of a villager's tenure. Moreover, various relationships, such as those through cross or parallel cousin marriage, may give him access to particular plots or arable land and productive services at great distances. A villager's land tenure may thus cover distances which exceed the length of the largest tribal territory or chieftaincy to which a high-veld hamlet belongs.

A resident of a high-veld hamlet is more limited in the reach of his land tenure. The smallest administrative unit—i.e. a ward of hamlets—is the widest political community within which domicile counts for his rights to work land.[6] In a village the ward is also the smallest administrative unit, but it is not similarly the limiting division for land rights. This difference in villages and hamlets goes beyond a matter of span. In each kind of settlement domicile applies to a sociologically quite distinct unit: the ward of hamlets is an economically diversified, territorial division, while in a village a ward may be a component unit of residence. Moreover, a hamlet resident's right to work land within his ward is qualified by a second legal limitation. It depends on the location of his hamlet. The site of his hamlet locates a man within a set of neighbours who have moral claims along with legal and economic interests which are not those of a political or administrative unit.

Unlike a villager, a hamlet resident is legally barred from having fields in several localities. The restriction applies even if these are within a wider political unit, such as a chieftaincy or a section that includes a man's ward. Neither he nor his descendants lose title to fallows after they abandon residence and cease to work land, and if they leave behind land which has not reverted to bush, they may grant it to a person of their choice. They have a right to resume cultivation when they resume residence.

No single political unit is defined by a locality. Indeed, it covers an overlapping of administrative divisions, and is not a bounded territory. A locality is a named expanse of land near or surrounding a landmark, such as a knoll or kopje, a river or another distinctive feature, a great stand of trees for example. As an area of cultivation and land use, it may overlap two or three wards, without embracing their total territory or even the whole of one ward. I know of no term in Kalanga for a locality. Kalanga may express their conception of it, when they refer to "over here" (*muno*),

6. This does not imply that a person can hold land only in terms of his *current* domicile. See below (p. 115) where I discuss implications of the fact that a man is not necessarily limited to his current ward.

in contrast to "over there" (*yeno*), or sometimes when they speak of "at our home" (*kanyi kwedu*). To be more explicit, they mention the name of the locality; for example, *Goba Malala*, Collect Rubbish, *Dombo Shaba*, Red Rock, *Danga le Shumba*, Pen of Lions, *Mazvilasha*, You Cast Yourselves Aside. Such a name is relative, in that a speaker's reference depends on where he is, and on the context. Speaking in an adjacent chieftaincy to an outsider, he might refer to several localities at his home collectively, by the name of a well-known one; to a neighbour he could distinguish these specifically. One must be a neighbour to know clearly the ambit of an area of land use; indeed, one cannot remain a neighbour without this knowledge. There is, however, a usual extreme in distance between a man's hamlet and his fields, about two or three miles, and a locality is estimated within this distance.

In some villages too, a land law of locality is recognized. It makes a man's rights in any locality conditional on his continuous cultivation there; but it lets a man spread his cultivation over several localities. This law is found among Ngwato villages: a man loses the right to work his fallows or grant them to others once he abandons a locality; his title lapses, when he ceases to work nearby (Schapera 1943a: p. 178). Significantly, few Ngwato families are reported to have spread their holdings over several localities, compared to other villagers elsewhere, such as the Kgatla or Kwena, in the sample which Schapera reports (1943a: p. 147). Thus the law of locality for villagers is associated with a tendency towards concentration of a family's cultivation within a single locality, though in none of the large villages does there appear to be complete localization of every family's plots.

What is distinct is not so much the village or hamlet law as the component of locality to which it applies. In a village this component is a stabilized belt of production which is usually a specially compartmentalized part of the economy; in a hamlet the component is an area of highly varied production with its diverse resources and combined services.

The distinction can be seen more clearly by a look at localities in the dispersed and nucleated settlements. Activities kept somewhat separate in a village are coordinated in a locality of hamlets. Consequently, a locality of hamlets is a more comprehensive arena of neighbourliness for its residents and, in a sense, they have greater opportunity, and also need, to bring pressure to bear on neighbours in defence of their interests in land. They expect others in the locality to pool their labour, and at certain peak periods of the year competition arises for co-operative services, so that who actually turns up for a particular work-sponsor depends on various factors including the nature of the task, a past history of services, the sponsor's local prominence, his (or her) kinship and personal relations with neighbours. Nevertheless, within such a locality neighbours are mobilized for services which, in a large village, may be given by people from distant localities. Hamlet neighbours work in one another's fields, (primarily clearing, hedging, weeding, harvesting and threshing) when beer is laid on for the invited workers. They are also called on for domestic production, such as brewing beer, when a set of women share the task of stamping grain, each preparing a basketful of meal for the brewer. Moreover, joint arrangements are made among some of the same people for herding away from the home valley. Borrowing of goods for brief use, such as bicycles, pots or drums for beer and ploughs, is constant within a locality. Other relationships of debt and credit, including marriage and the loan of livestock, are contracted for longer periods between people of a locality, so that their interests in basic resources and in services for these are shared along with other linked interests of varying duration.

A locality for residents of hamlets is an arena of neighbourliness *par excellence*, by comparison to the locality where villagers live. Residents in hamlets must cooperate and compete with the same people, their fellows in a locality, throughout a year or from year to year. Villagers need not, since their residential neighbours need not have adjacent fields or pasture. For residents of hamlets interdependence with their neighbours is continuous for a variety of purposes, including consumption and production. However, no feast is attended exclusively by people of a locality. This primary area of production is not demarcated from others by a special occasion for consumption. In this it is unlike a ward or other territorial division whose members may feast as a group, receiving a distinct portion of meat from their headman.

People of the territorial or political unit should be invited along with people from the locality when meat is shared in a hamlet after a slaughter of cattle. Kalanga do distinguish between local and territorial relationships, but they also bring them together under the same obligations and conceptual idiom, "We live with them" (*Togala nabo*), and "We have one plate with them" (*Tina ndilo ngompela nabo*). At a feast, distinctions are made in the portions given and where these are eaten, at the cooking compound or among the crowd at the hamlet's forecourt. But there is an obligation to invite the people of the locality, even if the bull or cow is sacrificed at an ancestral shrine. Cattle may be butchered for sale. Otherwise people of a locality gather to share in the slaughter. Similarly, a slaughter of small stock, whether a sacrifice or not, is an occasion for sharing meat among the closest neighbours. (One way closest neighbours reject relationships with each other, despite spatial proximity, is to cease sharing the meat of small stock, goats and sheep.) Such a distribution forges neighbourliness. Indeed, it declares who are neighbours, and for what purposes: to fulfil a duty to distribute beer or meat, and consume it with neighbours is to generate obligations over further production.

It is important to distinguish between a locality and a set of neighbours centred on one hamlet. I refer to such a selection as a neighbour set and to those considered the closest neighbours as an inner set. Every hamlet is at once within a locality and also the focus of its particular set of neighbours. Kalanga speak of the inner set of closest neighbours as "the cooking places" (*mabiko*). Hamlets of the same locality invite one another's residents to major feasts but do not invite all of each others "guests" (*bezi*, *mwezi* in the singular), this divergence represents the area of variation from one hamlet's neighbour set to the next. In effect, a locality covers mutuality, it includes certain relations in common among diverse neighbour sets focused on different hamlets.

Although a locality is not a bounded territory, it limits its inhabitants' prospects and rights of land use. A man may exercise his right or expect to keep several fields in production, to resite his hamlet, and extend cultivation only so long as he remains within a locality. Such expectations vary over time and with the options open to neighbours in contiguous localities. My impression is that, where neighbours appreciate that shortages are severe, a locality is most restricted, and a man cannot expect and is not allowed to distribute his cultivation and residence so widely as elsewhere. Claims of "people of over here" (*bathu be muno*) are expected to prevail over those of "people of over there" (*bathu be yeno*). When and where this expectation is fulfilled much depends on the density of occupation and on the mutual investment which neighbours make in providing one another with productive services, meat at feasts, and other goods.

The distribution of land in a locality is primarily controlled through negotiated adjustments of rights and claims between neighbours. Neighbours assert an overriding moral premise in such adjustments which I refer to as a "premise of beneficial tenure." This is a premise that, until recently, could not be enforced legally or in court. The premise assumes that interests in production—in the beneficial use of land—ought to take precedence over interests in the security of tenure. Neighbours act on the assumption that an owner should not be allowed an unrestricted security of title, irrespective of his use of the land; and they consider it immoral for an owner to deprive anyone and everyone of cultivation and residence on arable land, while the owner reserves it securely for an indefinite period. Until very recently, like most villagers, high-veld hamlet residents did not have a legal prescription to limit a title to land and define the application of their premise by a specific rule. Schapera, who calls this premise a "principle" among villagers (1943a, p. 181) records that some of their chiefs legislated about this, before 1916 in one community (1943: p. 178). Their legislation fixed a statutory period limiting non-productive tenure, after which a man forfeited his rights. National legislation since 1968, the Tribal Land Act of 1968 and an Amendment of 1968,[7] has prescribed a statutory period for all, both villagers and hamlet residents. In 1969 I recorded one instance of special pleading, apart from a moot or court, in which a man who justified himself to his neighbours mentioned the new national legislation as one of several grounds for his clearing and taking possession of land that was held in non-productive tenure, despite the owner's objections. The national legislation has set a legal standard and public limits, but it has yet to eliminate, if it can, the negotiated adjustments which have prevailed while neighbours could not sue in court to insist on beneficial tenure, but had to resort to measures which they themselves considered harassment and encroachment.

Under conditions of great land shortage, some villagers do not keep home sites in the central residential area. Rather, they "settle down beside their fields", as at Mochudi (Schapera 1943: p. 175). According to a lawyer's recent observations, "In some areas surrounding the central part of Mochudi, many instances of 'self-allocation' of land have taken place with the acquiescence of the tribal land authorities. It is not clear whether the persons occupying such plots can be considered as having any legal right to do so." (Roberts n.d.c. 1970: p. 11). This and other evidence suggests that there is a direct correlation between the strict separation of belts of production, restricting the arena of neighbourliness, and the extent of effective direction of the allocation of land by a superior and central authority. Such direction seems to be least, and the scope for negotiation between neighbours greatest, where residential land for permanent home sites directly reaches arable land, allowing a person to control fields from his residence and its frontage.

7. The legislation also provides for Land Boards which would replace or regulate tribal rulers in the administration of land tenure. At the time of my fieldwork in 1969, however, this change was planned but not effective in the high-veld. Once founded, the Tati Land Board was headed by a chieftain, and by 1974 he and certain other tribal rulers had extended, rather than lost, their importance in the administration of land tenure.

In order to demonstrate this point in relation to the kind of negotiation and competition for land which takes place among high-veld hamlets, I must first of all further clarify key conceptions of Kalanga. Some Kalanga see an analogy between their strategic occupation of land and playing games. Kalanga play checkers. Quick strategic moves, commanding several critical places at once and made boldly, along with a line of dazzling chatter (You stray from the breast, *Watsambuka zhamu*; I free cattle from the pen, *Ndozhula ngombe mu danga*; I devour from cattle, *Ndojila ngombe*; I make an "airplane"; *Ndotama "frai-machina"*) are admired. An analogy to checkers was first pointed out to me among Eastern Kalanga, in the low-veld of Southern Rhodesia, by Ta Mfundisi, an elder who had lived in the high-veld until his middle-age when ranchers displaced him. I had asked Ta Mfundisi why a man should have two or even three plots separated from one another, though in the same locality, since he then has greater difficulty in watching them against birds and pests.

Ta Mfundisi explained by comparison to checkers. As in checkers so too in cultivation, a man has to gain spaces for the future and for expansion. A man finds his yield poor and the soil getting bad, so he begins a new garden, while still cultivating the old:

Small gardens (*niba* in Eastern Kalanga, *ntiba* in Western) are plans for the future. When a man wants to move his garden, he'll not go to the man who controls the land in front, and say "I want to plant and plough fields (*minda*) near you". He'll say, "I want to plant a small garden of groundnuts; for you know that groundnuts do not grow well in old soil, and mine is getting old." Once he has the garden, then he gains control of the land in front. He has a foot in, and he can go forward to a big field, bit by bit; and the one who used to control the land in front can say nothing now, for the owner of the garden is now in control.

Little land lies long in the high-veld without someone claiming it. A newcomer is usually sponsored by an old neighbour or a kinsman of his; for he may come to the head of a ward and ask for land, but the ward head, in turn, cannot grant a plot, unless he has permission from those who claim it, because it is their frontage (*sholo*, head) or their fallows (*makula*, sing. *gula*) or their fathers' fallows and their hamlet ruins (*madongo*). Among all these claims, frontage, whether of a hamlet or a field, is fundamental, and a man who lacks it must appeal to a person I refer to as a "contact", that is one who controls frontage and with whom the man has a personal relationship. The limits of frontage must always be defined in relation to the nearest neighbours of the hamlet or field. Kalanga recognize the right of the hamlet's head or the field's owner to take priority before all others.

Whoever controls the immediate frontage must give his permission—or their permission if several owners' frontage is impinged—before others may cultivate or build or cut and clear on it. Therefore, one way that Kalanga insure access to land during its regeneration is to clear within new growth, and build a hamlet. And bit by bit, gardens, then fields, follow.

The conversion from fallows to cultivation and hamlets, so vital on the granite sands of the high-veld, is often not so straightforward a process, because many neighbours anticipate needs that will grow. They sometimes get permission from only a single neighbour on the frontage and ignore other neighbours' claims so that they build new hamlets or clear new gardens without the consent of all who should give it. For not all neighbours are willing to give it and welcome a particular immigrant or relocated neighbour, especially when he comes as the friend, kinsman, and ally of rivals. To clear the scrub and cut a major field, a man usually draws on a pool of local labour, and mobilizes his neighbours for a co-operative work bee. In effect, the occasion becomes one trial of support for or against a man's claims to the land. Neighbours whose claims are neglected need not make an immediate crisis of it, however, by fighting and quarrelling over the issue at hand. Instead such neglected neighbours may retaliate later, and they may block an intruder's expansion, by clearing another garden near his goat pen, not far from his hamlet, and even neglecting the hedge, so that there can be a suit for a goat's damage. After discussing such an instance, a neighbour remarked; "They provoke one another like little gnats".

Some claim to have the status of "owners of the country", and thus, heirs to the fallows and hamlet ruins of their fathers. Others admit that they are not natives and came as children or recently. Occasionally, they take possession of land, then they gain permission to use it, by appealing to the generosity of the owner of the frontage or by submitting to a fine, fixed by the owner during a moot or at a headman's court. All seek bases for staking claims. Some do so to the point of violence, a crime which they consider to be a grave offence against God also, for "it is taboo (*goila*); soil, is not fought over (*mavu hatogwigwa*)".

II

There is a basic identity between men and land, Kalanga maintain. This means, in one aspect, that the wildness of human kind and the wildness of the land—of thickly overgrown bush, *denje*—are one; as a proverb puts it, "The wilderness is the human being (*Denje unthu*)." A further aspect was put to me most forcefully by Ta Ndiwa, who knew about foreign modes of land tenure, having served about four years with the British Army in the Middle East. Ta Ndiwa told me:

There is no grass. Yet when you get to the European farms [in the middle-veld elsewhere in the District] there is grass, and grass, and grass. Now, how can they buy that soil (*mavu*), and call it a farm? The soil is the soil of Mwali (God). They say they bought the land. From whom did they buy it? To whom did they give that money? Can land be bought or can a person be bought? No, land cannot be bought, for Mwali is the owner of the land.

A counterpart to this is that a man's status must be as a dependant, a "child", or he cannot hold the basic resources he requires for production. But, ultimately, it is as a "child" of God, Mwali, that a man and all men hold land. A man's choice lies in whose dependant he becomes, and this choice, like the range of others who may become "children" of his, is limited. One measure which Kalanga take of a man's status is the measure of his dependence: "Chiefship means people" (*Busha kodha bathu*). It is in determining their dependence and these statuses that Kalanga move their hamlets and gardens, having to make decisions and plan for the future, somewhat—to use Ta Mfundisi's analogy—like checker players.

Whoever has land owes a share to his "child", *mwana*. In this notion, Kalanga include any dependant within a hamlet—indeed, any subject of a ward head or a chieftain. A share is his by right. Normally, his mother gives it to him from hers, first; and from adolescence onwards a child becomes entitled to a plot in his own name to be cultivated on his behalf, and its produce to be set aside for his disposal. Children away at work in towns do not lose this right; their plots are worked for them, if possible. A man does not buy his land.[8]

In his status as a child, a man may be the dependent of those who are unable to give him land where he needs it. Service to those who can give it to him secures it. A man, wherever he goes is a child, yet everywhere he is not an heir of fallows and sites in ruins or an "owner of the country" and a relative of the holder of a territorial title; and he may have to become a "client" (*nlanda*). Usually, when Kalanga speak of a man as a client, it is not to his face. Inferiority of status is implied, and it is provocative. The

8. The nearest that I recorded to a cash transaction over land was an attempt by a well-owner, on leaving his ward and section, to transfer his manured and improved field to the buyer of his well, in effect as part of the sale of the well, and without the permission of the ward head. The ward head refused to allow the buyer to use the land, and the owner who had improved it continued to insist that it must go to the person of his choice. At the end of my first field trip, it had remained fallow for over a year; and even four years later, on my return, there was still backbiting over it, since the ward head had been unable to allocate it to anyone else. Eventually, a close relative of the owner took it over.

conventional meaning Kalanga most readily mentioned is that a client is a person "tamed" by another. This is a meaning connected with a proverbial notion of a payer of bridewealth, "The tamer of a bachelor is whoever gets him to pay bridewealth" (*Watuiwa sumbolume nde wailobodza*). But Kalanga also see present relationships of inferiority and dependence in terms of laws which they say are no longer enforced.

Legally, they say, in the past a client owed much service without direct compensation, slaughtering, cooking meat, and cultivating for a patron and being protected by him. A client was one who lacked kinsmen to help him or had left them; he or his fathers came in need, hunger and poverty, and were given political status, land, the use of cattle, and perhaps eventually a wife, by an "owner of the country", who was not a relative. Kalanga say, too, that his children succeeded him in his legal and political status, unless they became the wife-givers (*bakalabga*) of the "owners of the country", (thus altering the status and debt relation), or could find land in a ward headed by their patrikinsmen.

An implicit obligation to provide labour in return, in future years, goes along with the grant of the use of such productive resources as land and, in some circumstances, livestock also. Whether a man "begs" (*kumbila*) a piece of land from a contact who is a relative, borrows it from a neighbour and friend, or is given it as a client, he gets it with this obligation. A man cannot stay in one place from one decade to the next, if he is to avoid this obligation. He must move on or expand his assets in order to keep his own dependants and provide for the possibility of having others in the future. A man is led to encroach on land which others claim, and this, in turn, provokes them to countermeasures, particularly when further grievances, such as damage done by stray goats and cattle, must follow in the trail. Eventually, disputes may be carried forward to the chieftaincy's or District's court, in order to determine the adjustment between competitors advancing on areas of future development, as members of rival wards. Or, to win a respite from squabbles, the men in a ward along with their neighbours in a locality compromise their claims among themselves, agreeing to rest disputed areas for the time being. But as an oft-repeated proverb puts it, "Meat rots, a matter of blame does not rot" (*Gobola nyama, luposva haguto bola*). As time passes, claims are re-asserted, and the old disputes aroused in new ones; and this, too, Kalanga expect and presage proverbially: "An old boil is revived by the new" (*Londa gulukugwi lomusiwa ne litsva*).

A man and his neighbours do not always agree on the exact location of past boundaries, on which paths, ridges, kopjes, streams, gullies or specially marked trees were the historic dividing landmarks. "The country has many boundaries," they observe, somewhat wryly. But they do agree on change and movement: they know the present territorial divisions and areas of landholding do not coincide with those of the past, just as some present rulers, chieftains and headmen, have replaced their predecessors and have not succeeded according to patrilineal rules. Moreover, some titles are suspended in particular places or partially transferred elsewhere; past divisions and areas of landholding are considered to have lapsed for some but not for all purposes.

Neighbours are virtually unanimous, also, about which titles were held over major divisions in land half a century or more ago, though some shrug their shoulders at the folly of asking them, directly, to tell all they know, in others' hearing. An area is often spoken of as if it were the ancestral estate or perpetual domain of a prior title, one no longer held by a chieftain or headman in that area.[9] By reference to these prior titles, a locality's residents assert other titles and various claims which they neither derive from the contemporary hierarchy of political authority nor sustain within its currently recognized divisions.

Neighbours recall a spread of titles and political relations between them from times unlike the present. Tales are told of when and where a title was founded and of its vicissitudes over time. That the tales have some basis in historical facts can be seen by an inspection of a list[10] recorded in 1910–11, of those tax headmen having more than ten tax-paying followers and under the Khurutse Chief Rauwe (see Werbner 1971: p. 33f), who then ruled much of the District. This list is proof that nearly half of the titles now recognized by the chieftains have survived several generations.[11] These are all titles which are said by Kalanga to have been founded prior to the present chieftaincies. The claim which neighbours make that some titles have not only endured through several generations but also antedate the present superiority of the chieftains' titles, is not a complete invention

9. For example, "This is the country of Mswazi", or "This is the country of Cizhina (Sebena)", I was told in chieftaincies now ruled by others. Presently, these titles are held in the adjacent District, where some headmen claim to be the descendants of the title-holder who left such ancestral domains within the lifetime of elders.

10. Professor I. Schapera kindly gave me a copy of this list, which he found in the files of the Protectorate Administration.

11. At least twenty-six of the fifty-seven titles listed are currently held in the District's Reserve. There may be more which I could not recognize because of spelling or the use of alternative or personal names. The list also covers two kinds of headman that I do not consider here: (a) those that have been renting land directly from the Tati Company, and (b) heads of wards that left with the Khurutse Chief and are now in the adjacent District.

or a simple fiction: it has a basis in fact. But what is not subject to proof is the titles' force or the precise territorial coverage of titles over time. Indeed, their value for Kalanga invests titles with an ambiguous, changing force.

III

Their disputes and many of their casual remarks highlight that Kalanga have an explanatory scheme about landholding and the local titles of groups and persons which is quite simple in terms of a legal order of administration. They conceive of matters which do not fit the scheme as due to historical contingencies. Moreover, they categorize and, thus, comprehend some acts in characterological terms, as instances of gross opportunism and, ultimately, anarchic or of an order fit for gnats or wild animals, not human beings. Yet behaviour which they understand as exceptional, deviant, and disorderly is regular from a sociological point of view. This is not to dismiss their conceptual scheme or to fall back, analytically, on that gross and most overworked of dichotomies, the "ideal" v. the "real". My aim is to take into account how they interpret and apply their scheme when they have to give various acts moral and legal value; and my argument agrees with one which Peters (1967) and Moore (1969: 1972) have advanced about people's conceptual schemes and rationalizations or justifications of behaviour. Thus Peters observes that Bedouin explain away some of their behaviour which seems inconsistent with what Moore would call their "constitutional theory" (1969: p. 383), and they do so through rationalizations in terms of contingencies. Peters points out, however, that "What they fail to appreciate is that these 'contingencies' are ecologically, economically, demographically, and politically essential." (1967: p. 275).

Kalanga usually resorted to a rudimentary serial scheme, when they tried to explain to me their basic legal ideas about land tenure: that is, how the granting of land fits estates in administration, to use Gluckman's terminology (1965: p. 90). Their scheme represents relationships towards land as if in a single progression, from the widest to the narrowest span: an arrangement somewhat like the general one Gluckman presents after he observes that Lozi "landholding is formulated in a straight-forward

---

The surviving titles are distributed among the District's, mainly Kalanga, chieftaincies in the following proportions (I show in parentheses the current number of ward headmen): Habangana 9 (18); Musojane 4 (11); Masunga 5 (11); Ramokate 8 (20). This does not imply constant affiliation: some of the headmen have gone from one chieftaincy to another. Moreover, the list covers a period prior to the establishment of the chieftaincies, and thus does not indicate which ruler, if any, was a tax headman's immediate superior.

series of allocations" (ibid.: p. 85). For example, to illustrate this rudimentary scheme, Ta Mbatili, an elder, drew for me two roughly parallel lines in the sand. These represented the *duthu*, the domain or "area of allocation" of a person "looking after the country" (*shango*) for the ruler, a chieftain. (Such a person would hold a territorial title and be the head of a section or a ward.) Ta Mbatili drew another line between the parallels,

thus 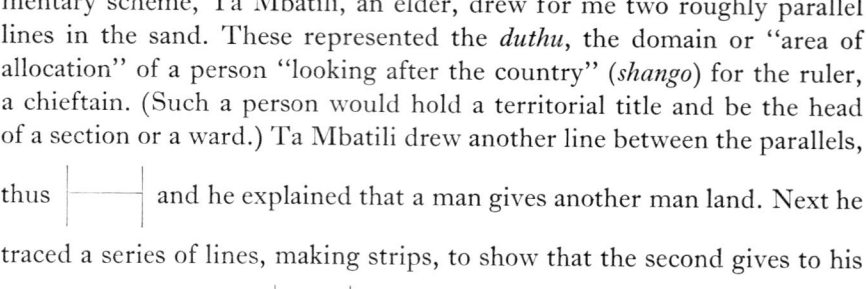 and he explained that a man gives another man land. Next he traced a series of lines, making strips, to show that the second gives to his children, in turn, thus . Significantly, when Ta Mbatili and others went on to discuss particular instances, known groups or persons and their estates or the lands to which their titles referred, lines continually had to be redrawn; and as others came to join us in our conversation, lines were smoothed over or re-interpreted to represent different periods in time.

Similarly, a ward headman in the very densely populated chieftaincy of Habangana recounted for me, in great detail, a history of localities where his ward had held land and the movements of the chieftaincy itself, and then he observed, sadly, "Now there is no domain (*duthu* or 'area of allocation'), because there is no place where there are no fallows." In a like manner, also, one of my closest neighbours, who disparaged the pretensions of others to having their own domain, appealed to history and explained that "An area of allocation (*duthu*) means country which has never been cultivated (*shango usatongo limiwa*)."

The Kalanga scheme is what they chart for rudimentary legal purposes; indeed, rudimentary almost as if in a state of nature. They take for granted unconditional titles along with virgin country, unencumbered by a long history of landholding. Cite any specific territorial title, however, and there is almost always someone in the locality who regards it as qualified, in some respects even dubious; and all deny that unencumbered land can now be found. Moreover, what their scheme seems to eliminate, namely competing legal interests in the same land, it nevertheless tolerates, and even facilitates, because they conceive of sociologically quite distinct spans of relationship by reference to a single kind of status relation, that between "father" and "child". Given such flexibility in their concepts, any title stretches so that heterogeneous and varying congeries of neighbours and kin can be attached to it. A title is personified, and should pass in patrilineal succession; thus Kalanga speak of a "name dying", when none in a locality claim patrilineal descent from the eponymous ancestor, the first to hold the title and land. However, birth, rearing, or dependence through a voluntary contract, all give a man the status of "child" and thus claims to benefit and share in the title's estates. Moreover, the same person may be the "child" of more than one "father", and not restricted to parcels of land he may claim in terms of his current political affiliation or dependence. The very nub of ancestral estates is over-riding interest, crucial for the legal tenure of areas that overlap adjacent units of territorial administration which are independent and, even more, whose officers are competitors for men and basic resources. Structurally, such over-riding interest is of great significance for essential processes: for necessary micro-adjustments and local adaptations, for movement and the continual redistribution of people, and for the undertaking of risks due to fluctuations in the demand for land and in its serviceability within a locality. These are the processes which a rudimentary scheme explains away—or rather which Kalanga in their use of it explain away—however much the scheme may fit select aspects of territorial divisions associated with a hierarchy of authority.

An example is necessary to demonstrate these points in detail. I discuss the following one, since I know it best, because a hamlet in this area was my home for most of my fieldwork; but I know of comparable examples elsewhere. The territories of two adjacent sections, North and South, are publicly defined, and each section's headman is acknowledged by the chieftain to be the administrator of a valley divided from the adjacent one by a sand river. Map 1 shows the distribution in 1964 of some of their places of cultivation and residence, along with territorial boundaries. (The map is based on aerial photography and my survey of cultivation and my house to house census.) Within his valley, each section headman calls on communal work groups—the age-sets[12] of men and women—for public service, building the school, clearing and maintaining paths. Each headman holds court (*kuta, lubazhe*) and tries cases in which the defendant is his political dependent: a fault of a "child" is brought to his "father". Each headman, acting in court, also has the authority to banish or to order a person to abandon land, should he repeatedly disturb the peace or menace public order. Legally, also, any dispute over land within one headman's territory could be brought to that headman's court, if the plaintiff chose to do so, irrespective of the political affiliation of the defendant: in this respect, each headman has an estate of administration over his territory.

---

12. Later, after Botswana's Independence, age-sets or "regiments" were no longer called upon, and communal service was organized on a self-help basis.

Distribution of Cultivation and Residential Units

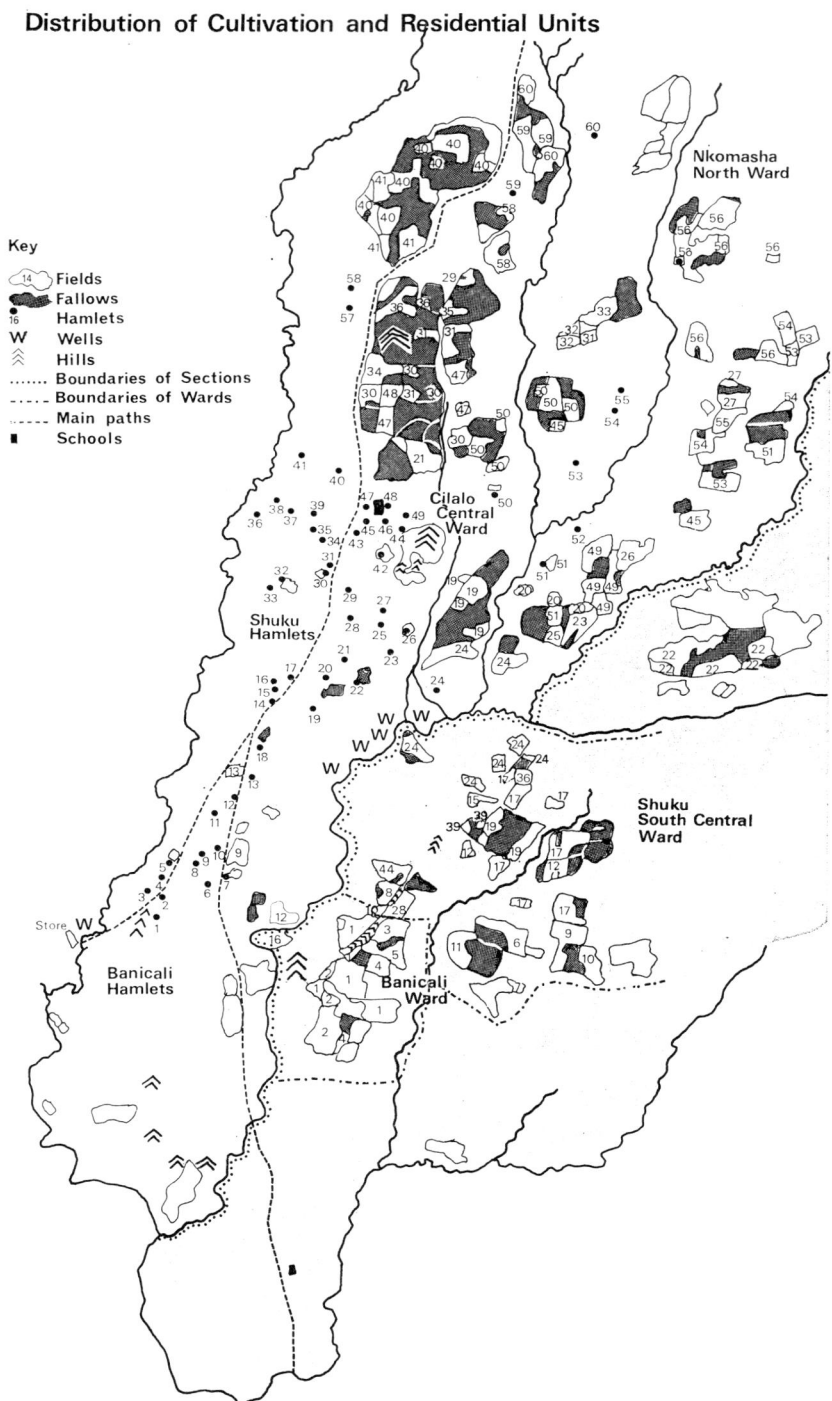

However, neither headman has all his political dependants on estates held on grant from him solely, for all his dependants do not live within his valley or cultivate exclusively within it; indeed, some insist that their tenure of an estate antedates his, and they do not hold land from him.

A similar interspersion along with estates derived from ancestral holdings is found between many wards; and when I pointed such interspersion out to an elder who had drawn a diagram of strips for me, like Ta Mbatili's, he remarked, "Being like wild animals (*puka dze shango*, animals of the country), we crossed over, each one was going in his own way, so and so and so (crossing his hands, over and under)." Heads of wards and sections also complain that there is too much opportunity for individuals and groups to vaccilate between wards, and they roundly condemn it: "The day they get at odds with those at (their present ward), they come over here; the day they get at odds with people here, they say they are people of over there and are going out; and again."

Neighbours trace a history which amplifies this in greater detail. One ward, Banicali South Ward, moved far to the south of the chieftaincy, about forty-five years ago. Shuku South-Central Ward remained, and was "left" (*siwa*) the area by Banicali South Ward to which it formerly belonged. Indeed, neighbours, when justifying their own claims and landholding, sometimes disparaged this ward's founding ancestor and title, "Shuku (the eponymous ancestor) came from Botletle (in another District) carrying rocks on his head, he was a client." Shuku South-Central Ward eventually resited its own hamlets and fields, cultivating over the ruins of Banicali South Ward. Banicali South Ward had had other sub-wards besides Shuku, and members of these gradually returned along with some patrikin of the head of Bancali South Ward. They built anew. However, they did not resume direct administration over the whole of their old estate or the increased estate of Shuku South-Central Ward. People of this former sub-ward now far outnumbered those who returned, the heir to the title of the old ward was not among them, and they were a minority of the old ward. They reclaimed land within their old estate, independently of Shuku South-Central Ward, chose hamlet sites, cultivated gardens, without requiring or seeking the permission of Shuku South-Central Ward. "We returned to our ruins", one explained to me.

A serial scheme suits, without rationalizations, no more than a fragment of wards like Shuku South-Central and Banicali South, their present estates of production, and some of their immediate estates of allocation such as the areas around their field. The rest of their estates, along with the location of both wards' hamlets, some of their fallows and the fields and hamlets of their former sub-wards which now overlap wards and sections, cannot be so simply fitted within the scheme; this distribution and these relations are either irrelevant or specific exceptions, seen in terms of the scheme. Along with Shuku South-Central Ward, the revived ward of Banicali South now holds its fields in South Section's valley. Their hamlets and some of their fallows are within North Section's adjacent valley. Similarly members of Banicali South Ward's former sub-wards, who are now affiliated to the adjacent section, have fields and hamlets in a complementary distribution. Their fields are within the South Section; their hamlets, in the North Section. (See hamlets 19, 24, 36, 39, 44 on Map 1.) As for the people, they are themselves, at present, political dependents of the headman of North Section and in Cilalo Central Ward; they join age-sets in this ward, and defend suits there, near their hamlets. Their situation complements that of people of Shuku South-Central and Banicali South Wards who belong to the South Section, and they do not give communal service or join the age-sets of the valley surrounding their hamlets; nor do they come as political dependants in the court of the section where they reside. Both these complementary situations fit together as ancestral estates, and both over-ride, in some respects, a contemporary hierarchy of administration.

Heirs to ancestral estates, though no longer dependants in an old administrative unit (or perhaps, *because* of their independence) insist on taking precedence over those current dependants of an administrative unit who are recent immigrants. Heads of wards, on the other hand, are subject to the pressing demands of new dependants to meet their needs and find them land or else lose their political affiliation. Blocking former dependants from future expansion and allocating fallows they claim as part of an ancestral estate are some of the tactics which headmen resort to where demand for land is pressing. To be able to bring to bear on one dispute a multitude of others which concern a wide range of neighbours, chronically, not ephemerally, is a capacity which differentiates the standing of "owners", "heirs", "people of over here" from that of those who can still be treated as "immigrants". Indeed, the assumption of this capacity is tantamount to becoming an "owner", able to derive benefit from longstanding debts, and faults. Every locality has its heritage of a dubious past, continually revived and nurtured as a force against the narrowing of a dispute to a single or immediate fault. The administration of estates in land could be straightforward or unequivocal, only if it applied to "immigrants" without any pretensions to being "owners", that is, to people who can be dealt with without recourse to old scores and memories of usurpation. In other words, a rudimentary scheme like that of Ta Mbatili is legal and holds true only insofar as no dubious acts provide a basis for an appeal against it. It cannot be comprehensive, without exceptions, because there is ever and always an accumulation of unwarranted acts and other faults, a persistence of prior interests and ancestral estates, a recurrence of presumption, vaccilation in the affiliation of dependents: "The wilderness is the human being".

Particular parcels of land come to be covered by competing claims and legal interests under conditions of increasing shortage of land and of necessity for moves to allow for soil impoverishment. These claims are understood by the people themselves in terms of histories of past landholding, so that a contemporary patch of land is seen as having a time dimension represented by ancestral estates. No cult is made of an ancestral grave and thus other memorials, primarily ruins and fallows, must anchor attachments to land. Yet the interest in ruins and past occupation goes beyond the mere validation of present land-holding, since ancestral estates, like other credits and debts, project statuses into the future. The units of land use within which negotiated adjustments of claims between neighbours take place—localities—cannot correspond with the hierarchy of administration over territorial divisions. Consequently, territorial divisions, localities, ancestral and other estates all represent distinct aspects of land and land tenure, and one aim of this essay has been to show what are the systematic relations between them.

To carry this analysis a stage further, it is necessary to examine the strategies which neighbours use to secure their legal interests in land and mobilize productive services along with personal support. The processes by which bounded zones of relationships are defined so that some neighbours are excluded from rights and claims while others are brought into preferential attachments must also be considered. Moreover, since critically important claims over persons are established between neighbours through affinity, patterns of marriage need to be discussed, as well. These problems, though so crucial for further argument, call for discussion well beyond the limits set by this *Festschrift*, and will be considered in a forthcoming essay elsewhere.

References

Allan, W. (1965). *The African Husbandman*. Oliver and Boyd, Edinburgh.
Bawden, H. G. and Stobbs, A. R. (1963). *The Land Resources of Eastern Bechuanaland*. Directorate of Overseas Surveys, Tolworth.

Biebuyck, D. (ed.) (1963). Introduction. *African Agrarian Systems*. Oxford University Press for the International African Institute, London.

Bohannan, P. (1960). "Africa's Land". *The Centennial Review* 4, pp. 439–449. Reprinted 1967. *Tribal and Peasant Economics*, Dalton, G. (ed.) pp. 51–60. The National History Press, New York.

Colson, E. (1971). "The Impact of the Colonial Period on the Definition of Land Rights." In *Profiles of Change: African Society and Colonial Rule*. Turner, V. (ed.) pp. 193–215. Cambridge University Press, Cambridge.

Gluckman, M. (1965). *The Ideas in Barotse Jurisprudence*. Yale University Press, New Haven and London.

(1969). "Property Rights and Status in African Traditional Law". In *Ideas and Procedures in African Customary Law*. pp. 252–265. Oxford University Press for the International African Institute, London.

Lloyd, P. C. (1962). *Yoruba Land Law*. O.U.P. for the Nigerian Institute of Social and Economic Research, London.

Mayer, P. and Iona (1965). "Land Law in the Making". In *African Law: Adaptation and Development*, Kuper, H. and L. (eds), pp. 51–78. University of California Press, Berkeley.

Moore, S. F. (1969). "Descent and Legal Position". In *Law in Culture and Society*, Nader, L. (ed.), pp. 374–400. Aldine, Chicago.

(1972). "Legal Liability and Evolutionary Interpretation: Some Aspects of Strict Liability, Self-Help and Collective Responsibility". In *The Allocation of Responsibility*, Gluckman, M. (ed.), pp. 51–107. Manchester University Press, Manchester.

Peters, E. L. (1967). "Some Structural Aspects of the Feud Among the Camel-Herding Bedouin of Cyrenaica". *Africa* 37, pp. 261–282.

Ranger, T. O. (1967). *Revolt in Southern Rhodesia, 1896–7*. Heinemann, London.

Richards, A. I. (1939). *Land, Labour and Diet in Northern Rhodesia*. Oxford University Press for the International African Institute, London.

Roberts, S. n.d.c. (1970). *A Restatement of the Kgatla Law Relating to Land and Natural Resources*. Government Printer, Gaborone.

Schapera, I. (1943a). *Native Land Tenure in the Bechuanaland Protectorate*. Lovedale Press, Lovedale, South Africa.

(1943b). "The Native Land Problem in the Tati District. Mafeking". Reprinted 1971 in *Botswana Notes and Records* 3, 219–268.

Werbner, R. P. (1971a). Local Adaptation and the Transformation of an Imperial Concession in North-Eastern Botswana. *Africa* 41, 32–41.

(1971b). Symbolic Dialogue and Personal Transactions Among the Kalanga and Ndembu. *Ethnology* 10, 311–328.

(1972). "Sin, Blame and Ritual Mediation". *The Allocation of Responsibility*. Gluckman, M. (ed.), pp. 227–235. Manchester University Press, Manchester.

White, C. (1958). "Terminological Confusion in African Land Tenure". *J. Afr. Admin.* 10, pp. 124–130.

(1963). "Factors Determining the Content of African Land Tenure Systems in Northern Rhodesia". In *African Agrarian Systems*, Biebuyck, D. (ed.), pp. 364–373. Oxford University Press for the International African Institute, London.

Wilson, M. (1963). "Effects on the Xhosa and Nyakusa of Scarcity of Land". *African Agrarian Systems*, Biebuyck, D. (ed.), pp. 374–391. Oxford University Press for the International African Institute, London.

8 | Preferential Marriage and Polygyny among the Tswana

Adam Kuper

Isaac Schapera's publications on the Tswana of Botswana constitute perhaps the most complete and scholarly of contemporary ethnographies. Those who have worked in the same ethnographic area will be particularly aware of the quality of his achievement, but it has become something of a legend throughout the ranks of Africanists and social anthropologists. Despite his emphasis upon the ethnographic enterprise, Professor Schapera has also developed a number of theories to explain particular aspects of Tswana social organization, and these have also stimulated research workers studying other societies in the same culture area.

The present essay attempts to indicate something of the richness of the material, by reviewing the problem of close-kin marriage among the Tswana. This is a problem which Schapera has explored in a number of papers (1949, 1950, 1957 and 1963) and, while I accept his central thesis, I shall try to use his meticulous data to develop a few points in partial contradiction to him. This is a risky thing to try at the best of times, for Schapera's arguments are always carefully weighed and tested. Nevertheless the attempt will at least serve to indicate the extraordinary quality of the data which Schapera has provided.

The Tswana (and most other Sotho-speaking peoples) are remarkable in Bantu Africa for their tendency to marry close kin, including lineal kin. In exploring this issue, Schapera has been concerned to demonstrate four main propositions:

(i) Nobles marry close kin more frequently than do commoners. (Close kin are defined as kin who share a common great-grandparent, or who are more closely related.) In particular, they marry first kin more frequently than do commoners. (First kin are relatives who share a grandparent, or who are more closely related.)

(ii) Among close kin, nobles show a preference for marriages with agnates, and their kin marriages are much more heavily biased in favour of such marriages than is the case with commoners. In particular they show a decided preference for marriage with a genealogical FBD, a preference not shared by commoners. Schapera explains this, convincingly, as a function of the political system. The Tswana are patrilineal, and by marrying close agnates nobles maintain their access to power, and also restrain conflict within the inner circle of the powerful.

(iii) Polygynists marry close kin of all kinds more frequently than do monogamists.

(iv) There has been a decline in all categories of close-kin marriage in the past four generations. This decline has been most marked in the case of noble marriages with first kin and close agnates. Schapera argues that this decline is associated with the parallel decline in the incidence of polygyny.

I accept Schapera's demonstration of the differential marriage strategies of nobles and commoners. However, I dispute his suggestion that there has been a marked decline in close-kin marriages and that this is associated with the decline in polygyny. Indeed, if this were true, his more important hypothesis about the political function of close-kin marriages would require considerable modification. I shall examine this objection, before discussing the first two propositions.

The broad features of Schapera's sample should be apparent in Table I, which I have constructed from data he provides (1957: pp. 139–44). As the layout of my table indicates, one may choose between two measures of the tendency to marry kin. The first measure takes married men as the unit, and shows what proportion of married men have married at least one kinswoman. The second measure takes marriages as the unit, and shows the proportion of marriages which are between kin. Schapera is primarily concerned with the first measure in his paper, and as he points out this introduces certain distortions, since some men have married more than once. The second measure cannot be directly deduced from the first—indeed, using Schapera's figures I have had to leave some boxes blank in section (b) of the table. Moreover, a decline in the first measure does not necessarily imply a decline in the second measure. That is to say, the fact that fewer men are married to close kin than was the case in the past does

TABLE I. Schapera's sample of marriages in nine Tswana tribes
(a) *Number of men marrying close kin*

Class	No. married men	No. men marrying close kin	Percentage	No. men marrying first kin	Percentage
Nobles:	691	287	42	157	23
Polygynists	251	157	63	93	37
Monogamists	440	130	30	64	15
Commoners:	917	199	22	97	11
Polygynists	202	63	31	33	16
Monogamists	715	136	18	64	9

(b) *Number of marriages with close kin*

Class	No. marriages	No. marriages with close kin	Percentage	No. marriages with first kin	Percentage
Nobles:	1144	365	32	?	?
Polygynists	704	235	33	?	?
Monogamists	440	130	30	64	15
Commoners:	1179	207	18	?	?
Polygynists	464	71	15	?	?
Monogamists	715	136	18	64	9

not necessarily mean that the rate of close-kin marriages, as a proportion of all marriages, has declined. This point should perhaps be spelled out.

Let us assume that in an imaginary society 50 per cent of all marriages are between kin. Half the married men are monogamists, half being polygynists with two wives each. The polygynist with two wives has two chances of 1/2 of marrying a kinswoman; which gives him three chances in four of marrying at least one kinswoman.[1] Therefore, three-quarters of the 50 per cent who are polygynists would have married at least one kinswoman =

1. The reasoning is as follows. A man makes two marriages. Each time he has an equal chance of making or not making a kin marriage. If a kin marriage = k, and a non-kin marriage = n, then his first marriage may be k or n, and his second marriage may be k or n. If the first marriage is k, then the possible combinations of spouses are kk and kn. If the first marriage is n, the possible combinations of spouses are nk and nn. Of these four equal possibilities, the first three would include at least one kinswoman as a wife.

38 per cent of the married men. Only half the 50 per cent who are monogamists would have married a kinswoman = 25 per cent. Therefore, 63 per cent of the men would have married at least one kinswoman. Assume now that polygyny is abolished, but the rate of kin marriage remains 50 per cent. Obviously now only 50 per cent of the men will have married a kinswoman. Schapera's first measure is drastically reduced, but the second measure remains constant.

Schapera shows that there has been a steady decline in the incidence of polygyny among the Tswana over the past four generations. Concurrently there has been a decline in the proportion of married men who have married at least one close kinswoman. The relevant data are arranged in the following table. Generation 1 (G1) was initiated between 1830–60; generation 2 (G2), between 1860–90; generation 3 (G3), between 1890–1920; and the contemporary generation (G4) began to be initiated in 1920 (Schapera, 1957: pp. 142, 146).

TABLE II. Decline in polygyny and the proportion of men married to at least one close kinswoman

Class	Average No. wives per married man	Percentage of married men who have married at least one:	
		Close kin	First kin
Nobles:			
G1	3·3	62	41
G2	1·8	55	33
G3	1·4	42	21
G4	1·1	20	7
Commoners:			
G1	1·9	30	17
G2	1·4	22	10
G3	1·3	25	13
G4	1·1	16	7

However, as we have seen, the decline in the proportion of married men who have married at least one close kinswoman may follow a decline in polygyny *even if the rate of close-kin marriage remains constant*. We must therefore examine Schapera's figures to abstract the second measure, the proportion of close-kin marriages out of all marriages. This measure can in fact be deduced by comparing Schapera's Table II (1957: p. 143), where he gives the number of relatives married per man in each generation, with

Table V (ibid., p. 146), where he gives the number of wives per man in each generation. This yields Table III (I am now concerned with nobles only, for his hypothesis applies particularly to them):

TABLE III. Noble close-kin marriages over four generations

| Generation | No. marriages | Percentage of marriages with | |
		Close kin	First kin*
1	242	29	14
2	316	41	18
3	404	34	15
4	182	18	6

* The figure for first kin must be taken from Schapera's tables VII and VIII—pp. 149 and 151. Unfortunately, it is impossible to deduce the precise number of marriages in each category from these tables, since men marrying more than one first kinswoman are only counted once. This excludes 5 per cent of first-kin marriages overall. However using the same tables to calculate second kin marriages in each generation, one arrives at the following percentages for all close kin marriages: G1 26%, G2 38%, G3 30%, G4 18%. Comparing these figures with the percentages of all close kin marriages in column three of the table above, it can be seen that the bias is fairly evenly distributed over the four generations.

It is clear from these figures that at least in the first three generations there has not been a decrease in the rate of close-kin and first-kin marriage —on the contrary, G2 and G3 score more highly than G1. Therefore the decline in polygyny has not resulted in a decline in the rate of close-kin marriage. Schapera writes: ". . . there seems no reason to doubt that kin marriages are on the whole becoming less common. This applies particularly to nobles, among whom, for every 100 men marrying near kin in G1, there were only 66 in G3" (1957: p. 142). The second statement is correct; the first is wrong, for there is no simple connection in a polygynous society between the rate of close-kin marriage and the number of men who have married close kin.

It is also not the case that there has been a marked decline in the rate of noble marriages with close agnates. This may be seen in Table IV, abstracted from Schapera's Table VII (ibid., p. 149).

Among first cousins the preferred order of marriages in every generation was FBD, MBD, FZD and MZD. Among second cousins the order from G1 to G3 was classificatory FBD, FZD, MBD, MZD. The only marked oddities are the behaviour of G4, and the preference in G1 for BD among first kin, and classificatory BD (FFBSSD) and FZ (FFBD). The odd

TABLE IV. Incidence of close kin marriages with specified
categories of kin—nobles

(a) *Categories of first-kin marriage as percentages of all first-kin marriages*
(First kin share a common grandparent) close parents

	G1	G2	G3	G4
FBD	35	55	38	36
MBD	26	20	26	18
FZD	12	11	13	36
MZD	0	7	10	0
BD	18	5	13	0
*Others	9	2	0	9
Total	100	100	100	99

* Others include 3 sisters (G1–2; G2–1) and 2 mothers' sisters (G1 and 4).

(b) *Categories of second-kin marriage as percentages of all second-kin marriages*
(second kin share a common great-grandparent, but exclude first kin)

	G1	G2	G3	G4
*FBD	21	28	30	19
FZD	18	20	24	29
MBD	7	17	15	29
MZD	0	2	3	10
BD	25	19	13	10
FZ	21	6	7	5
†Others	7	8	8	0
Total	99	100	100	102

* These are classificatory categories.
† Others include 4MZ—G1–1; G2–1; G3–2; and 9ZD—G1–1; G2–4; G3–4.

behaviour of G4 may be due to the small size and incomplete nature of the
sample, though I shall attempt another explanation later. The specific
preferences of G1 are due, perhaps, to the high incidence of polygyny in
the past, for this would certainly make it more likely that one had half-
brothers whose daughters once could marry. Overall, however, what is
striking is the maintenance of steady preferences for particular kinds of kin
marriage over the generations, at least until the contemporary generation,
despite the rapid decline in the incidence of polygyny.

Having said all that, one final point must be noted. Although the average rate of close-kin marriage was fairly constant for monogamists and poly-gynists, polygynists were more likely to take a close kinswoman as first wife, and much less likely to take one as a subsequent wife. (Cf. Schapera, 1957: table IV, p. 145).

TABLE V. First and subsequent close-kin marriages rates
(per cent)

Class	Average	Monogamists	Polygynists	Polygynists: first marriage
Nobles	32	30	33	40
Commoners	18	18	15	22

Moreover, few men who had married first kin on first marriage married another first kinswoman later (Schapera, 1957: table IV, p. 145): therefore most men who married first kin in their second marriages had not married a first kinswoman on first marriage. These facts indicate that, although the overall rate of first and close, kin marriage of polygynists approximated to that of monogamists, polygynists not only had a statistically higher chance, in any case, of marrying at least one close kinswoman, but they also increased this chance for their class as a whole by tending to marry only one first kinswoman each.

In sum, until the current generation, the Tswana displayed a consistent pattern of marriage preferences. However, polygynists showed a much higher tendency to make a preferred marriage in their first marriage than did monogamists.

The marriage strategies of nobles and commoners differed systematically, until the current generation. Taking married men as the unit of measure-ment, over four generations 42 per cent of nobles, as opposed to 22 per cent of commoners, married close kin. Moreover, 25 per cent of nobles married close agnates, as opposed to 6 per cent of commoners; while 19 per cent of nobles married cross-cousins, as opposed to 13 per cent of commoners.

Taking marriages as the unit of measurement, we can be even more specific about the range in preferences, since a higher proportion of nobles than commoners were polygynists. The figures in the following table are drawn from Schapera's tables VII and VIII (1957: pp. 149, 151). As men-tioned earlier, there is the drawback that men who married the same kin category twice are counted only once, a possibility which I calculate accounts for five per cent of noble close-kin marriages and one per cent of commoner close-kin marriages. It may be, of course, that the whole five per cent (in the case of noble marriages) should be added to one category of close-kin marriages. However, this is unlikely, and even if it were the case, as will be seen, the overall pattern would not be greatly disturbed, whichever category is favoured.

TABLE VI. Marriages with categories of first kin as percentages of
all first-kin marriages
(*same GP: all categories genealogical*)

	FBD	FZD	MBD	MZD	BD	Others	Total
Nobles (N = 162)	43	13	23	6	11	3	99%
Commoners (N = 98)	13	10	48	19	7	2	99%

Categories of second-kin marriage as percentages of all second-kin marriages
(*same GGP: classificatory categories*)

	FZ	FBD	FZD	MBD	MZD	BD	Others	Total
Nobles (N = 184)	9	27	22	16	3	16	7	100%
Commoners (N = 160)	3	19	20	35	13	8	2	100%

As Table VI shows, marriages made by nobles with FBD constituted over 40 per cent of their first-kin marriages and marriages with patrilateral kin constituted 67 per cent. Commoners married MBD in nearly 50 per cent of first-kin marriages, and agnates in only 30 per cent. Among second kin the contrast is similar, if less sharp. Nobles still showed a marked preference for FBD and FZD over MBD marriages, while commoners showed the reverse order of preference.

What is the explanation for this pattern? Schapera first explained that the Tswana state their preference in the order MBD, FZD, FBD, MZD, and he listed the reasons given by the Tswana in support of these preferences. In general, close-kin marriages are preferred on the grounds that since one knows the girl's family one can be sure of her quality; and furthermore, the existing close connections between the families would make the success of the marriage more likely. The MBD is preferred since:

(i) The MB's family has already shown that it provides good wives;

(ii) the mother's brideprice was used to provide a wife for her brother, and this gives her a claim on the return of her brother's daughter as a daughter-in-law, to work for her; and

(iii) the joking relationship between the cross-cousins eases the path to a good marital relationship.

In general, the attitude of the Tswana is summed up pithily in their phrase, *Ntsala wa motho ke mogatse*, "a man's cross-cousin is his wife". They may also add a particular preference for marriages between the children of a linked brother and sister.

The only other type of marriage which is explained in terms of specific advantages is that with the FyBD, in support of which the Tswana cite the saying, *ngwana rrangwane, nnale, kgomo di boele sakeng*, (FyBD, marry me, so that the (bridewealth) cattle may return to the kraal,) (Schapera, 1950: p. 151). This saying should not be read too literally. It is extremely unlikely that a man will share rights in cattle with his FyB. The saying rather defines a preference in terms of the value of agnatic solidarity, and this is expressed in a form familiar to Africanists where cattle = agnates.

Despite the fact that there are no specific justifications for FZD and MZD marriage, one might leave the problem here if the Tswana followed the stated order of preference. However, as we have seen, they do not. Nobles actually make kin marriages in the order FBD, MBD, FZD, MZD; while for commoners the order is MBD, FBD, MZD, FZD. Schapera has been particularly concerned to explain the preference shown by nobles for marriage with close agnates.

Schapera argues that the purpose of patrilateral marriages among nobles is to convert tense and competitive relationships in the ruling group into relationships of affinity and, later and more particularly, matrifiliation, which can be mobilized more readily for political support. Politically the critical alliances are those between the ruling groups of different wards, who are also members of the royal line. I quote his reasoning *in extenso*:

... it seems reasonable to contend that one function of agnatic marriage among Tswana nobles is to counterbalance the fissiparous tendency of the ward system (or, within the ward, of the "house" system) by establishing new sets of ties between groups that have become (or are likely to become) politically distinct. So far as the children are concerned in particular the effect will be to convert relatively distant paternal kin into closer maternal kin ...

Now among the Tswana disputes often occur in every local group of agnatic kin, from the household upwards, owing to arbitrary exercise of authority or rival claims to property or position. It is not fortuitous, for example, that most accusations of sorcery are made against relatives who are also close neighbours.

The proximity in which they live, and the rule of patrilineal succession and inheritance (complicated by the practice of polygyny), breed jealousies and rivalries that may prove stronger than the ties of mutual dependence and kinship solidarity. The usual outcome is that the group splits, some of its members moving away to establish their own household, ward, etc. In noble families, especially that of the chief himself, the stakes are far more valuable and consequently far more tempting, and on the whole they tend to break apart more frequently than those of commoners.

Such disputes are far less likely with maternal kin, who because of unilineal descent cannot be rivals for one's patrimony. Indeed, a person's maternal relatives are notoriously more attached and devoted to him than are his agnates, and it is to his mother's brother above all that he looks for disinterested advice and support in times of difficulty. Hence, by marrying an agnate whose father belongs to the ruling family of another ward (or to another "house" within the same ward), a man will generally ensure that at least some potential rivals of his sons are transformed into the partisans normally constituted by maternal kin. And he himself likewise often receives support from his wife's people . . .

Nor are the advantages one-sided. People benefit in many ways from the political eminence of uterine kin, and are therefore anxious to marry their sisters or daughters to men of rank.

(Schapera, 1957: pp. 197–198)

In his most recent paper on Tswana kinship and politics, Schapera takes this argument further, with respect particularly to "royals", i.e. chiefs, their sons and sons' sons. These are the élite among the nobles, who comprise all lineal descendants of the original ruling family of the tribe. (Schapera, 1963). He shows that they had a higher rate of close-kin marriage than the broader group of nobles considered in his earlier paper—and also an even more marked preference for real and classificatory FBD marriage. FBD's were married more frequently than all cross-cousins combined. (1963: pp. 105–106). Furthermore, over "twice as many agnates were married as all other relatives combined" (p. 106), agnates including real and classificatory Z, FZ, FBD and BD.

Schapera also divides the tribes under consideration into two cultural sets—the western v. eastern Tswana. These sets differed systematically. The western tribes married more royals than others—over 60 per cent of marriages were with royals in three of the five western tribes. The eastern tribes made only slightly more than 40 per cent of their marriages with royals. Similarly, as might be expected, royals of the western tribes show a greater tendency than the easterners to marry agnates. Royals of the western tribes made 47 per cent of their marriages with agnates, 17 per cent with cross-cousins, and 5 per cent with other kin; the easterners made

36 per cent of their marriages with agnates, 16 per cent with cross-cousins, and 2 per cent with other kin. (1963: pp. 104–7).

Schapera identifies the cause of this variation in the different mode of ward formation in the western and eastern tribes. In the west a new ward is created for each "house" of the chief. In the east all the chief's sons, except for the heir, are placed in one new ward. The western royals will thus want to make a number of alliances between the ruling groups of different wards, while the eastern royals, less threatened by fissiparous possibilities within the tribe, will be less highly motivated to do so. Another statistic which supports this interpretation is that in the east 29 per cent of marriages were within the ward, while in the west only 8 per cent were within the ward. The argument therefore strengthens his general reasoning about the noble preference for FBD marriage in particular and, more broadly, marriages with close agnates.

The difference between senior royals and other nobles, I suggest, is explicable in similar terms. Senior nobles wish to transform competitive power relations into supportive relations. They therefore marry brother's daughters, father's brother's daughters and other close agnates. More junior nobles, those more distantly descended from a ruling chief, will make some marriages of this kind, but will be more concerned to create closer relationships with the really powerful men—and so they will make marriage alliances, where possible, with senior royals. This will be most easily accomplished if their fathers or father's fathers were related by marriage to such royals—and so they will often be marrying cross-cousins. I believe that the cut-off point for the effectiveness of simple close agnatic relationship is equivalent to the point of Schapera's "close kinship", i.e. descendants, in this case, of a common great-grandfather. Beyond this point a family retains influence in the royal circles only if it is also connected to top royals by marriage. If my argument is correct, it would explain the peculiar behaviour of G4 in the table presented above (Table III). This is precisely the generation of nobles which will contain a majority whose connections by descent with the ruling core will have become too tenuous to be significant. They must therefore reinforce any matrilateral or affinal connection with the really powerful men. As may be seen in Table IV, nobles of G4 married five cross-cousins to every four FBD's in their first-kin marriages, while members of the other generations showed a marked preference for patrilateral parallel-cousin marriages.

My reasoning is as follows: Schapera's genealogies of nobles begin with tribes formed in 1807, 1820, 1830, 1834 and 1835 (1957: p. 133). The generation of nobles initiated from 1830 (G1) would therefore constitute sons of the chief, brothers and brothers' sons. By G4, however, the category of nobles would include many, perhaps a majority, who were only distantly related by descent to ruling chiefs. They might then be expected to behave like commoners—to rely upon their matrilateral and affinal links with the really powerful inner circle of the tribe. Including a majority of distantly connected nobles in the sample, as must occur by G4, will have exactly the contrary effect to sampling only those nobles most closely related to the chief, as Schapera did in his 1963 paper. In the former case one might expect behaviour approximating that of commoners; in the latter case, nobles' behaviour in an exaggerated form. This is precisely what one finds. The hypothesis assumes that there is a critical break after about three generations among the descendants of a chief, which would account for the distinctly noble behaviour of G2 and G3. This is consistent with the developmental cycle of family groups, where descendants of a common great-great grandfather are hardly ever found together, unless linked by marriage. It is also consistent with the assumption which underlies Schapera's definition of close kin as people who share a common great-grandparent or who are more closely related.

The preference shown by commoners for MBD marriage is capable of explanation in similar political terms. Many wards and family-group alliances include affines and matrilateral kin of the group head. They do not themselves hold any office—such as ward-head. Their path to political influence is therefore through marriage with the ruling group at every level of tribal government, but particularly at the lower levels. One's political strength is then most usually on one's mother's side of the family, and it is there that one seeks a wife.

The Kgalagari and Southern Sotho, whose political and territorial organization parallels that of the Tswana, show a similar pattern of ideal and actual marriage preferences. I have described elsewhere the political structure of a Kgalagari village, founded a generation ago, where all but one of the men in the ruling line had married at least one close agnate. Overall the aristocrats had made 45 per cent of their marriages with close agnates, and 11 per cent with other close kin, while the other villagers had made 13 per cent of their marriages with close agnates and 23 per cent with other close kin. (Kuper, 1970, especially p. 32).

Ashton has provided extremely detailed material on marriage patterns for the main Southern Sotho group. (Ashton 1952: pp. 327–337; cf. Jones, 1966: pp. 59, 69–71). He distinguishes two generations each of chiefs' and commoners' families. It appears from his figures that 25 per cent of "chiefs" made close-kin marriages as opposed to 20 per cent of commoners, but that both groups made a very high proportion of first-kin marriages— 21 per cent among chiefs, and 18 per cent among commoners. The chiefs also greatly favoured patrilateral marriages—21 per cent of their marriages as opposed to 13 per cent for commoners.[2]

By comparison with the other two groups, the Southern Sotho show a very much greater preference for marriage with first over second kin. This may be correlated with the much higher degree of mobility which characterizes the Southern Sotho. Their general marriage strategy is, however, of the same kind as that of the Tswana and Kgalagari.

Finally, Ashton makes an observation which throws light on some facts noted earlier. Studying the genealogy of a chief, he points out that "the senior wives of the senior males are kinswomen, whereas their junior wives and the wives of the junior males are usually not related. The former tend to be married to fulfil family and, occasionally, political obligations, the latter from personal choice . . ." (p. 332). The Tswana figures show similarly that polygynists exhibit a particularly high tendency to marry close kin in their first marriages. I would suggest the following explanation. Polygynists are most likely to be important men, e.g. heads of family-groups and family-group alliances. It is their marriage alliances which have the greatest political impact, and they are therefore most likely to make political marriages on first marriage. However, polygynists are not overall "ratebusters" in the field of close-kin marriage, since they seldom marry more than one first-kin; and over-all in their second marriages they are less likely than monogamists to make a close-kin marriage. The Sotho are reported in the literature as explaining this in terms of avoiding conflict over seniority of wives. A polygynist's first wife is normally the senior wife, and her eldest son is generally the heir. If a man was to marry, say, a FBD after marrying a non-kinswoman, or even a MBD, there might be disputes over which house was senior, and, later, over inheritance and succession.

These considerations are clearly important, but another factor may also be operative. Particularly in the case of nobles, every close-kin marriage cements a political alliance. By arranging a marriage the noble casts his lot with one faction rather than another. To multiply such marriages is to multiply possibly contrary allegiances. This may be advantageous in some

2. I have throughout abstracted Ashton's figures for close-kin only—i.e. those with a common great-grandparent, or, in Ashton's phrase, at most "two generations removed".

situations, but it is not generally so for the Sotho noble, particularly since factional allegiance normally implies coresidence.

A further deduction may be made. If polygyny declines, then the more politically influential men will have an extra incentive to make their only marriage as politically advantageous as possible. This may explain why the Tswana statistics show that in G2 and G3 the rate of close-kin marriage is actually rather higher than in G1, when with extensive polygyny there were a number of politically redundant marriages.

To sum up, I have tried to support Schapera's case that the preferred marriage strategies of the Tswana must be understood in terms of their political consequences. Seen in their proper light, Schapera's data about the effects of the decline of polygyny strengthen the basic hypothesis.

References

Ashton, Hugh. (1952). *The Basuto*. Oxford University Press for the International African Institute, London.

Jones, G. I. (1966). "Chiefly Succession in Basutoland", In Goody, Jack, (ed.) *Succession to High Office*, Cambridge Papers in Social Anthropology No. 4, Cambridge University Press, London.

Kuper, Adam. (1970). *Kalahari Village Politics: An African Democracy*, Cambridge University Press, London.

Schapera, I. (1949). "The Tswana Conception of Incest", In Fortes, M. (ed.), *Social Structure*. Oxford University Press, Oxford.

(1950). "Kinship and Marriage among the Tswana", In Radcliffe-Brown, A. R., and Forde, Daryll (eds), *African Systems of Kinship and Marriage*. Oxford University Press for the International African Institute, London.

(1957). "Marriage of Near Kin among the Tswana", *Africa*, XXVII, pp. 139–159.

(1963). "Agnatic Marriage in Tswana Royal Families", In Schapera, I. (ed.), *Studies in Kinship and Marriage*. Royal Anthropological Institute Occasional Paper No. 16, London.

9 | Early Travellers to Tristan Da Cunha

J. B. Loudon

In the summer of 1905 a clergyman of the Church of England named Barrow wrote a letter from his home in Worcestershire offering his services to the Colonial Office. "Knowing that the islanders of Tristan da Cunha have for 15 years been wanting clergyman or schoolmaster, my wife and I have decided to go and live amongst them if we can get to them. We have contemplated this step for some time, taking a special interest in the islanders because years ago my mother was wrecked off Tristan and cared for by them". (Cd. 3098, pp. 58–59). He added that they proposed going at their own expense and that they would be accompanied by Mrs. Barrow's maidservant. The reaction of the Colonial Office to this offer was notably cautious. The Assistant Under-Secretary of State wrote saying that there seemed very little possibility of a passage being provided in one of His Majesty's ships and observing that "the inhabitants raise difficulties in regard to providing a house". He enclosed a copy of a recent letter received through the governor of the Cape from one of the islanders in which it was said that Tristan people themselves could provide neither salary nor house but that "if a charitable man choose to come and stay with us for a short time he may be unmarried one which he may stay with one of the families". (Cd. 3098, p. 60). The Colonial Office proposed that the Earl of Crawford, who was shortly intending to pay a private visit to Tristan da Cunha in his yacht *Valhalla*, be asked to discuss the question of accommodation for a chaplain with the inhabitants. The Barrows, together with their maid, were however already on their way to Tristan. In November 1905 they sailed from Southampton to St. Helena. Failing to obtain a passage from there, they went on to Cape Town to await a ship bound for South America which might be induced to take them to their destination.

Meanwhile Lord Crawford had visited Tristan, as in due course he reported in a letter to the Colonial Office. Arriving on 17th January, 1906, he was unable to land "owing to stress of weather". A party of eleven island men, including Andrea Repetto, the writer of the letter already quoted, came off in two boats to visit the *Valhalla* shortly after her arrival. But after remaining "a few miles from the island for about three days, without any signs of the gale moderating", his Lordship was unwillingly obliged to go on his way to Cape Town without setting foot on shore and without further contact with the inhabitants. His information and opinions were therefore based on the little he could see of the place from his ship and on what conversation he was able to have with the men who came aboard.

Lord Crawford, then aged fifty-nine and a man of great wealth and some distinction in British public life, was no doubt accustomed to good manners, if nothing more, among those with whom he had dealings. It seems from his report that he was treated with scant respect by the island men. He writes that "they were not in the least glad to see us or obliged for the mails and stores I had brought them—but grumbled that I had not come from the Cape, and that I had not brought money to them from the French Government on account of a French barque which, some little while ago, put in on fire. She remained there for seventeen days, during which time the crew was supplied with fresh meat by the islanders. When she went away the captain said he had no money, and that it should be sent to them. I could not learn the name of this barque. Their chief wants seem to be clothing and gunpowder, but they ask without scruple for anything they fancy to be given to them, and for everything they bring off by way of trading they ask very high prices, excepting meat, which is 4d a pound. They have a large herd of cattle." Lord Crawford also reported that the men were so suspicious of one another "that they all had to go over the side to their boats together, for fear that one might get an advantage unknown to the others". Most of his conversation seems to have been with Andrea Repetto, himself regarded by native-born islanders as something of an outsider; for Repetto was an Italian, then aged 39, who had been shipwrecked at Tristan in 1892 and, having married an island girl, had remained there ever since. Repetto told Lord Crawford that he was only a spokesman for the islanders, largely on account of being able to read and write; but that he was in no sense a headman, for "they all resented the idea that one should be greater than another". Lord Crawford reports Andrea Repetto as confirming what he had earlier written to the Colonial Office, "that any chaplain coming there should be a bachelor, and arrange to lodge with one of the families, that no other way was possible", to which Lord Crawford adds the comment that "if all he said was true I quite agree with him". (Cd. 3098, pp. 61–62.)

The bad weather and the cool reception did not give the Earl of Crawford a very favourable impression of the place and its inhabitants. When he got to Cape Town he made a point of seeing Mr. Barrow; but he failed to persuade him to abandon his plans to go to Tristan, though he "most strongly urged him *not* to take his wife and maid with him". The Barrows were not deflected from their purpose and soon managed to arrange a passage in a ship bound for Buenos Aires, taking with them the stores for the islanders which Lord Crawford had been unable to put ashore. In a letter headed "S.S. Surrey, 100 miles E. of Tristan da Cunha, April, 1906", Mr. Barrow wrote in sober triumph to the Colonial Office, adding as postscript, "the receipt of this letter will mean that we have been safely landed at Tristan da Cunha with everything entrusted to us". (Cd. 3098, p. 63.)

The Barrows and their maid duly landed the following day, sang the doxology and were conducted up from the beach to a house which had been made available for them. Three years later, in April 1909, they left Tristan and returned to England. By the end of the following year Mrs. Barrow published a volume, based on her journal and on letters to a sister, in which she seems to have achieved her aim of giving "a simple and true description of daily life among a very small community cut off from the rest of the world". (Barrow, 1910.) More than fifty years after the Barrows left, when the Tristan people were temporarily removed from the island and most of them for the first time saw something of the outside world, many of the individuals who—as children, young persons or (in a few cases) young adults—figure in Mrs. Barrow's book were able to give their own account of daily life at the time it was written.

For the purposes of this essay I propose to regard the Barrows as the first of many recent travellers and visitors who have given some account of the place and its people. I therefore do not intend to use Mrs. Barrow's book in what follows but I have given a brief description of the events which led up to their visit as an introduction, because a number of matters which I intend to explore are clearly illustrated therein and because I am able to exploit a coincidence of time and place which is only partly of my own creation. As anyone willing to consult a standard work of reference may discover, Schapera was born in what was then Cape Colony at the time when the Barrows had decided to go to Tristan; and it is through the Cape that Tristan has its main lines of communication with the rest of the world and from the Cape that its first permanent settlers came.

*   *   *

The bravest procedure in selecting a title for a contribution to a *Festschrift* is to settle head-on for an area or topic in which the person it is intended to honour has long excelled. In that way the foolhardy are enabled to flatter him with affectionate sincerity while demonstrating his manifest superiority. Were it still a matter of real disagreement, Schapera's writings alone are sufficient evidence that an anthropologist can enrich his analysis of the social present by making use of oral tradition and written records. "He would be a poor scholar were he to ignore that additional information if it is in fact available". (Schapera, 1962.) If simply failing to ignore such material were the sole criterion, few works of poor scholarship have been published by anthropologists in recent years. While it is open to doubt whether all anthropologists possess the necessary skills and background knowledge to make the best use of documentary and other sources, few if any can match the standards of exact learning and meticulous scholarship established by such works as *A Handbook of Tswana Law and Custom*, first published in 1938, the series of Livingstone volumes edited between 1951 and 1963, and *Tribal Innovators 1795–1940*, produced in 1970.

In this latest work Schapera makes extensive use of documentary sources to conduct a comparative study of social change among the five largest Tswana tribes. He sets out to show how social change in any one tribe was not determined solely and rigorously by external influences and internal pressures but depended also upon what he calls "an unpredictable factor, namely, the kinds of person its chiefs happened to be", (op. cit., p. vii). And he proceeds to demonstrate the importance of that often neglected factor by carrying out careful intertribal comparisons.

My aim is to take these two themes—the use of written records and the neglected "unpredictable factor"—to look at certain descriptions of Tristan da Cunha and its people by early travellers, that is, by those who went there before 1905. I am concerned to show the extent to which the descriptions given by travellers, particularly regarding status differences among the islanders, can be related to the kind of person the traveller happened to be. At the back of my mind, and to be dealt with elsewhere than in this essay, is the notion that some of these early accounts of Tristan have had a marked effect upon the attitudes towards the islanders of other more recent travellers and visitors. I also believe that the views of early travellers have had some influence upon the islanders' own ideas about themselves and their place in the world.

*   *   *

"No event", wrote the Abbé Raynal in mid-eighteenth century, "has been so interesting to mankind in general, and to the inhabitants of Europe in particular, as the discovery of the new world and the passage to India by the Cape of Good Hope". Among the least important side effects of those events was the discovery and eventual settlement of Tristan da Cunha. The group of uninhabited islands in the South Atlantic was first sighted in 1506 by Portuguese ships belonging to a fleet bound from Lisbon for East Africa and India but following an unusual course. The islands were named after the admiral in command and made their first appearance on a map dating from about 1509, where they are shown under the inscription *Ilhas que achou tristam da cunha*. During the sixteenth, seventeenth and eighteenth centuries the islands were visited from time to time by Dutch, French and British ships prospecting for possible victualling and watering stations; but they remained without permanent inhabitants until the early years of the nineteenth century.

Tristan da Cunha consists of three small islands and two large rocks in mid-ocean about 1200 miles south of St. Helena, 1500 miles west of Cape Town, and about 1800 miles from the coast of South America. Tristan itself is the largest and only inhabited member of the group, with an area of about thirty square miles and a population at the present time of nearly three hundred. The tip of a submarine volcano, it is a roughly symmetrical cone rising almost 7000 feet above sea level from a base about seven miles in diameter. The other islands in the group, with a total area of about five square miles, are about twenty miles from the main island; although they are uninhabited, they are visited two or three times a year by people from Tristan collecting wild birds and their eggs.

We do not know when men first spent more than a few hours ashore on Tristan. The first record of a prolonged stay dates from 1790, when part of the crew of an American ship spent seven months on the island and amassed more than five thousand seal skins for the China market. But they found goats already established and it is therefore possible that earlier unrecorded visitors spent some time there. The first settlers arrived in 1810, when three men, led by one Jonathan Lambert of Salem, Massachusetts, made what proved to be a short-lived abortive attempt to set up an independent republic on what Lambert tried to rename the Islands of Refreshment.

During the Anglo-American war of 1812–14 Tristan was used as a base by United States warships and privateers. This demonstrated, contrary to earlier reports, that the island had a certain value to maritime powers as a source of fresh water, fresh meat and vegetables, provided that it had a small resident population. For this reason, and because of a fear that the French might use it as a base from which to attempt the rescue of Napoleon (by then incarcerated on St. Helena), the British decided in 1816 to take possession of Tristan and in due course established a garrison there under the command of a young South African officer who was to die sixty years later, full of honours, as General Sir Abraham Cloete. But within a few months of the setting up of a garrison there was a change of mind in London. The evacuation of the island was ordered and the soldiers withdrawn after less than twelve months' occupation. Three men obtained official permission to remain. Two were civilians who had been employed as stonemasons in the erection of fortifications; both left within a few years without having married or left descendants on the island. The third man, who had come to Tristan accompanied by a wife and child, was a Corporal in the Royal Artillery named William Glass, who remained on the island with his family until he died in 1853. William Glass and his wife Maria Leenders were the first of what may be termed the "settler ancestors" of the present population.

The Tristan people of the present day are the descendants of fifteen "settler ancestors" (eight males and seven females), all of whom arrived on the island between 1816 and 1908 and of whom only two (one male and one female) did not remain on the island until their deaths. The following list will serve to indicate something of their backgrounds and the dates and circumstances of their arrival:

1. William Glass, born in 1787 in Kelso, Scotland: arrived on Tristan in 1816 as a member of the original garrison and remained there until his death in 1853 at the age of 66. He had married in 1814, in Cape Colony, Maria Leenders and by her had 16 children, of whom three have descendants among the present population.

2. Maria Magdalena Leenders, born in 1802 in Cape Colony and des-

scribed as a Cape creole: she came to Tristan with her husband William Glass in 1816 and after his death left for the United States in 1856 with a number of her children: she died in New London, Connecticut, in 1858 aged 56.

3. Alexander Cotton, born in Hull, England, probably before 1790: he had been a seaman in the Royal Navy and came to Tristan as a settler in 1821: he married Maria Williams on Tristan in 1827, by whom he had 12 children, of whom two have descendants among the present population: he died on Tristan *circa* 1865 at the age of about 75.

4. Maria Williams, born on St. Helena, probably before 1810: described as "coloured": came to Tristan as a settler in 1827, when she married Alexander Cotton: died on Tristan in 1892 aged about 90.

5. Thomas Swain, born in Hastings, England, in 1774: a sailor who had served in the Royal Navy: settled on Tristan in 1826: married in 1827 on Tristan Sarah Williams, by whom he had 10 children, of whom four have descendants among the present population: he died on Tristan in 1862 aged 88.

6. Sarah Williams, elder sister of Maria Williams: born on St. Helena, probably before 1897: described as "coloured": came to Tristan as a settler in 1827 with her sister Maria and accompanied by a daughter by a previous union (see Mary Williams, below) and married Thomas Swain: died on Tristan after 1875 aged over 80.

7. Peter William Green (formerly Piet Willem Groen), born Katwijk, Holland, in 1808: a sailor on a ship wrecked on Tristan in 1836, he married in that year Mary Williams, daughter of Sarah Williams Swain, and decided to settle on Tristan: he had eight children, of whom two have descendants among the present population: died on Tristan in 1902 aged 94.

8. Mary Williams, born on St. Helena, probably in 1815: came to Tristan as a settler with her mother in 1827, married Peter Green in 1836: died on Tristan in 1900 aged 85.

9. Jack Rogers, probably born in the United States, probably before 1815: a sailor on an American whaling ship: came to Tristan in 1836, in which year he married Jane Glass, a daughter of William Glass and Maria Leenders, by whom he had one child who has many descendants among the present population: he left Tristan in 1838 and never returned: place and date of death unknown.

10. Andrew Hagan, born in New London, Connecticut, U.S.A. in 1816: master of an American whaling ship: settled on Tristan in 1849 when

he married Selina Glass, a daughter of William Glass and Maria Leenders, by whom he had 10 children of whom two have descendants among the present population: died on Tristan in 1898 aged 82.

11. Susannah Martha Philips, born on St. Helena, probably in 1844: married Samuel Swain, son of Thomas Swain and Sarah Williams, in 1862, probably on St. Helena: arrived on Tristan as a settler in 1862: had 11 children, of whom six have descendants among the present population: died on Tristan in 1932 aged 87.

12. Gaetano Lavarello, born in Genoa, Italy, in 1867: a sailor, shipwrecked at Tristan in 1892: decided to settle there and married in 1893 Jane Glass, a grand-daughter of William Glass and Maria Leenders and of Thomas Swain and Sarah Williams, by whom he had six children, all of whom have descendants among the present population: he died on Tristan in 1952 aged 84.

13. Andrea Repetto, born in Genoa, Italy, in 1867: a shipmate of Gaetano Lavarello and shipwrecked with him at Tristan in 1892: settled on Tristan and married there in 1893 Frances Green, a granddaughter of Peter Green and Mary Williams and of Alexander Cotton and Maria Williams, by whom he had seven children of whom six have descendants among the present population: he died on Tristan in 1911 aged 44.

14. Elizabeth Smith, born in Ireland in 1883: emigrated as a child to South Africa where in 1898 she married Robert Glass, a grandson of William Glass and brother of Jane Glass, wife to Gaetano Lavarello: she lived with her husband in South Africa where he was working at that time, and came to Tristan as a settler in 1908 when he returned to the island: she had eight children, of whom seven are still alive and have descendants among the present population. She died on Tristan in 1916 aged 33.

15. Agnes Smith, sister of Elizabeth Smith, born in South Africa in 1888: married twice, first in South Africa in 1905 Joseph Glass, elder brother of Robert Glass (her sister's husband), with whom she came to Tristan as a settler in 1908 when he returned to the island. He died in 1915 and she married as her second husband in 1919 William Rogers, a great-grandson of Jock Rogers. She had a total of nine children by her two husbands, of whom eight are still alive and have descendants among the present population. She died on Tristan in 1970 aged 81.

A complete list of "settler ancestors" has been given in order to indicate the varied origins of those from whom members of the present population trace descent. The list also serves to show that the process of settlement was continuous over a period of more than ninety years, from 1816 to 1908. Since the latter year there have been no further settlers; and only six individuals left the community in the fifty-three years that elapsed between then and 1961, when a volcanic eruption led to the temporary total evacuation of the island. What the list cannot show is the size and composition of the population at different points in time over the long period of settlement; nor can it indicate that the present inhabitants are descended from what is in fact a minority of those who came to the island. A number of individuals arrived, some by design but most by chance or accident, at intervals over the whole period, and many spent some time there before eventually changing their minds and leaving; some of these individuals founded families who either departed with them or left later.

The number of inhabitants fluctuated a good deal during the first ninety years of the settlement's existence. When the garrison finally withdrew in November 1817, the initial resident population consisted of six persons: William Glass and his wife with two small children, and the two stonemasons. By the middle of 1821 the two stonemasons had left but the population had increased to fourteen through the birth of further Glass children and the arrival of a number of unmarried men. Later that year the number of inhabitants increased dramatically to nearly sixty with the rescue of over forty survivors from the wreck of the *Blenden Hall*, bound from London to Bombay; among those rescued was a small girl who later became the mother of Mr. Barrow. Within a few months the population had gone down again, following the departure of most of those rescued from the *Blenden Hall* and of a number of others. In 1824, when there arrived the first traveller to leave a detailed account of the place and its inhabitants, the population consisted of four men, two women and a number of young children. An influx of women (including the Williams sisters) in 1827, together with a number of children, led to a steady increase in the size of the community. Over the next thirty years or so a combination of reproduction and immigration brought about a net growth of population to a figure of nearly one hundred. In 1855 there were ninety-five inhabitants, ranging in age from under one year to over seventy, and organized into twelve "families" or domestic households, the married men at the head of each comprising three Englishmen (including Cotton and Swain), three Americans (including Hagan), two Danes, one Dutchman (Peter Green) and three young men, natives of Tristan and the sons of Englishmen. The wives in all cases were of mixed ancestry, described as "mulattoes" or as native island women.

Emigration on a large scale then took place, reducing the population by December 1857 to a total of thirty-five persons living in six households. The male heads of households were Cotton, Swain, Hagan, Green and two young island men, sons of Swain and Green. Twenty years later, however, the population had again risen to about ninety and by February 1880 there were 109 inhabitants, the highest total achieved in the nineteenth century. A few individuals left in the next year or two, most of them young men who joined whaling ships and went to the United States.

In 1885 an island longboat, together with its entire crew of fifteen men, was lost under circumstances which remain mysterious. The men had pulled off in uncertain weather to attempt to make contact with a passing ship some nine miles distant from the settlement. Some of those watching from the shore believed that the longboat had been swamped by a wave, or had been run down by the ship, and that in neither event did the ship make any attempt to rescue the crew. Among other islanders the belief persisted that the men had been shanghaied. Whatever happened they were never seen again. This event reduced by about two-thirds the adult male population and had an effect on some of the people's attitudes to outsiders; it also led to another large-scale exodus over the next five or six years, in which not only the widows and orphans but also a number of young adults of both sexes left the island and settled in South Africa. By 1894 the population had fallen to a total of sixty-one. Vigorous but unsuccessful attempts were made by the authorities in Britain and in the Cape to induce the remainder of the people to leave. With the arrival of new blood in the shape of the two Italians, Gaetano Lavarello and Andrea Repetto, numbers again began to rise. By the time the Barrows landed on Tristan in 1906 there were over seventy inhabitants, including a growing number of young children. Many of these children, the offspring of those who would not leave, survive as the old people of to-day. They have not forgotten the boat disaster of 1885. Although born after it happened, they were brought up on stories about it and many of them are the grandchildren of men who were lost.

*   *   *

Few of the nineteenth century inhabitants of Tristan were literate and few documents survive which were written by those who were. The most important exception was Peter Green, who seems to have maintained a lively correspondence: some examples of his letters were published in Imperial Blue Books (C. 4959, 1887: Cd. 3098, 1906) and other extracts may be found in more recent accounts of the island and its history (Brander, 1940: Mackay, 1963: Munch, 1945 and 1971). The latter also print a number of documents written or signed by William Glass and other individuals in the early years of the settlement's existence, and a few other letters may be found in the Blue Books. Apart from sporadic attempts to keep an account of ships which passed, called or were wrecked at Tristan, no systematic records seem to have been kept by the inhabitants. A register of births, deaths and marriages was introduced in 1880, but most of the entries were made by visiting outsiders. The most important source of information about Tristan da Cunha in the nineteenth century is a series of accounts written by early travellers and visitors. The writers may be classified according to how and why they went there. First there are those who went because they were ordered to do so, but probably would not have gone there otherwise; most were officers commanding ships of the Royal Navy who were required to prepare reports of their visits but the category includes a Commissioner from the Cape Government who produced a full and valuable account (Hammond-Tooke *in* Cd. 3098, 1906). A second category consists of those who went there of their own volition, including one or two traders and prospectors; but the most important were two ministers of the Church of England who served on the island as missionaries, one of whom wrote an account of his stay (Taylor, 1856). A third category comprises those who went there involuntarily, among whom was the writer of the first extended account of the place and its inhabitants.

Augustus Earle, a wandering artist of English birth but American origins, was aged thirty when he embarked in February 1824 on a ship bound from Rio de Janeiro for the Cape of Good Hope. Ten years earlier he had spent some time at sea in a gunboat commanded by his half-brother, William Henry Smyth, who became an admiral and a well-known scientific writer. Earle was now on his way to India after four years wandering in South America. The ship called at Tristan in the course of a very stormy voyage across the South Atlantic and Earle seized the opportunity of landing, partly out of curiosity and partly because he was "completely tired of being tossed about so long on a rough sea, and rejoiced at the prospect of spending a few hours on shore". (Earle, 1832: p. 290). But the bad weather blew up again and his intended visit of a few hours became an involuntary residence of eight months. He was eventually taken off at the end of November 1824 by a ship bound for Tasmania. This led him to spend the next four years in Australia and New Zealand before going on to India in 1828. There his health broke down and by the end of 1830 he was living in London. Two years later a volume was published, three quarters of which consists of a narrative of his nine months in New Zealand and is an important source of material on the early history of that country. The remaining quarter of the text, possibly added "as a makeweight to what would otherwise have been a meagre volume" (McCormick, 1966: p. 16), consists of a journal of his time on Tristan, which contains nothing contentious and is written in plain but vivid English.

The New Zealand narrative is another matter. There Earle indulges a fancy for what McCormick calls uninformed theorizing and is highly critical of the activities of missionaries from whom he had accepted help and hospitality. He also shared to a considerable extent in the life of the Maori while disapproving very strongly of some of their customs. It is no wonder that the book was extensively reviewed at a time when very little was known of the early stages of systematic colonization in New Zealand. Earle's account gave rise to considerable discussion and controversy; and before long it became clear that he was guilty of the suppression and distortion of facts. He certainly did not attempt to be an impartial reporter; it was his involvement, together with his skills as a writer and draughtsman, which no doubt enabled him to convey his experiences with force and immediacy. But his reliability as a witness cannot be taken for granted. One of those to question it was no less skilled an observer than Darwin.

Towards the end of 1831, before his book was published, Earle had joined *H.M.S. Beagle* as personal draughtsman to the commander, Captain Robert Fitzroy, for the expedition on which the young Charles Darwin served as naturalist for five years. Earle and Darwin were colleagues for the first two years of the venture. While they were in South America Earle's health again broke down and he was forced to resign and make his way back to England, where he died in 1838 at the age of forty-five. At the time of his departure Darwin wrote affectionately of him as an "eccentric character": but by the end of 1835 Darwin had not only read Earle's account but had himself visited the same area of New Zealand and met some of those so bitterly criticized therein. In a letter to his sister, Darwin wrote that he and his companions were "quite indignant with Earle's book; beside extreme injustice it shows ingratitude. Those very missionaries who are accused of coldness I know without doubt always treated him with far more civility than his open licentiousness could have reason to expect" (Barlow, 1945: quoted by McCormick, 1966: p. 25).

Even with the most renowned agnostic of the nineteenth century ranged against him on the side of a group of missionaries, there are no good reasons for mistrusting the material presented by Earle in his Tristan narrative. His situation there was very different from what it came to be in New Zealand and he had no particular axe to grind as far as the Tristan settlers were concerned. In his defence it should also be recalled that Darwin in 1835 had not yet abandoned orthodox Christian beliefs and still, by his own account, accepted the Bible as the unquestionable authority on matters of right behaviour. And Taylor, himself a missionary and the only writer who had read Earle and who knew personally most of the individuals described by him, commends his account as very life-like (Taylor, 1856).

Earle appears to have written up his experiences from a journal kept at the time. He also made a number of sketches, some of which he later worked up into water-colour paintings; one of these is reproduced in the published narrative. The most interesting and informative passages are those based on entries made in the first weeks of his stay, in which he not only gives a vivid picture of the place and of his reactions to it but also describes the people, tells us something of their daily life and relates what they told him about their backgrounds and how they came to be there. There is no mistaking the enthusiasm with which, after an exile from England of six years or more, he greeted the Union Jack flying at the tiny settlement; the houses impressed him as having "an air of comfort, cleanliness and plenty truly English; and which was highly gratifying . . . from the contrast it formed to those I had lately seen in South America."

But before long he grew disenchanted. The weather is described as frequently dreadful, with whole weeks "a succession of tempests, one immediately following upon another, and scarcely any possibility of going out of the house". In the course of eight months, which spanned a southern winter, he saw only seven ships, each of which either ignored his efforts to attract attention or was unable to haul to and take him off because of the weather. Before his rescue by the eighth ship, which with some difficulty he succeeded in boarding, Earle regarded his stay as "a miserable imprisonment on this wretched island" and refers more than once to his "great depression of spirits". Although he writes with unaffected gratitude of the unremitting kindness and generous treatment shown him by "entire strangers", it is clear if one reads between the lines that he came to find his hosts a trifle tedious. Their unvarying cheerfulness was increasingly hard to bear as his anxieties mounted and his spirits sank. "I force myself", he writes, "to struggle against dismal thoughts . . . so I take my seat by the fire, shut out the night, pile on a cheerful log, and tell my tale in turn. I must confess that, amongst my companions, I never see a sad or discontented-looking face; and though we have no wine, grog, or any other strong drink, there is no lack of jovial mirth in any of the company".

The company consisted of no more than a dozen persons. Apart from Earle himself, there were five men, one of whom had come ashore with him; all were ex-servicemen who, with the exception of Corporal William Glass, were formerly seamen and said by Earle to "partake greatly of the honest roughness of British tars" with "all their characteristic warmth of feeling and desperate courage". The men are described as having decided to settle on Tristan because of "the comfortable prospect that island offered them of independence . . . at a time of peace, when it was almost impossible for the most prudent and industrious to gain their bread" in England. In addition, there were two women, the wives of Glass and of one of the seamen, together with a number of children the oldest of which, William Glass junior, was aged nine. Mrs Glass is described as a Cape creole, the other woman as "a half-cast Portuguese from Bombay". We hear very little of the women since Earle says that their time was so fully occupied with cooking and looking after their offspring that he seldom saw them.

Although himself thankful to escape from the island, Earle took it for granted that the settlers were justified in believing themselves better off there than elsewhere, despite the isolation, the privations and the harshness of the environment. Unlike later visitors, he was not particularly concerned about the future of the community and did not therefore feel the need to ask himself the kind of questions they did. Essentially what may be called an artist-journalist, his main concern in writing about Tristan and New Zealand was to make a living and to promote the sale of his pictures by bringing his name before a public hungry for first-hand accounts of little-known parts of the world. It cannot be claimed that Earle was in the first rank of the many British topographical artists active in the first decades of the nineteenth century. Better known contemporaries included his close friend C. R. Leslie, like him the London-born son of American parents: G. R. Lewis, another traveller and illustrator specializing in landscapes of remote places; and Samuel Daniell, an artist and traveller who took part as secretary and draughtsman in a mission of exploration to Bechuanaland. What can be said of Earle, however, was that he was an "eager participator in life as he found it" (McCormick, 1966: p. 26). This characteristic matches his main activity, the production of a form of genre-painting for which there was at that time a ready market; he painted informal interiors in which a number of persons are depicted going about their ordinary affairs. There are several good examples of his work in the National Maritime Museum at Greenwich, showing scenes on board ships of the Royal Navy; their chief interest lies in what would now be called their essentially "documentary" nature. A similar water-colour, showing the interior of one of the houses on Tristan with most of the inhabitants grouped round a table, is reproduced (as Plate 21) in McCormick (1966).

In answer to the historian's first questions about any piece of documentary evidence, "who wrote this" and "why did he write it", it seems reasonable to say that Earle was primarily a producer of accurate visual records of surface appearances and that his written account of what the early settlers told him was a version unvarnished by any need to accommodate a particular audience. What he quotes William Glass as saying has the ring of truth: "Why, you know, sir (said he to me), what could I possibly do, when I reached my own country, after being disbanded? I have no trade, and am now too old to learn one. I have a young wife, and a chance of a numerous family; what could I do better for them than remain?". Glass was, of course, speaking for many thousands of demobilized soldiers suffering unemployment and distress in post-Napoleonic war Britain. The Navy had been cut in one year from 100,000 to 30,000 men. Twenty ship-loads of so-called 1820 settlers had taken up residence in Cape Colony. It is not too fanciful to say that the handful of settlers on Tristan were deposited there by the furthest ripples of the deflationary policies of Lord Liverpool's government.

Within three years of Earle's departure the number of settlers on Tristan increased with the arrival of more British seamen and of a small group of women and children from St. Helena. A common assumption among later commentators seeking to explain the early settlement of the island has been that the men, all of whom were "white", went there and remained there because their wives and children, all of whom were "coloured" in the South African sense, would have been at a relative disadvantage elsewhere.

There is no evidence that this view was ever held by the next visitor to publish an extended account of the Tristan community. On the contrary, the Reverend William Francis Taylor, who arrived in February 1851 and lived there as "missionary" until March 1857, an uninterrupted stay of six years, became convinced that the entire population should be removed. This conviction was later to be shared by the only other Anglican clergyman to reside on the island in the nineteenth century, the Reverend Edwin

Heron Dodgson, who spent a total of some six years there in the 1880's. Both men believed that the people were in grave danger of physical, mental and moral degeneration if allowed to remain there. The fact that they held such views became known to the islanders and, reinforced by attitudes expressed from time to time since then by other outsiders, has had a complex and enduring effect on island ideas and values.

During the nineteenth century a number of other clergymen made brief visits to Tristan. Most were naval chaplains who went ashore to baptize children while their commanding officers were carrying out what may be termed informal inspections. The first recorded landing on Tristan by a clergyman, however, was that of a missionary named Applegate, bound for India on a ship which called at the island briefly in 1835; he baptized twenty-nine persons. In 1848 another clergyman named Wise, also bound for the East as a missionary, visited the island for a few hours. He later wrote to the Society for the Propagation of Christian Knowledge in London, praising the efforts being made by William Glass to hold religious services and teach the children; he urged the need for books, and, if possible, a teacher to be sent to Tristan. His letter was seen by Taylor, at that time training for missionary work in London, who thereupon determined to go there as soon as he was able to do so.

Not very much is known about Taylor. He was unmarried and aged about thirty when he went to Tristan and seems to have been of relatively humble origins. After leaving Tristan in 1857 he worked in the Cape as a clergyman in various places, dying in Stellenbosch in 1903. His book on Tristan, the thirty-fourth in a series published by the Society for the Propagation of the Gospel under the general title *Church in the Colonies*, appeared in 1856, while he was still on the island. His first impressions of the settlement were very similar to those of Earle nearly thirty years before; he was struck by the resemblance to an English village, with the houses all looking clean and tidy and the people dressed neat and clean and orderly. But the population had changed; not only were there now getting on for a hundred inhabitants, they were predominantly "coloured" people with only a few white men among them. He describes the men and women as living together "not very happily", though one or two of the women who came from St. Helena in 1827, he says, proved better than could reasonably have been expected, given their background; though all, he says, were "very ignorant" and some were "viciously enough disposed".

During the 1830's and 1840's the development of the whaling industry resulted in Tristan becoming for a time one of the South Atlantic's more important supply stations for American whalers, some of which called there regularly every season. This greatly diminished the isolation of the islanders from the outside world; it also, according to Taylor, led to evils which he was unable to root out. He does not go into details, referring only to "drunkenness, and other vices" resulting in the neglect of "the highest duties of life" and in the children being badly cared for and being allowed to grow up "mostly very ignorant". It is clear that some of the children were the offspring of illicit and casual unions between visiting American sailors and island women. At the same time, a number of island girls married men from whalers and Taylor welcomed this and the opportunities offered by the industry to young island men wishing to leave home. His concern about the future of the community arose in part from the decline in the whaling traffic already evident in the 1850's, in part from signs that the population would soon outstrip natural resources, in part from what he saw as the dangers of a growing imbalance between the sexes. "The families now here", he writes, "consist almost entirely of females. The boys are continually enticed away, by the natural desire of seeing the world, which they can easily gratify, the whalers being always glad to obtain lads who are well used to boating. The girls have no such opportunity of escape. There are now more than a dozen adult females here, with no prospect of a comfortable provision for life" (Taylor, 1856: p. 89).

Unlike Earle, who wrote with no well-defined audience in mind and no specific aims apart presumably from making a living, Taylor's book was intended for a particular readership, mostly Anglicans of the professional and middle classes who were subscribers to the Society for the Propagation of the Gospel and hence supporters of men like Taylor committed to the care of souls in distant parts. Apart from the general aim of ensuring the continuance of such support, Taylor was anxious to explain the need, as he saw it, to get the people off the island and to gain for his efforts the particular backing of Bishop Gray of Cape Town, in whose diocese Tristan was then included.

In a narrative both modest and readable, lacking neither humour nor plain-speaking, he manages to convey his affection for individual islanders, and his anxiety about the future of the community, without being patronizing. Convinced of the inherent degenerative tendencies of man if left to himself without the Gospel, he sought to indicate to his readers that the people deserved help, without going so far in describing the moral dangers to which he believed they were exposed that he risked losing the patronage on which his work depended. It is reasonable to suppose, reading between the lines of what he wrote, that Taylor feared that Tristan might become, if not a brothel, at least a notoriously easy lay for visiting whalers. A good illustration of the skill with which he endeavoured to appeal to those of property among the faithful in parishes in England without arousing alarm is provided by the meanings conveyed by his discussion of women's clothing. "The females", he writes, "dress just like those of their class in England—in cotton print, made always according to the latest fashion". Cotton print in the 1850's was what was thought suitable for respectable maid-servants when off duty and was within reach of a slender purse. But lest the mention of the latest fashion might be taken to imply extravagance or immodesty on the part of Tristan girls, or that they were attempting to ape their betters, he goes on to stress that for Church on Sundays they did not wear hats or bonnets, like their counterparts in "more civilized portions of the world", but each had "a kerchief (a silk one if she has it) folded neatly over her plainly-braided hair", a style which Taylor considered "a far more becoming covering for the head".

Taylor's efforts to gain the support of the Bishop were successful. The latter wrote in April, 1856 that he hoped that "in a few days a large ship will be sent to bring them all away". But to no avail. By the time Taylor himself left Tristan a year later he had only managed to induce half the population to emigrate, some to the number of about forty-five accompanying him to the Cape, others going to the United States. The remainder were adamant in their determination to stay on.

Thirty years later, Taylor's successor Dodgson was as determined as he was that the island should be evacuated, and as unsuccessful. Born in 1847, the son of Archdeacon Charles Dodgson of Croft in Yorkshire and younger brother to C. L. Dodgson, better known under his *nom de plume* of Lewis Carroll, Edwin Dodgson does not seem to have written a systematic account of his time on Tristan; but his views were influential among officials dealing with policy regarding the future of the island, being made known in numerous private letters and in at least one pamphlet in which he referred to the inevitability of degeneration among the islanders if they were allowed to remain. For more accessible accounts by visitors in the second half of the nineteenth century one must turn to the published reports of naval officers.

Between the departure of Taylor aboard H.M.S. *Geyser* in 1857 and the arrival of the Barrows fifty years later some thirty ships of the Royal Navy paid official visits to Tristan. Some of the commanding officers produced reports which were later published in Government Blue Books and which provide information about the place and its inhabitants at that time which is of the greatest value. Some wrote brief factual accounts which were published but are too impenetrably thin to be of much use; though these reports, less elegant and vivid than others, sometimes contain very revealing asides in which a whole set of attitudes and reactions on the part of the writer are expressed. Some commanding officers wrote no reports other than those which formed part of their ship's log and hence remain unpublished. Few, if any, naval vessels spent more than forty-eight hours at Tristan and this fact inevitably sets limits on the extent of the information obtainable from such short visits; perhaps the most important material is contained in lists of the inhabitants which provide census data for certain years and make it possible to work out the comings and goings of the people as well as the approximate dates of births, deaths and marriages. Most of the visiting vessels were either on training cruises or on their way to or from Britain, St. Helena and the Cape. On some occasions it appears that the commanding officer did not go ashore but surveyed the island from the bridge and received a deputation of island men who came aboard from their boats. On other occasions the commanding officers were entertained ashore in one of the houses, when they were usually accompanied by the ship's chaplain or the medical officer; the latter sometimes prepared a special report on the health of the people which was annexed to the main report.

Something is known about the identity and background of most of the officers commanding these visiting naval vessels. The most eminent name is that of H.R.H. Prince Alfred, Duke of Edinburgh, the second son of Queen Victoria, who visited Tristan in 1867 in command of H.M.S. *Galatea*. He was then aged thirty-three. None of the other commanding officers with whom we are concerned was as young or as illustrious.

They were all in their late thirties or early forties, and drawn, with only a few exceptions, from a relatively small section of British society having important ties through kinship or marriage with senior service officers and, in many cases, with aristocratic or landed families. This was almost invariably the case with naval officers until the end of the century; naval careers, certainly until the 1870's, were almost a monopoly of certain families. And many of those who commanded ships which visited Tristan in the 1870's and 1880's rose to high rank. If we consider the officers commanding ten ships of the Royal Navy which called there over a period of twenty years following the visit of H.M.S. *Galatea*, the following individuals appear:

H.M.S. *Challenger*: Captain G. S. Nares, the son of a Naval Captain; retired as Vice-Admiral Sir George Nares, KCB.

H.M.S. *Sappho*: Captain N.S.F. Digby, the son of a Captain in the Grenadier Guards, a cousin of Lord Digby, and sister's son to Lord Lanesborough; retired as Vice-Admiral.

H.M.S. *Diamond*: Captain G. S. Bosanquet, a member of a well-known family of landed gentry; married to his cousin; retired as Admiral.

H.M.S. *Wolverene*: Captain L. Brine, a member of a well-known family of Irish landed gentry and cousin of a Baronet; retired with the rank of Captain.

H.M.S. *Miranda*: Captain E. S. Dawson, a younger son of Lord Dartrey, an Irish peer, and through his mother a kinsman of Lord Derby; his wife was a daughter of Lord Clanwilliam; retired with the rank of Captain.

H.M.S. *Sapphire*: Captain J. R. T. Fullerton, son of a Yorkshire clergyman and, through his mother, a kinsman of Lord Plymouth; his wife was granddaughter of one of Queen Victoria's chaplains; he retired as Admiral Sir John Fullerton GCVO, having commanded the Royal Yacht.

H.M.S. *Opal*: Captain A. T. Brooke, a member of a well-known Irish landed family and kinsman of a Baronet; his mother was a daughter of Lord Huntingdon; retired as Captain, CB.

H.M.S. *Thalia*: Captain D. H. Bosanquet, a cousin of Captain G. S. Bosanquet and brother of Bernard Bosanquet the philosopher; retired as Admiral Sir Day Bosanquet, KCB.

H.M.S. *Curacao*: Captain R. Stopford, a member of a prominent naval family and kinsman of Lord Courtown, an Irish peer; retired as Admiral.

H.M.S. *Swallow*: Captain R. J. Fortescue, a member of a Devon family of landed gentry and grandson of a General.

Although not a wholly representative sample, in that it excludes one or two ship's captains about whom information is not readily available, this list serves to indicate something of the social characteristics of those upon whose official reports the authorities depended for first-hand information and whose opinions and advice were certainly influential in determining the policy of the Colonial Office. For, although not primarily responsible for Tristan affairs, the Admiralty was the department of Government most closely involved in maintaining contact with the island, and the naval Commander-in-Chief of the Cape of Good Hope station was for some years more directly concerned with the island's inhabitants than those nominally responsible, namely the Governors of St. Helena and of Cape Colony.

Although the reports of the ships' captains reveal occasional differences of opinion on relatively minor matters, it is not surprising that the general impression given by what they wrote is one of considerable uniformity. Not only were they themselves mostly drawn from a particular minority in Britain, their reports were originally intended only for the eyes of officials, most of whom were members of the same social category. It was therefore possible for them to convey meanings as much by how they said what they said, and what they did not say, as by what in fact they did say. To take one example, in his report of 1875 Captain G. S. Bosanquet writes of the Dutchman Peter Green's position as an informal leader on the island as being due not only to "his superiority in years, but also from having greater force of character, being a European, than the rest of the community, who are half-castes and of more plastic materials. There are two exceptions, one an Englishman who . . . is now desirous of leaving with his family, and going to New Zealand, or first to the Cape of Good Hope, and the other an American, who settled here of his own choice in 1849. The first of these, Joseph Beetham, I was willing to have removed to the Cape, as he evidently was dissatisfied, and is probably a disturbing element in the settlement; unfortunately, the principal female member of the family was not in a condition to make a hasty move". In the list of the inhabitants which Captain Bosanquet included with his report he has a footnote concerning Beetham in which he says the latter "came voluntarily to the island in 1866, because his wife is a native" and adds that the reason Beetham gives for wishing to go to New Zealand was that "he thinks he could 'better himself' ". The implications of whether an inhabitant came voluntarily or was a castaway were important when it came to the provision of a free passage; and the overtones of meanings conveyed by the reference to Mrs. Beetham as a "native" and "the principal female member of the family", as well as the suitably restrained manner, by the then current standards, in which it was indicated that she was heavily pregnant, no doubt spoke for themselves when read by the recipients of the report.

Pursuing a little further the matter of the mixed racial origins of the inhabitants, we find Thomson (1877) writing of the visit of H.M.S. *Challenger*, and remarking that a few of the islanders were what he regarded as "fine-looking, sturdy young men, somewhat of the English type", though noting with evident sorrow that most had "a dash of dark blood". The same themes recur again and again in the accounts written at that time. Captain Brine, looking forward to the time when some kind of judicial authority might have to be provided on the island, writes that "the children now growing towards manhood will have less European blood than their parents, and will probably therefore be less self-reliant, less manly, and less capable of self-government". Some writers refer to Tristan as "this distinctively British community"; others emphasize the inevitable problems which they believed would arise from "in-breeding" and racial admixture. Many visitors did not know quite what to make of the Tristan people. In the earlier years they are most frequently described as "settlers" or "the inhabitants"; later they are usually referred to as "islanders" or "natives". Some writers clearly regarded them as what one observer called "riff-raff and beggars", the coloured descendants of coloured women and a few eccentric, if engaging, white wastrels. Others were more impressed by their sturdy independence and by the fact that many of the islanders regarded themselves as in most cases the descendants of British pensioners, entitled to support from outsiders in consideration of past services to visiting ships and distressed mariners. They also saw themselves as guardians of a British colonial outpost and the potential rescuers of the victims of inevitable future shipwrecks. This view was reinforced from time to time by the receipt of gifts from the outside world in recompense for particular rescues; and the fact that one of these gifts was a signed photograph of Queen Victoria, sent by Her Majesty in recognition of their loyalty, amply confirmed their view. However unfriendly some of the naval officers might be, and sometimes were, the regular visits of inspection by Her Majesty's ships were seen by the islanders as repeated assurances of their special importance to the Crown.

The small number of visitors to Tristan whose accounts of the place were published in the first eighty years or so of the community's existence are only a tiny fraction of those outsiders who went ashore over that period. It is probable that some thousands of people had at least a few hours of first-hand acquaintance with the place and its inhabitants; and one can only guess at the accounts they gave of their impressions. It is possible, however, to make some informed guesses by attempting to do what I have indicated may be possible: that is, to read with caution between the lines of what was written by those who, for whatever reason, wrote of their experiences. If careful attention is paid to the kinds of person who wrote and whom they wrote for, and to the mental equipment which it may be inferred was shared by them, additional information is available which, as Schapera suggests, no careful scholar should ignore.

The notion that it was possible to reform the moral character of a population by altering their environment, which runs through so much of what was written of Tristan by early visitors, was an important element in the groundswell of nineteenth century thinking; the more recent history of the

Tristan people shows clearly that it still persists in many quarters.

References

Barlow, N. (1945). (Comp.) *Charles Darwin and the Voyage of the "Beagle"*. London.

(1958). (ed.) *The Autobiography of Charles Darwin*. Collins, London.

Barrow, K. M. (1910). *Three Years on Tristan da Cunha*. Skeffington, London.

Brander, J. (1940). *Tristan da Cunha 1506–1902*. George Allen and Unwin, London.

Earle, A. (1832). *A Narrative of a nine months' residence in New Zealand in 1827; together with a Journal of a residence in Tristan D'Acunha, an island situated between South America and the Cape of Good Hope*. London.

Hammond-Tooke, W. (1906). See Cd. 3098.

Mackay, M. (1963). *Angry Island: the Story of Tristan da Cunha*. Arthur Barker, London.

McCormick, E. H. (1966). (ed. with an introduction) *Narrative of a Residence in New Zealand: Journal of a Residence in Tristan da Cunha: by Augustus Earle*. Oxford.

Munch, P. A. (1954). *Sociology of Tristan da Cunha*. Oslo.

(1971). *Crisis in Utopia*. New York.

Parliamentary Papers (Imperial Blue Books)

    1876. C. 1445.

    1887. C. 4959.

    1897. C. 8357.

    1903. Cd. 1600.

    1906. Cd. 3098.

Schapera, I. (1938). *A Handbook of Tswana Law and Custom*. London.

(1962). "Should Anthropologists be Historians?" *J. R. Anthrop. Inst.*, 92, pp. 143–156.

(1970). *Tribal Innovators: Tswana Chiefs and Social Change 1795–1940*. London.

Taylor, W. F. (1856). *Some account of the settlement of Tristan D'Acunha in the South Atlantic Ocean*. London.

Thomson, C. W. (1877). *The Voyage of the Challenger, 1873–6*, (Vol. 2). London.

Some Speculations on the Status and Role of the Free People of Colour in the Western Cape

10

Sheila Patterson

"Should anthropologists be historians?" asked Professor Schapera in his Presidential Address to the Royal Anthropological Institute in 1961. He concluded:

The time may yet come when some anthropologists, unable or unwilling to do intensive fieldwork, or content with what they have already done, may, like economic or social historians, pay special attention to social systems of the past.

This time was near at hand, at least insofar as the new phase of scholarship on slavery was concerned. Anthropologists studying the social present in New World societies formerly involved with slavery were impelled to seek illumination from a knowledge of the more recent social past of those societies and of the disparate racial and cultural groups which had been brought together there, some by force. Some became interested in the comparative study of this social past as a social present, in which library research and the evaluation of sources largely replaced fieldwork, although some elements of the latter remained in the search for oral tradition and archaeological remains.

I first met Schapera in 1949 when he was Professor of Anthropology at the University of Cape Town and I was an L.S.E. postgraduate student in search of a thesis subject. Firmly and rightly discouraging my over-ambitious notion of making a study of the Afrikaners, he suggested that I should make a mainly library-based study, with some fieldwork, of the Cape Coloured People, focusing on their contemporary situation and their recent history, only briefly touched upon by Professor Etienne (J.S.) Marais in his great historical study of the Cape Coloured People (1939). This I did over the next three years, with much generous advice and encouragement from Schapera, and the immediate outcome was *Colour and Culture in South Africa* (1953).

A later outcome is this essay, for how better could one endeavour to honour one's mentor and friend of long standing than by reviewing, however inadequately and tentatively, some unexplored aspects of the history of the people to which he first directed my attention. Schapera must, however, also bear some responsibility for encouraging my historical bent and my library-orientation to the point that now, content with the field-work already done, I have turned my attention to the recent "social past", seen as the "social present".

As first planned, this essay was to compare the salient features of a New World slave society, Barbados, where I had carried out fieldwork in recent years, with the situation prevailing in the Cape in the pre-Emancipation era, and to test in the latter area some of the interpretations arising out of recent scholarship on New World slavery. In order to do this, it was necessary that the basic primary research should be available. It was also necessary that those who provided this material should have been looking for answers to the kinds of questions that scholars of a legalistic, philanthropic or ethnocentric bent used not to ask; the evidence may therefore still be locked in the archives, if it is available at all. Such questions are concerned with the slave as a person as well as a chattel, with everyday relations between masters, slaves, servants and freedmen, and with the patterns of life created by slaves from a synthesis of elements transferred from their home cultures and elements in the new society. They are also concerned with the status hierarchies which grew up on and off the estates and with the situation of the freedmen groups which emerged.

Such research has been carried out in Barbados, as elsewhere in the West Indies, but only that relating to freedmen is as yet available. For Barbados, the principal researcher (with Arnold Sio) as Jerome Handler, to whose meticulous and wide-ranging scholarship and generous cooperation, particularly in providing an advance copy of his study, *The Unappropriated People*, profound acknowledgements are due.

When I turned to the Cape material, including research done in the last two decades, the picture was much bleaker. The existing studies of Cape slave society have for the most part failed to ask or answer the kind of questions posed above, and their approach has tended to be consciously or unconsciously albocentric and, even in the case of the white liberal historians, more or less disinterested in the lives of the subordinate communities, which were seen as the objects of disruption, discrimination, philanthropy or other processes imposed by the dominant élite.

The initial project had therefore to be radically modified. A more modest but possibly useful exercise was to focus on the comparative situation and role of the free blacks and coloureds in the two societies, taking Handler's very full documentation for Barbados as a model and reference point—although the Barbados summary had in the end to be omitted here for reasons of space—and using such evidence as could be teased out of the existing published studies relating to Cape slavery and the early history of the Cape Coloured People. This approach would, it was hoped, serve, firstly, to indicate what sort of material should be sought in the primary sources, and secondly, by presenting at least a tentative picture of the free coloured people in the Western Cape, to extend the geographic range of recent comparative studies of such groups in the New World.[1]

The most comprehensive set of such New World studies, ten in all, has recently appeared in the symposium *Neither Slave nor Free* (1972). Of the volume's general approach the editors Cohen and Greene write:

> . . . It has two related points of focus: first, the degree to which the experience of the free colored can serve as a measure of the character of slavery and race relations in each of the slave societies here discussed, and, second, the special— and sometimes effectively pivotal—roles of this group in the evolving societies in which they lived.

The second point of focus is obviously concerned with a growing appreciation of the importance of the free coloured in their own right, as an intermediate or marginal group in a socially and culturally stratified society. This could presumably operate not only in the pre-Emancipation social present, but in the development of relations up to the present day, taking into account the intervention of new and extraneous factors.

The first point of focus derived from the Tannenbaum and post-Tan-

1. To my knowledge only one short comparative study of Cape and New World slavery has been published, by Greenstein (1973). In it he takes issue not only with Tannenbaum's thesis but also with the tendency by many contemporary observers of Cape slavery and later historians to present South African slavery as milder than either South American variety. In his rather simplistic view, the Cape slave system was "a complete microcosm of that in the Americas" and "one would be hard put to justify saying that it was less inhuman in one place than the other."

nenbaum scholarship on the nature and variations of New World slave systems. (For outlines and assessments of this cf. Sio (1965, 1967); Foner and Genovese (1969); Lane (1971); and Hoetink (1973).) In his essay *Slave and Citizen: The Negro in the Americas* (1947), Frank Tannenbaum maintained that variations could be found in the character of slavery and race relations from one society to another, according to their differing historical and cultural backgrounds (i.e. the Anglo-Saxon, the Iberian and the French traditions). He took as a principal index of variation the relative status of free people of colour within the slave societies, and gave particular attention to legislation and practice relating to the ease and availability of manumission.

More recently, this idealist perspective, shared by Freyre and Elkins, was challenged by Marvin Harris (1964), presenting a materialist alternative, that economic and demographic conditions determine social relations and necessarily prevail over counter-tendencies in the historical tradition. In Brazil, for example, he suggested that, because of the unequal ratio of whites to non-whites, there was a severe shortage of white labour; consequently an intermediate free group of half-castes had to be created to perform essential services which in the United States were performed by an intermediate class of whites.

Winthrop Jordan, whose *White Over Black* (1968) provides a massive survey of the attitudes towards Negroes and slaves imported and developed by Anglo-Saxon whites in the North American colonies in the first two-and-a-half centuries of settlement, also considers the divergencies which arose between the status and treatment of the freedman in the United States and two other societies with English backgrounds, Jamaica and Barbados. He points to the differing demographic patterns, i.e. the much lower proportion of non-whites to whites in the American colonies, as helping to maintain a biracial society, combined with the non-acceptability of mulattoes and escape for some by the "silent mechanism of passing". In the British West Indian colonies, on the other hand, where the proportion of blacks to whites was high, and there was initially a high ratio of white men to women, there was also acceptance of concubinage, a toleration of mixed offspring (especially in Jamaica, where the high white sex ratio continued) and a three-caste division into white, coloured and black (ibid., pp. 171–8). Degler, in his comparative historical study of slavery and race relations in Brazil and the United States, *Neither White Nor Black* (1971) re-examines Tannenbaum's interpretations, and finds the key to understanding the differences and similarities in race relations between the two countries in the position of the mulatto—a Negro in the United States, but in Brazil a large group with a separate place, which he calls the "mulatto escape hatch".

The idealist and the materialist approaches, taken on their own, seem inadequate and it would appear more profitable to attempt a synthesizing approach between the historical-traditional and the ecological processes in relation to a given slave society (cf. Genovese, 1969: pp. 238–55, for a discussion of this whole issue).

In view of the fragmentary evidence at present available about the free coloured of the Western Cape, it is impossible to evaluate the relative importance of the historical-cultural, the economic, demographic and other factors stressed by scholars of New World slave societies. All that can properly be done in this essay is to organize the available evidence for the Cape under a set of headings similar to those used by Handler and Sio for Barbados (and Jamaica, Sio, 1974), and also by other contributors to the symposium *Neither Slave Nor Free*, and to conclude with some brief and extremely tentative comments on any comparisons and contrasts which emerge or seem to merit further enquiry.

The Handler/Sio headings relating to freedmen are as follows:

(a) Demographic patterns;
(b) Manumission;
(c) Miscegenation;
(d) Legal status and the politico-judicial system;
(e) Occupational roles and the economic system;
(f) The freedman in the social order.

Handler and Sio are concerned with two slave societies with an Anglo-Saxon tradition and thus say little about the historical-traditional background. This aspect is also little stressed in *Neither Slave Nor Free*, which contains contributions relating to societies with French, Spanish, Portuguese, Anglo-Saxon and Dutch traditions. There has been relatively little discussion of the Dutch tradition,[2] insofar as it differs from the Anglo-

2. Hoetink (1967) classifies the Dutch tradition under the North-West European variant (British and Dutch), as distinguished from the Iberian or Latin variant. He also (1973) shows how slavery and race relations evolved differently in Surinam and Curaçao despite the common tradition, because of differing economic, geographical and demographic factors. Even if we accept, however, that British and Dutch fell within the same variant, there would seem to have been some differences in socio-economic and cultural background between British and Dutch settlers in the West Indies (and in the Cape). Nor should we assume without further enquiry that the Dutch tradition was or remained identical in the West India Company (WIC) territories and those governed by the VOC (cf. Boxer, 1973a; Chapter 2).

Saxon one, or is subsumed under an overall northern Protestant label, and it is impossible to examine and compare the Dutch and English traditions systematically here. The nature of the Cape material, at least until after the British occupation, did however influence me to add some more headings; a brief introductory note of major historical, geographical and economic factors; a note on the ethnic origins of the white and non-white groups in the society, (not overlooking the influence of linguistic pluralism); and religious adherence and educational participation as a separate heading. The sixth heading above has not been included because there was insufficient material, and the available material is included under earlier headings.

The Cape of Good Hope

The distinctive flavour of the early Dutch settlement at the Cape of Good Hope is well conveyed by the term "tavern of the two oceans". Whatever was to evolve in the hinterland, Cape Town was and remained a half-way house between Europe and the East Indies and beyond. The seventeen Directors of the Dutch East India Company (here called for convenience the XVII and the VOC) regarded it as "the frontier fortress of the Indies", and in ambience Cape Town at least was nearer to Batavia than to Amsterdam or the Hague.

There were a number of similarities between the Cape and the colonies set up in the Caribbean area by the Dutch, Portuguese, Spanish, French and English. This applied particularly to the colonizers' objectives—gain, gospel-spreading, or glory—and to their firm conviction of their superiority as Christians and Europeans over the peoples they dispossessed, conquered or enslaved.

But there were some important points of contrast which made the Cape virtually unique. These included a temperate climate suitable for white settlement, and a seemingly near-empty and unbounded hinterland which favoured the cultivation of grain, fruit and vines or, further north and east, the grazing of cattle and sheep. It also encouraged the evolution of a new and centrifugal Boer community of cattle-owning pastoralists, set in an Old Testament mould and intolerant of all outside controls.

In terms of men and cultures, moreover, the Cape was distinguished by a multi-cultural, polyglot pluralism, deriving not only from its position as a unit in the farflung Dutch seaborne empire of the East but from the variegated ethnic origins of its white officials, servants and settlers on the one side and its imported slaves on the other, and, lastly, from the presence on the expanding frontiers of a number of Khoisan, and later Bantu-speaking, tribes. Finally there was the advent of an alien and centralizing metropolitan power in 1806. British rule brought attempts to enforce law and order in the frontier areas, British settlers, the introduction of English as the official language and the Church of England as the establishment denomination. It also brought and buttressed the humanitarian and liberalistic ideas of the British philanthropists and missionaries. Amelioration and emancipation for the slaves, and the extension of equal legal and political rights to Hottentots and other free people of colour—these were imposed by an outside power, in seeming haste and with no regard for local conditions, and were thus the more resented.

The Cape was much more than a slave society on the New World pattern. Thus it is not altogether surprising that most historians of South Africa have devoted only brief sections to the topic of Cape slavery before going on to deal with the establishment of broader master-servant relationships, the dispossession, destruction or assimilation of the Khoisan peoples,[3] the expanding and turbulent frontier, relations between Boers and Bantu-speaking peoples, Boers and Britons, whites and blacks, the establishment of the Boer Republics and the Union of South Africa, and the rise of Afrikaner and African nationalisms and the apartheid society.

Slavery at the Cape was developed by circumstance rather than by necessity, as de Kiewiet observes (1941, p. 217). It was an early and increasingly a minority problem, and one which was seemingly solved by the 1850s. Yet the slaves, along with the Hottentots, were to help shape the later institutions and customs of South African society well before the end of the eighteenth century. "Slavery", wrote J. S. Marais in the preface to his classic study of the Cape Coloured People (1939, p. ix), ". . . deserves

3. In the historical sources the yellow-skinned hunter-gatherers were called "Bushmen" and were distinguished from the yellow-skinned pastoral "Hottentots". The reports were in fact describing ways of life rather than distinctive racial or linguistic groups, but gradually the assumption (so characteristic of South African "racial compartment" thinking) grew up that physical type, language and economy were necessarily correlated. To get away from this, the *Oxford History of South Africa* (1969) uses different terms for physical type, language and economy (pp. ix–x). In later sections the "Bushmen" hunter-gatherers are referred to as "San" and the "Hottentot" pastoralists as Khoikhoi (i.e. in linguistic terms) (pp. 20–24; pp. 40–74). Other writers (e.g. Marks, Legassick, Ross) use the blanket term "Khoisan" (despite the reservations of linguists as to the connexion between the two language groups) to cover the historical "Hottentots" and "Bushmen". Shula Marks (1972) further challenges the traditional division between the hunter-gatherers and the pastoralists, not only racially but in terms of economy, arguing that there was little to distinguish Khoi who had lost their cattle from San, or San who had acquired cattle from Khoi. While bearing in mind these changes of terminology, I have on the whole, in no spirit of derogation, preferred to retain the traditional terms "Bushmen" and "Hottentots" where found in contemporary historical reports. The standard work on the two peoples has long been Professor Schapera's own *The Khoisan Peoples of South Africa* (1930).

more detailed study[4] than it has received. It helped to produce the urge of the colonists to spread into the interior of the Cape Colony; it influenced the laws passed to regulate the position of free persons of colour and the attitude of the law courts towards them; and it left a mark on the descendants of the slave-owners which time has not yet effaced."

Ethnic Origins of the Free People of Colour

The ethnic composition of most slave societies in the Caribbean area was relatively simple—a West European white minority, a black West African majority mostly from similar culture-areas, and an intermediate mixed coloured group. Thus the contributions to *Neither Slave Nor Free* contain little or nothing under the heading of "origins".

In the Cape, unlike Barbados, it seems essential to examine this aspect, in view not only of the wide variation of ethnic components within each initial component (whites, slaves and indigenous peoples) but also of the persistence of ethnic distinctiveness between major groups up to the present day. The pluralistic situation at the beginning of the eighteenth century was outlined by Valentyn (Vol. II, p. 171):

The inhabitants of this land are either Servants of the Hon. Company; or Burghers, also called Freemen; or Hottentots . . . all Nations are found here, Dutch, English, French, Germans from all parts, Savoyards, Italians, Hungarians, Malays, Malabaris, Sinhalese, Macassar-folk, Banians, Amboinese, Bandanese, Buginese, Chinese, men of Madagascar, Angolese, inhabitants of

4. Such detailed research is still lacking, except for the short and interesting study by Cruse (1947) and *Those in Bondage* (1950) a cosy, anecdotal and popularizing book by Victor de Kock, who worked in the Cape Archives for many years. There are also two unpublished theses on late and limited aspects of slavery and Emancipation (see under van Rensburg and Hengherr in Bibliography). See also Hugo (1970) on the Cape domestic slaves. Edwards' study (1942) contains a good deal on the everyday life of slaves, as well as on the slave laws. She was not, however, concerned with the free coloured minority before Emancipation. Some valuable illustrative material is to be found in MacCrone (1937), who also discusses the changing status of the free coloured. Valkhoff (1966; 1972), in two socio-linguistic studies of creolization in relation to Portuguese Creole, Low Malay and Afrikaans, opens up new and non-albocentric vistas of everyday life and relationships in the multi-ethnic Cape society of the seventeenth and eighteenth centuries by asking the simple but essential question: in what language or languages did these very diverse groups communicate within and between themselves, given the presence of the Portuguese *lingua franca*, Low Malay and some Hottentot, various forms of Dutch and Low German, as well as French and later English? Valkhoff is concerned with the influence of these languages on the transformation of Cape Dutch, but his evidence, drawn from contemporary sources, not only dispels some of the linguistic fog and assertions of a "Babel" of confusion at the Cape, but also gives an extra dimension to the usual flat picture of public and private relationships between white and coloured, slave and free, at work, in the lawcourts, in places of worship, in the street and market-place and at home.

Guinea and the Salt Islands, with whom one can get along in Dutch, Malay and Portuguese.

The historical heritage of the Europeans at the Cape was not seigneurial, but bourgeois at best. The available material on the origins of the European population at the Cape indicates that most of the early burghers were poorly educated Hollanders or Germans, many of them former Company servants and mercenaries.[5] Hoge (Valkhoff, 1972; p. 100) quotes the unfavourable opinions which the first Governors of the Cape expressed about their laziness, drunkenness, ignorance and loose sexual morals (in relation to slave women).

There were also some *knegte* or indentured white servants of similar origins, some of whom married burghers' daughters and became burghers themselves. Others may have become poor whites or merged with the free coloured. This easy-going burgher core was stiffened by the arrival around 1688–1689 of something under 200 Huguenot refugees, or about one-sixth of the free burgher population. These newcomers were genuine colonists, characterized by their knowledge of viticulture, their industriousness, their stern Calvinist fanaticism and by a rejection of Europe and all its ways. The authorities wanted "no Quebec at the Cape" so the Huguenots were not allowed to settle *en bloc* and preaching and instruction in French were discouraged. Their amalgamation with the rest of the burghers was speeded by their common opposition in 1706 to the arbitrary behaviour of the Governor, William Adriaan van der Stel (Walker, 1947: pp. 53–57).

The comfortable, leisurely life-style already achieved by some Western Cape farmers[6] is illustrated in the journal of Adam Tas, a well-educated Stellenbosch burgher who led the 1706 protest. Thereafter assisted white immigration was stopped, but the Cape settlers' numbers were augmented by natural increase and a steady flow of Company employees,[7] mostly Germans, who married Cape Dutch girls, and also as we shall see, by some Asian wives and their mixed offspring. In the 1770s Stavorinus commented on the thorough blending of nations and the emergence of a new national character (Boxer, 1973a: p. 280). May Katzen (OHSA, Vol. I, pp. 231–232)

5. In 1691 one-third of the VOC's army and civil service were foreigners, half of them German. By 1778 the total had risen to two-thirds, all Germans (Colenbrander, II, 216). Cf. also Ross, 1974: pp. 4, 20–21.

6. Visitors in the eighteenth century easily discerned the differences between the urban free burghers of Cape Town, the settled wine and corn farmers of the West and the wandering cattle-farmers of the East (for references see Walker, 1947: pp. 84–89, 94–104; Edwards, 1942: pp. 11–22).

7. Cf. Ross, 1974: p. 15, for some figures for the period 1657–1807.

also comments on the fundamental difference between this mainly rural, backwater, complacent settler community with a Dutch stamp and the rich, confident, cultivated merchant class of the parent Dutch Republic.

A new English-speaking element was added to the white population after 1806. Up till the 1820s, however, there were only a few thousand officials, military personnel and merchants, mainly in Cape Town. Thereafter some 5,000 settlers arrived in the Eastern Cape. Little information is available about their interaction with the free coloured in the pre-Emancipation period, although some were a potent force in the amelioration and emancipation of slaves and coloured servants. (For the early English-speaking settlers cf. Edwards, (1924); Hockly (1957); Bond (1956).)

The other three components of the early population of the Cape were: the slaves, the Hottentots and the Bushmen. Within the slave category there were also groups of widely differing ethnic origins and socio-cultural levels. These included slaves imported from East Africa (Mozambique and Madagascar)[8] and from the Dutch East India Company's sphere of influence in the East (India, Ceylon and the Malay Archipelago). The Asian group also included some high-ranking Indonesian political exiles with their entourages, and convicts sentenced to varying terms of servitude with banishment.

The "Africans" were in the majority, and were mainly used for hard work in the vineyards, orchards, vegetable gardens and grain-lands. Those from Mozambique were apparently Bantu-speaking and negroid.[9] Those from Madagascar, who constituted a majority,[10] were presumably negroid with more or less of an Indonesian strain and may have spoken some Malagasy, an Indonesian language with remnants of a few Bantu words.

The Eastern component of the slave and freedman population of the Cape was drawn from the Indian mainland (Bengal and the Malabar and Coro-

8. A few hundred slaves from Angola arrived in 1658 and 1659, but they proved intractable, and many absconded with the object of returning home. The West African experimen was not repeated and in 1704 the Dutch West India Company pointed out that trade on the West coast of Africa was strictly forbidden to all but them.

9. J. S. Marais, writing in the 1930s, commented: "Coloured people of obviously Negroid stock are still today spoken of as *Masbiekers* ('Mozambiquers') in Afrikaans." (p. 1, n. 1).

10. Shiploads of slaves from Madagascar, mostly young men, were regularly brought in by VOC vessels, or sometimes by English and Portuguese ships, throughout the seventeenth and eighteenth centuries. (cf. de Kock, 1950: pp. 17–30 and Theal, II, p. 77 for more detailed information on the conditions of the passage, mortality, etc.) Coincidentally, a communication from the XVII in 1676, advocating the extension of the slave-trade with Madagascar, backed this with the comment that the English "appear . . . to be in the habit of supplying the island of Barbados from that island".

mandel coasts), Ceylon and the East Indian islands.[11] This component was numerically smaller than, but qualitatively superior to, the Africans and its members were generally employed as highly prized house slaves or artisans. Details of the nature of the trade, the manner of enslavement and the socio-cultural backgrounds of these slaves are hard to come by. The Indonesian "Malays",[12] many of them Muslims, seem to have come from most parts of Indonesia except Java, where enslavement was forbidden as it was for Hottentots, (Boxer, 1973a: p. 269–270). On the other hand, there were some Javanese exiles and convicts. Indian and Ceylonese slaves presumably came from poorer and lower-caste groups. Some may even have been Eurasians and there were some Roman Catholics (Valkhoff, 1972: p. 88).

Precise numbers are not available, though the origins of non-Cape born slaves and freedmen were indicated by their names: Parkat of Timor, Flora of Bengal, April of Ceylon, Leander of Malabar and, in the case of the African-born slaves, Eerst of Guinea, Hector of Madagascar or Leander of Angola. Slaves born at the Cape were so named, e.g. Paul or Maria of the Cape. Asian slave women were either employed in the Company's Slave Lodge or in private households, as domestic servants, childrens' nurses (*aias*) and needlewomen. The Eastern slaves were concentrated in Cape Town and the rich settled areas of the Western Cape.[13]

Other components of the early Cape population and the present Cape Coloured group were: Hottentots and Bushmen, slave-white, Hottentot-white, Bushman-white, Hottentot-slave and Hottentot-Bushman crosses. Here we are, however, concerned primarily with those elements which, in conjunction with the slaves, contributed to the free black burghers and the free black and coloured population in Cape Town and the Western Cape before Emancipation.

11. Valkhoff (1966: p. 186) maintains that the influx of slaves from the East actually increased from 1730 onwards (cf. also *ibid* pp. 148–149). The entry of Eastern male slaves and convicts was forbidden in 1767; the convicts in particular had been described as "these dangerous people" and the "Malay" habit of running *amok* caused considerable alarm. The inflow, however, did not stop, since the proclamation was repeated in 1784. Here is yet another instance of the wide gap between legislation and actual practice in Cape society.

12. On the "Malays" generally (*Slameiers* in Afrikaans), see I. D. du Plessis (1946/1947), du Plessis and Lückhoff (1953). They spoke Low Malay, in addition to Portuguese Creole, up to at least the middle of the nineteenth century.

13. Cf. Hugo (1970: p. 17, n. 57) for the inventory of a modest Stellenbosch wine farm in 1761. This employed only Asian and locally-born slaves: two male Malabaris, three men and one woman from the East Indies, one Bengali woman and a locally-born man and woman and four children. The occasion for the inventory was that one of the Malays had run *amok* and murdered the farmer and his wife!

This means in practice the whites and the slave-white crosses. Hottentots and Bushmen, and Hottentot-slave crosses, were to be found in the Western Cape, mainly on farms. Technically Hottentots and Bushmen were free, while Hottentot-slave crosses became "apprentices"; their status was however low even within the slave-servant hierarchy, and there is no evidence to show that any members of these groups achieved "free black" status in the West.

The only record of a European-Hottentot marriage is that between the Hottentot interpreter Eva and Pieter van Meerhoff, surgeon and explorer in 1663. There were three children of this marriage, and despite Eva's subsequent irregular life, they were educated at the Company's expense and one of the girls married a well-to-do-farmer (MacCrone, pp. 43–44). Further mixed marriages in the West were inhibited by the Europeans' contempt for the Hottentots and their way of life (history abounds in derogatory stereotypes of the Hottentots, whom Jan van Riebeeck described as "dull, stupid, lazy, stinking natives").[14]

Later miscegenation, occasionally legalized but more often not, occurred on a large scale on the expanding frontier, where cattle farmers often went unaccompanied by European women. Some of these unions were permanent, and by the end of the eighteenth century,[15] there were sizeable communities of Bastards in the north-west and the north-east, living alongside but separately from the whites whose language, religion and way of life they otherwise shared, including the possession of horses and guns. For a while these Bastards or Griquas and similar acculturated or semi-acculturated people, some of whom were land-holders, played a vital pioneer and military buffer role on the frontier. As Legassick points out (1972 p. 9), opportunities for non-whites on the frontier were greater than they were in the West. Later, they were to decline, as the need for these services waned and Boer hunger for land and labour increased.

Demographic Patterns

The Council of XVII strictly forbade the formal enslavement of the "indigenous" Hottentots and Bushmen. These peoples, in any case, proved evasive or recalcitrant, and unsuited to heavy and regular manual work.

14. Cf. Marks, p. 55. *Hotnot* is still a perjorative term in use within the Cape Coloured community (cf. Patterson, 1953: p. 140).
15. For the period up to the mid-nineteenth century of relative equality or independence of some Bastard or Griqua and Hottentot communities, see J. S. Marais, passim; MacCrone, pp. 120–1; Halford, passim; Marks, 1972: p. 77; OHSA, pp. 68–70, 226f, 248–9.

Not long after the settlement, therefore, a need for labour was felt and the debate as to the respective merits of white labour or coloured slave labour began. In 1657, however, there were only 134 Europeans in all (100 Company servants, 10 free burghers, 6 married women, 12 children and 6 convicts). There were also 10 privately-owned slaves—3 males and 7 females.

For most of the seventeenth century the settlement increased in size very slowly. Table I shows the very uneven male-female ratio among the free population throughout this century. The totals for children apparently included an unspecified number of mixed children, who thereafter passed into the European population. The same was presumably true of the adult groups, particularly the women. From 1666 the male group also included a minority of "free black burghers" and possibly "free blacks", so categorized in the records, but mostly Asian or "mixed", and thus not necessarily "black" in pigmentation.

TABLE I Cape Population Figures 1672–1694*

| | Europeans/freemen | | | Dutch servants | Slaves (privately owned) | | |
	Men	Women	Children	(*knegte*)	Men	Women	Children
1672	64	39	65	53	Total, 63		
1679	87	55	117 (Dutch or mixed)	30	133	38	20
1687	254	88	231	39	230	44	36
1691	378	145	313	63	285	57	44
1694	446	195	431	87	325	64	58

* Source, MacCrone, 1937: p. 59.

The slave totals (which do not include an average total of about 600 Company slaves)[16] rose moderately over this period, but remained well below the European figures. The uneven male-female slave ratio reflects the VOC policy (and that of the slave trade in general) of importing young males and as few female slaves as possible. It may also screen some manumission and "passing" among female slaves, as may the low figures for slave children.

16. In the Cape, unlike British West Indian territories, slaves fell into two main classes: Company slaves, employed on public works and housed in the Slave Lodge, and privately-owned slaves belonging to officials, burghers and farmers.

TABLE II. Population of the Cape: 1710-1845

Year	A. Whites/Free Burghers					B. Knegte	C. Free Blacks			D. Slaves					E. Hottentots (and Bastards)		
	Men	Women	Boys (Children)	Girls (Children)	Total		Male	Female	Total	Men	Women	Boys (Children)	Girls (Children)	Total	Male	Female	Total
1710	656	338	458	470	1,922	94	Not separately enumerated during VOC period, but included in A.			1,299	260	99	122	1,780	Hottentots and Bushmen not enumerated in VOC period.		
1718	691	390	490	484	2,055	92				1,885	321	124	106	2,436	Figures for "Bastards" not available.		
1723	679	433	544	589	2,245	119				2,224	408	139	151	2,902			
1728	737	493	706	777	2,713	122				2,867	560	234	212	3,873			
1733	793	547	839	895	3,072	117				3,384	711	314	300	4,707			
1738	901	641	993	1,077	3,612	136				4,199	810	403	345	5,757			
1743	1,075	700	1,025	1,172	3,972	124				3,804	815	377	365	5,361			
1748	1,294	830	1,086	1,298	4,508	81				3,322	821	419	360	4,922			
1750	1,364	902	1,216	1,378	4,860	72				3,591	888	465	383	5,327			
1753	1,478	1,026	1,396	1,519	5,419	114				4,137	1,031	491	386	6,045			
1760	1,756	1,166	1,599	1,634	6,155	128				4,451	1,100	463	373	6,387			
1763	1,563	1,064	1,481	1,467	5,575	101				4,105	1,021	460	346	5,932			
1770	2,147	1,486	2,184	2,132	7,949	78				5,650	1,537	548	369	8,104			
1773	2,300	1,578	2,318	2,269	8,465	89				7,102	1,707	564	529	10,002			
1780	2,873	1,918	2,861	2,817	10,469	68				7,894	2,283	834	761	11,772			
1783	3,158	2,042	2,821	3,019	11,040	24				7,808	2,533	804	805	11,950			
1786	3,238	2,407	3,022	3,148	11,815	23				8,497	2,735	878	788	12,898			
1793	4,032	2,730	3,466	3,602	13,830	12				9,046	3,590	1,132	979	14,747			
1795					14,927	—								16,839	*1796 End of VOC Rule*		
1797																	
1800					21,746									25,754			
1806	14,074	12,694	included under adults		26,768	—	"Negro Apprentices" also given here in brackets after 1814			19,346	10,515	included under adults		29,861	9,784	10,642	20,426
1807	13,624	11,990	„	„	25,614	—	599	605	1,204	18,990	10,313	„	„	29,303	8,496	8,935	17,431
1810	16,546	14,648	„	„	31,194	—	—	—	—	18,873	10,521	„	„	29,394	9,553	10,302	19,855
1814	18,019	16,814	„	„	34,833	—	(154)	(29)	(183)	19,730	11,344	„	„	31,074	9,202	9,365	18,567

1806 Second British Occupation

Note: In the table below the first value-group is headed *Free Persons (White or Black/Coloured)* for 1817–1834/5 and *Whites* for 1840–1845; the second value-group is headed *(All Free Coloured (including E))* (1828) / *Coloured Population* (1840–1845).

Year	Free Persons / Whites — M	— F	— Total	—	Free Coloured / Coloured Pop. — M	— F	— Total	Slaves — M	Slaves — F / D. Apprentices (1834–8)	Slaves — Total	Whites — M	— F	— Total
1817	20,750	18,884	39,634	—	918 (411)	958 (132)	1,876 (543)	19,481	12,565	32,046	11,640	11,796	23,436
1820	22,592	20,505	43,097	—	905 (1,061)	1,027 (492)	1,932 (1,553)	19,081	12,698	31,779	13,445	13,530	26,975
1823	25,487	23,212	48,699	—	891 (1,118)	1,098 (652)	1,989 (1,770)	19,786	13,412	33,198	15,336	15,213	30,549
1828	29,264	26,091	55,355	—	16,561	15,394	31,955 (All Free Coloured (including E))	18,383	13,860	32,243	included under C		
1829/30	45,023	41,426	86,449	—	included under A			18,312	13,754	32,066	included under A / 1834 Emancipation		
1834/5	56,786 [60,440]	54,017 [56,418]	110,803 [116,858]	—	included under A (or in a few cases under D)			18,815 [19,580]	15,426 [16,589] (D. Apprentices (1834–8))	34,241 [37,169]	included under A / 1838 End of Apprenticeship		
1840	35,966 [60,440]	34,809	70,775 [116,858]	—	40,612	38,868	79,480 (Coloured Population)				included under C		
1845	35,474	33,557	69,031	—	39,343	35,143	74,486				,, ,,		

SOURCES

1. *Eighteenth Century*

(a) 1710, 1750, 1760, 1780, 1786. From Cruse (pp. 203–4) based on Leibbrandt's *Précis of the Cape Archives, Annual Returns 1688–1792*, except where otherwise stated. The garrison figures are not included and the data for slaves refer only to privately-owned slaves, not those in the Company's Slave Lodge.

(b) 1718–93. Five-year statistics (drawn from the *Opgaafrolle* of the Cape burghers) from Beyers (pp. 240–49).

(c) 1795 and 1797 figures from de Kock (p. 237).

2. *Nineteenth Century*

(a) 1806–1823. From G. Thompson, vol. II, p. 256.

(b) 1828–1834/5. From the *Cape of Good Hope Almanacks* (produced by the South African Library). *The Cape of Good Hope Blue Book* for 1834 gives somewhat higher figures, which are included here in square brackets.

(c) 1840–1843. From the *Cape of Good Hope Blue Books* (produced by the South African Library). Figures for later quinquennia include an unspecified but increasing number of Bantu-speaking tribesmen under the "Coloured" heading.

N.B. There are minor statistical discrepancies in the sources, but the general trends remain constant.

Only in the 1690s did the large influx of privately-owned slaves begin, which was to convert the Cape community once and for all into a slave-owning society. By 1708 there were 1,298 privately-owned slaves (981 men, 166 women and 151 children). Just two years later, according to Valentyn (II, pp. 239 and 243) they numbered 1,775 (12,294 men, 260 women, 99 male children, 122 female children), in addition to another 440 Company slaves with a very different sex ratio (127 men, 183 women and 130 children). Burghers still just outnumbered slaves, with an overall total of 1923: this was made up of 656 adult men (about half the slave total), 339 women, 458 male children and 470 female children. Other persons at the Cape included Company servants and soldiers (some 500 of the latter), 51 deportees on Robben Island, including two girls, 18 Europeans and 31 Chinese, Malays and men from Ceylon and Macassar.

In 1713 came the great smallpox epidemic, which decimated and broke the Western Cape Hottentot clans and took more slave than European lives. Despite this latter depletion, by 1718 the numbers of slaves exceeded those of the free burghers, and continued to do so, though only by a smallish margin, until the end of the century (see Table II). The increase was due mainly to importation, not natural increase (van Ryneveld, 1797: p. 6). The decision of 1717 by the Governor in Council to opt for slave labour instead of white immigration was to some extent a confirmation of the existing trend, which in turn reflected the way in which "all the work is done throughout Asia and in all the colonies, in the West Indies, Surinam, etc." (quoted by Boxer, 1973a: p. 293). The XVII agreed with this, and thereafter no further efforts were made to encourage large-scale immigration of European peasants.

The available VOC statistics did not, for the most part, distinguish free black burghers or free blacks, and there were no definite estimates for Bushmen, Hottentots or Bastards, although the latter could probably be extracted from the *opgaaf*-rolls of certain drostdys (cf. Marais, p. 12). After the second British occupation, the population statistics became more detailed and systematic, (see Table II). With the abolition of the slave trade in 1806, the European population began to outstrip the slave population, rising from 26,768 in 1806 to 48,699 in 1823.[17] This increase was helped

17. Later statistics were, as can be seen, complicated by the fact that in the years preceding Emancipation, the returns usually distinguished only between "free" (i.e. white, free blacks and free coloured/Hottentots) and "slave" or "apprentice". By 1840, however, the distinction was between "white" and "coloured", so that all free coloured, including the emancipated slaves, were now classed together. It may be noted here that the white predominance over the free blacks in the Cape was paralleled in Barbados, alone of all the British West Indian colonies (Wesley, 1934: pp. 139–140).

by the arrival of nearly 5,000 British settlers in the 1820s. The slave population, on the other hand, increased by less than 4,000 in the period
1806–1823; the total of men remained more or less steady, while the
number of women, though always lower, rose. Here some allowance must
also be made nor manumissions, if not for "passing".

The pre-Emancipation population statistics for the Cape Colony present a quite different picture from that in Barbados (see Table III) or
any other West Indian plantation society. The Cape whites were never
greatly outnumbered by the slave population and although, over the eighteenth century, the number of male slaves increased until it was nearly
three times higher than that of adult white males, there was always the
reinforcement of the resident garrison. Moreover, few farmers or house-

TABLE III. Population of Barbados

| | Number | | | | Percentage | | | Freedmen as percentage of Total | |
| | | | | | | | | Total | Non- |
Year	Freedmen	Whites	Slaves	Total	Freedmen	Whites	Slaves	Free	White
1748	107	15,192	47,025	62,324	0·1	24·3	75·4	0·6	0·2
1768	448	16,139	66,379	82,966	0·5	19·4	80·0	2·7	0·6
1773	534	18,532	68,548	87,614	0·6	21·1	78·2	2·8	0·7
1786	838	16,167	62,115	79,120	1·0	20·4	78·5	4·9	1·3
1801	2,209	15,887	64,196	82,292	2·6	19·3	78·0	12·2	3·3
1809	2,663	15,566	69,369	87,598	3·0	17·7	79·1	14·6	3·6
1810	2,526	15,517	69,119	87,162	2·8	17·8	79·2	13·9	3·5
1811	2,613	15,794	69,132	87,539	2·9	18·0	78·9	14·1	3·6
1812	2,529	15,120	68,569	86,218	2·9	17·5	79·5	14·3	3·5
1813	2,412	15,561	65,995	83,968	2·8	18·5	78·5	13·4	3·5
1814	2,317	15,920	66,663	84,900	2·7	18·7	78·5	12·7	3·3
1815	3,139	16,145	69,280	88,564	3·5	18·2	78·2	16·2	4·3
1816	3,007	16,072	71,286	90,365	3·3	17·7	78·8	15·7	4·0
1825	4,524	14,630	78,096	97,250	4·6	15·0	80·3	23·6	6·0
1826	4,777	14,584	78,543	97,904	4·8	14·8	80·2	24·7	5·7
1827	4,896	14,687	79,383	98,966	4·8	14·8	80·2	25·0	5·8
1828	5,020	14,824	80,050	99,894	5·0	14·8	80·1	25·2	5·9
1829	5,146	14,959	80,086	100,191	5·1	14·9	79·9	25·5	6·0
1833–34	6,584	12,797	80,861	100,242	6·5	12·7	80·6	33·9	7·5

Sources: 1748 (CO 28/29); 1768, 1786 ("Report of the Lords," pt. 4, no. 15 and 3rd suppl. to
no. 15); 1773 (CO 318/2, no. 16, cited in D. Makinson, *Barbados: A Study of North-American–
West-Indian Relations, 1739–1789* [The Hague, 1964], p. 15); 1801, 1809–11 (*PP*, 1814–15, vol. 7,
rept. 478); 1812–16 (compiled from statistics in: CO 28/86; *PP*, 1823, vol. 18, rept. 80; *ibid.*, 1826,
vol. 26, rept. 350); 1825–29 (*ibid.*, 1830, vol. 21, rept. 674; the 1825 slave population is given as an
estimate for all parishes); 1833–34 (M. Martin, *History of the Colonies of the British Empire* [London,
1843], p. 64; statistics on the white population of Saint Peter and Saint Thomas are not included).
This table was originally published in the article by Jerome Handler and Arnold Sio on "Barbados" in *Neither Slave Nor Free* (eds, David W. Cohen and Jack P. Greene, pp. 218–9), John
Hopkins University Press, Baltimore and London, 1972. It is reproduced here by courtesy of the
authors and the publishers.

holders had more than a handful of slaves, and none had as many as one hundred. At the time of Emancipation and compensation there were 3,344 claimants in relation to only 38,427 slaves (Hengherr, 1953: pp. 17, 45 n.2, 63f.). Nor did the ill-enumerated Khoisan present a menace, at least on numerical grounds. As the 1828 figures indicate, the whites, exclusive of troops, were not greatly outnumbered by the whole non-white population, including free blacks and Hottentots (enumerated together) and slaves.

The number of free blacks rose over the period 1806–1823 from 1,204 to 1,989. Between 1816 and 1824, the annual number of manumissions only twice exceeded fifty (Edwards, 1942: p. 153). Thereafter it slightly increased: the total number of manumissions in the decade before Emancipation was something over 1,566. The free black group was also enlarged by the accession of the Prize Negroes or Negro Apprentices, of whom there were 1,118 men and 652 women in 1823 (for these cf. Marais, p. 161; MacCrone p. 70f; Edwards, pp. 50–53). In 1823–1824 virtually all the free blacks and over half the Prize Negroes lived (and had always lived) in Cape Town (Thompson, 1827: vol II, pp. 255–256). They thus had few contacts even with the surrounding Western Cape areas. The free blacks alone comprised one-tenth of the town's total population, and stood in a ratio of about 2:9 to the white population, and nearly 1:4 to the slaves.

Miscegenation and Manumission

In most New World slave societies it is easy to set out the relative proportions of whites, slaves and freedmen and to look for some sociological relevancies. In the Cape, it is much more difficult to decide to which other ethnic or geographical group or groups the free blacks of the Western Cape or Cape Town should be related for any meaningful purpose. If we consider the whole free non-white category, there is little or no evidence of any significant connexions between the free blacks and Malays of the West and the Bastards and Hottentots of the East and North. On the other hand, about three-quarters of all slaves lived in the West in 1830, as did the majority of the 3,344 slave-owners. This essay is therefore primarily concerned with the free coloured people of Cape Town, seen in relation to the whites and slaves of Cape Town and the Western Cape.

Most white South African historians have been understandably reluctant to dwell on the subject of large-scale miscegenation in the Cape under Dutch rule. This applies particularly to intermarriage and the "passing" of the mixed offspring, and even the coloured wife, into the white community —something which recent generations have seen as contaminating the purity of the white race. The contemporary reports of a high incidence of miscegenation in the shape of mulatto and lighter children could not be disregarded, but there has been a tendency to put the major responsibility on soldiers, seamen and other outsiders, and not on the free white burghers. Yet the very uneven European sex ratio, which lasted into the nineteenth century, (for tables see Beyers, 1929: pp. 240–249) could only have inclined white men to cohabit with non-white women, just as the uneven slave sex ratio inclined male slaves to cohabit with Hottentot women.

The evidence of widespread miscegenation between whites and slaves as well as between slaves and Hottentots, both in the Slave Lodge and in private households, was reported by van Riebeeck and his successors with increasing concern. Successive though not very effective regulations were passed against debauchery, fornication and prostitution in public and private places. The scandalous situation in the Slave Lodge in 1685 was described by Baron H. A. van Rheede:

Men and women, young and old, dwell there together. In this country the animals are separated in better order according to sex than are human beings. Slave girls let themselves be used by whites in exchange for a dress or a blanket.

The whites—free burghers, soldiers and sailors (*onse natie, vryluijden, matrosen en soldaten*)—were, in van Rheede's view, the main seducers. In the Slave Lodge he found 32 boys and 26 girls who were the children of European fathers and slave mothers. He gave instructions for the Christian instruction and baptism of these children who, "being indisputably children of our nation, cannot be made slaves" (de Kock, 1950: pp. 119–120). Van Rheede's endeavours to prohibit further concubinage in the Slave Lodge were, however, fruitless, as visitors throughout the eighteenth century were to attest (Hoge, 1939: pp. 105–107).

Many instances of faithful concubinage in private households were also reported from the first settlement up to Emancipation. In such cases the man would often buy his concubine or at least their children free. Numerous christenings of illegitimate bastard children were recorded in the baptismal registers of the Reformed Church in Cape Town in the eighteenth century. Intermarriage was less frequent than faithful concubinage but nevertheless occurred more often than is generally supposed. Hoge (q.v. *passim* for miscegenation) mentions twenty-two cases of mixed marriages in the seventeenth century, recorded in the marriage registers of the Reformed Church in Cape Town, and a markedly increased number in the eighteenth century, almost all between white men and non-white women.[18] Taking the recorded white ancestresses of South African families given in H. T. Colenbrander's (1964) *De Afkomst der Boeren*, Hoge lists the names of at least 140 women given there as having "non-white blood in their veins" (on evidence taken from baptismal and marriage registers, wills and other sources).

If we take into account the fact that there were fewer than 250 adult European women and 319 female children at the Cape in 1700, and over ten times that many by the 1790s, the injection of at least 140 child-bearing non-white women into that community over the period must have had an appreciable effect. At the end of the century, Cornelius de Jong commented: "Even many of the oldest and most respected families in Cape Town have black blood in their veins" (1802–3, vol. I p. 126).

The considerable incidence at the Cape of intermarriage and "passing", (both virtually unknown in Barbados, although miscegenous unions were common), may be attributed to such factors as the shortage of white women, the attractiveness of the Asian and half-caste slave women and the early lack of race-consciousness among VOC servants. There was, however, a growing tendency to conceal such unions even during the eighteenth century, although they did not yet lead to social ostracism. Concealment was facilitated by the woman's adoption of a European name at marriage.

As time passed and attitudes hardened in the nineteenth and twentieth centuries, early coloured antecedents were either forgotten or never referred to, although genetic accidents have been known to embarrass the best-documented families.[19]

Manumission was fairly common in the early period, the laws which governed it being vague for some decades. It was often linked with mis-

18. In 1685, to check miscegenation, Baron van Rheede forbade marriage between whites and full-blooded "blacks", though not between whites and half-breeds. It is not clear whether this ruling was actually complied with. Here it should be noted that mixed marriages could occur among high-ranking VOC officials at this period. The early commanders or Governors of the Cape included two men of mixed origins: firstly, (1679–1969), the magnificent Simon van der Stel, son of Adriaan van der Stel of Dordrecht, once Governor of Mauritius, and of his Indian wife, Monica of the coast, and secondly, his more ill-fated son, William Adriaan.

19. In his 1935 booklet on *Miscegenation*, George Findlay estimated that between 500,000 and 733,000 coloured persons had passed into the European group since 1652. He pointed to the still noticeable lack of light-coloured persons in the Coloured group, and concluded that all who could pass did so, and that the line between coloured and white was in fact that between "half-caste" and "quadroon-white", with over 500,000 "play-whites" in the officially white population. (Cf. also S. Patterson 1953: pp. 330–332 and 334 for early and later details of "passing", and pp. 141–142 for continuing intermarriage and miscegenation).

cegenation, intermarriage and the freeing of the children of mixed unions. There were also manumissions by will; manumissions on the occasion of the master leaving the Cape; and an increasing number of self-manumissions by skilled slaves in Cape Town, who were allowed to hire themselves out and thus earn sufficient money to purchase their own freedom.

The number of freedmen apparently increased sufficiently fast in the first decades after the settlement for some restrictions to be imposed (Walker, p. 76). In 1685, as has been noted, van Rheede laid it down that Christian, Dutch-speaking half-breeds could claim freedom as of right on attaining the full legal age of 25 for men and 21 for women. Moreover, "foreign slaves" could claim freedom after thirty years' service and slaves born in the colony could, when forty years old, offer their owners 100 guilders and ask for freedom as a favour. During the eighteenth century, owners were asked to guarantee that a manumitted slave would not become a charge on public funds, first for ten years, then for twenty, and to pay a certain sum to the Dutch Reformed Church funds for this purpose (10 rixdollars after 1765, 50 rixdollars after 1777) (Cruse, 1947: pp. 250–251; de Kock, 1950: pp. 200–203). One reason for these measures, as in Barbados, was that certain owners were manumitting their aged or sickly slaves in order to be rid of their maintenance. There were also some cases of freedmen being re-enslaved, either voluntarily, because they could not support themselves, or on moral or criminal grounds.

When the Company manumitted its slaves—following van Rheede's injunction that they should not be compelled to "sigh under constant slavery"—some were taken into the Company's service on salaries. The Company also gave freedom to slaves for special bravery and service, such as the uncovering of a crime or a slave escape. Slaves taken to Holland automatically became free as soon as they set foot there, although complications could arise for those who returned to the Cape. In general there seems to have been some obligation on non-whites to prove that they were not slaves, at least by the end of the eighteenth century and later.

It is worth noting that, in contrast to Barbados and other West Indian islands, slaves freed in the Cape had the chance of returning to their homes. According to de Kock (1950: p. 199) some apparently did so, provided that they could pay the *double* passage; others who were too poor were apparently allowed to work their passage home. How many actually did return, and how many free coloured persons went to other VOC territories or to Holland, is not known. Another differing circumstance was the open land frontier, which encouraged slave escape rather than rebellion.

TABLE IV. Manumissions 1715–1792: by whom manumitted and numbers manumitted

By whom manumitted (*vrygestel*)	Number manumitted	Group	Total
Testamentary bequest by whites	196 ⎫	A	240
Testamentary bequest by Free Blacks	44 ⎭		
Company slaves—freedom self-purchased (*vrygekoop*)	32 ⎫		
Company slave children—freedom purchased by their mother	29 ⎪		
Company slave children—freedom purchased by non-white fathers	4 ⎬	B	86
Company slave mothers—freedom purchased by their children	2 ⎪		
Company slave children—freedom purchased by whites	19 ⎭		
Slaves manumitted by whites	361 ⎫		
Slaves manumitted by Chinese*	40 ⎪	C	567
Slaves manumitted by their mothers/owners	10 ⎬		
Slaves manumitted by Free Blacks	156 ⎭		
	893		893

* The mysterious category of "Chinese", who freed 45 slaves in all, were almost certainly never slaves, but had been brought to the Cape as convicts or exiles. When they had served their term, most returned to the East, freeing their concubines and children on departure (Cruse, p. 265).
Source, Cruse 1947: p. 253.

In the early decades, burghers were not obliged to notify the authorities about acts of manumission, and the small number recorded clearly does not reflect the actual numbers freed (Cruse, 1947: pp. 246–250). Rather more satisfactory data for the period 1715–1784, (derived from Leibbrandt, 1905–1906) are to be found in Cruse (ibid. pp. 251–273). These show that a minimum of 893 slaves were manumitted (see Table IV), 585 requests for manumission being involved. The number of manumissions rose absolutely and in relation to the total number of slaves for the first five decades of this period: 12 in 1715–1724; 32 in 1725–1734; 93 in 1735–1744; 111 in 1745–1754; 188 in 1755–1764. Thereafter the numbers fell away somewhat: 152 in 1765–1774; 174 in 1775–1784; and 131 in 1785–1794.

According to Cruse, these figures do not support the supposition that slave-owners at the Cape were greatly influenced by the libertarian ideas of the French philosophers in the late eighteenth century (ideas which were to flower somewhat sparsely and ephemerally during the period of the

Batavian Republic in 1803–1806). Of the total manumitted, 576 were given their freedom by white slave-owners, but Cruse does not tell us how many of the 585 requests came from whites and how many from non-whites, or at what date. The white manumitters were certainly in the majority and, while they constituted a minority of the total number of white slave-owners, there may have been proportionally more of them than in Barbados. The relatively early incidence of manumissions by non-white slave-owners in the Cape is also worthy of note.

Economic considerations were particularly important for manumission in this domestic, non-plantation, slave economy. A modest household of slaves could be a free burgher's main capital and form of investment (sometimes used for mortgage purposes or hiring out): manumission thus involved not only immediate expenditure but also a diminution of capital. Expense was probably the main consideration for non-white manumitters: the records indicate that the purchase and subsequent manumission of relatives was spaced over a number of years. The categories in Table IV give us an idea of the different types of manumissions and the relationships involved. Cruse estimates (p. 272) that at least 57 out of the 585 requests for manumission involved miscegenous unions and their offspring, some occurring late in the eighteenth century.

Thirty-two Company slaves are shown as having bought their own freedom. The records do not, however, indicate how many of the privately-owned slaves were also self-manumitted, although this certainly happened fairly often in Cape Town, where the opportunities for earning money and purchasing one's own freedom were relatively good.

A further instance of the disparity between regulations and their application is afforded by the fact that the records relating to Company slaves contain no mention of the complex system laid down by van Rheede in 1685 for freeing different categories of slaves at a certain age. Instead, adult slaves were given their freedom if another healthy and acceptable slave was provided in their place, despite Goske's prohibition of this practice in 1671, and children were freed for a payment of 100 guilders.[20] In Barbados, the white administration periodically raised manumission fees in an unsuccessful attempt to limit the number of manumissions, but there is no evidence for this at the Cape.

20. For the slave laws in force at the Cape in 1797, including brief references to those relating to manumission, see van Ryneveld, 1797, p. 4. The situation in 1813, and that following the ameliorative measures of the 1823 proclamation and Ordinance 19 of 1826 are set out in Edwards, (1942), Appendices I and II (the latter also outlines the differences between the West Indies and Cape situations).

Cruse's data indicate the geographical origins of the freed slaves. The majority of those manumitted were Cape-born, but 290 had been born elsewhere. Of these the great majority came from Asia: 140 from the East Indies, 106 from India, 26 from Ceylon and 3 from the Philippines. Only 15 were of African origins, 11 of them from Madagascar. Of the "Asians", the majority of the East Indians came from Macassar (34), Batavia (37), Bugis (Celebes) (29) and Bali (12); of those from India 71 were from Bengal, 11 from the Coromandel Coast and 7 from Malabar. There is little here to tell us how many of these manumitted slaves "passed" into the free European community and how many became "free blacks". Most of the 140 from the East Indies may have been Muslims, as may some of the Cape-born freedmen, and thus swelled the ranks of the "Malays".

There is a gap in the available manumission figures between 1793 and 1815. Isobel Edwards (1942: p. 153) provides figures for the subsequent pre-Emancipation years under British rule. There were 430 manumissions in all in the period 1816–1824, and at least 1,566 in the period 1825–1834. The relatively low total for the first period probably reflects the steep rise in the price of slaves and the cessation of imports following the abolition of the slave trade. The rise in the last decade may be attributed primarily to the increasing certainty of eventual Emancipation and also to the falling value of slaves as restrictions on their use accumulated (Walker, 1947: p. 178).

Edwards does not tell us what proportion of the second total gained their freedom as a result of Ordinance 19 of 1826.[21] Marais (p. 167), basing his statement on the Report of the Guardians of Slaves, however, writes that "a small, though by no means negligible, minority" of the 1200-odd slaves manumitted over the period 1816–1830 bought their own freedom. If an owner refused to manumit the slave or demanded an unfairly high price, the matter went to court for appraisal and decision. The institution of compulsory manumission was of real benefit only to the wage-earning slave artisans of Cape Town. It was, however, part of the whole new climate of increasing slave amelioration and reform, with the examination of claims to manumission passing into the hands of the Guardians of Slaves.

21. This was based on the Trinidad Ordinance of 1824, passed by Canning as a model of amelioration for the slave-owning colonies. Ordinance 19 provided for a registrar and guardian of slaves. It also provided for compulsory manumission, removing the master's privileges of conceding or denying freedom by allowing any slave to purchase his own freedom and that of his wife or child provided that he could prove to the newly appointed Guardian of Slaves that the money had been obtained by lawful means (Edwards, 1942, pp. 152–153). Barbados refused to adopt such a measure until 1831.

The reaction of the masters to Ordinance 19 was predictably hostile: memorialists maintained that it struck at the roots of the acknowledged rights of property, and that those who applied for manumission would prove to be "the most cunning in vice and lasciviousness", who had successfully robbed their masters. In the vain hope of getting Ordinance 19 repealed, and also of securing a representative assembly, the colonists produced schemes for gradual emancipation. Such a scheme was adopted in 1828 by the Philanthropic Society in Cape Town, the aim being to bring about the ultimate abolition of slavery by the purchase, manumission and apprenticeship of female slave children between the ages of three and ten. Because of local apathy, only 127 slave children were emancipated during the five years of the Society's existence.

The decade before Emancipation witnessed a flood of memorials and representations from anti-libertarian and pro-libertarian white interests in the Colony relating to slave amelioration and emancipation and the protection of the nominally free Hottentots. By contrast with Barbados, however, few initiatives towards improving their own status seem to have emanated from the free blacks, although the Hottentots and Bastards and some slaves[22] were more vocal in their own cause.

Legal Status and the Political–Judicial System

Most South African secondary sources are permeated by an albocentric climate of disinterest, which makes definite, unqualified statements about different aspects of the legal status, rights, privileges and responsibilities of free people of colour—in practice as well as in law—impossible without further recourse to the primary sources. Nevertheless, free blacks and other free people of colour undoubtedly had a separate status by usage and custom, differentiating them from slaves and, increasingly, from white burghers. This differential status may indeed have been imposed by the white burghers rather than by the VOC authorities.

VOC rule at the Cape was for the most part arbitrary, corrupt and inefficient. Government remained largely in the hands of the XVII in the

22. Hengherr, when making the point that many slaves could read and write, refers to some letters written to the Governor by slaves in Worcester in 1830–1 but gives no details about the contents. In general, the number of complaints made by slaves against their masters to the Guardians and Protectors suggested that a spirit of lively or dogged protest was widespread among them, even in the harsher conditions of the eastern districts. After Emancipation several addresses of gratitude by the former slaves were published, thanking the King, Parliament and the British people, the Governor and their friends in the Council (*Commercial Advertiser*, 3, 10 and 27. December 1834) (*op. cit.* pp. 9, 19f, 43 n5).

Netherlands and, until 1743, of the Governor General in Council in Batavia. Day-to-day government was in the hands of the Council of Policy (the Governor and seven senior officials), whose overriding aim was to protect and support the commercial interests of the VOC, not those of the burghers—the "illegitimate children of the Company." This Council legislated for all who participated in the Cape polity, VOC servants, burghers (including a minority of "free blacks") and slaves.[23] The rule of law did not exist during the Company period. In practice only freemen and Company servants had access to the courts. The central courts were largely controlled by Company officials, the local ones by white farmers; in neither case were the judges (other than the Fiscal) trained or familiar with the over-detailed and often contradictory Cape laws. Sentences were often partial and capricious, related to the legal status of the offender or the person offended against; the Bible was frequently cited in this regard, as when, in a 1685 case of a master being tried for murdering his slave, the Stellenbosch *landdrost* quoted a passage from Exodus xxi, 20–21, which distinguishes between freemen and servants in the matter of punishment for a crime.

Burghers were not represented on the local Council of Policy. The burgher councillors chosen to sit on the Council of Justice to help try cases involving burghers were, however, traditionally consulted on matters affecting that class. The only qualifications required were that they must be members of the Dutch Reformed Church (i.e. Muslims, Catholics and others would be disqualified) and not too closely related to one another. The Council also appointed burghers to various administrative boards. There is no mention of any non-white burgher serving in such positions, nor—after the van der Stel era—of any persons of known mixed origins serving as higher VOC officials. Some lower Company servants were however non-whites, notable the uniformed "Caffres", usually Indian exiles or slaves, who served as executioners' assistants and constables: they carried out arrests and floggings of whites as well as non-whites. In 1780, following a request by the *Patriotte* that the Fiscal should be made to

23. Slave law at the Cape was essentially derived from the Roman code, as varied by the Statutes of India and befogged by a flow of detailed Cape *placaaten*. For the letter of the law and its frequently arbitrary application, including the increasingly harsh punishments during the eighteenth century, see Edwards, (1942). Chapter VI and *passim*, de Kock, 1950: Chapter VIII and J. S. Marais, (1939, 173f). As for the indigenous peoples, in the eighteenth century the Cape Government claimed jurisdiction over all pure-blooded "Hottentots" within its boundaries. Technically they were free men living in the Colony but not of it. In practice, most had become vagrants or virtual serfs on Boer farms (Walker, 1947: pp. 134–135 and MacMillan and Marais *passim*).

employ white men to arrest white burghers, some European constables were placed at the Fiscal's disposal.

The burghers selected to attend the Council of Justice also constituted the Burgher Council, Cape Town's municipal authority. It had no legal existence but was given *de facto* recognition by the government.[24] As the eighteenth century passed, this Burgher Council reflected the increasingly exclusive attitudes of the white burgher class, and stressed the distinction between burgher and non-burgher status. MacCrone (1937) writes of the last decades of the eighteenth century: "One had to be born free, of free-born parents who were themselves of Christian, that is, of pure European descent, in order to be accepted as a fully qualified burgher on an equal footing with other members of the same class" (p. 133).

There was a clear legal concept of burgher status (Botha, 1926: p. 33) but it is not clear whether MacCrone is here discussing a legal or a social set of requirements. In the 1780s, however, some effective moves were made by the burghers to exclude free blacks and children of various types of mixed unions from full burgher status. Male burghers had to serve in the burgher companies, and in this decade a "Free Corps" was formed, at the suggestion of the Burgher Military Council, for the enrolment of all those not born in wedlock and those whose parents had not been born in the state of freedom. Such persons, it was stated, "cannot be enrolled among the burghers doing service; also . . . they cannot very well be employed with those at the Fire Engines and Public Works, who have been born in slavery." (MacCrone, ibid. pp. 133–134).

The evidence relating to this intermediate status, and to any restrictions which impinged upon free blacks or freed coloured as opposed to whites (or slaves), is fragmentary and confusing. Marais (p. 162) writes that until the passing of Ordinance 50 of 1828 the free blacks of Cape Town were subject, by order of the Burgher Senate (formerly Council), to restrictions upon their freedom of movement, to compulsory service as a sort of fire brigade, and to interference on the part of the police, especially at night. Elsewhere (p. 126) he refers to passes for slaves, Hottentots, Malays and other free blacks. It is not clear when these restrictions on movement were

---

24. For other local authorities see OHSA I, p. 223f, p. 298f. Those in the West were more involved with VOC policies and towards the end of VOC rule were making modest demands for full political rights for free burghers (not of course for non-white freemen). The frontier Boers were less concerned with the VOC, particularly as it failed to defend them and their property. They became increasingly self-sufficient, resentful of authority, and inclined to administer their own domestic justice in relation to slaves and other non-white dependants.

introduced for Malays and free blacks (they did not apply to Bastards). Pass regulations had been in force for slaves from 1760, and for Hottentots, in the Stellenbosch district at least, since 1797. Passes for Hottentots were introduced by Lord Caledon in his 1809 proclamation, which brought them under colonial law, and was aimed both at affording them some legal protection from ill-treatment and at providing a settled supply of labour for the farmers. This proclamation apparently referred only to the Hottentots. On the other hand, Ordinance 50 of 1828, while repealing the Hottentot legislation of 1809–1819, also made all free people of colour equal before the law with Europeans. The second clause, which swept away *inter alia* the pass laws, opened with the following words:

And whereas *by usage and custom* [my italics] of this Colony, Hottentots and other free persons of colour have been subjected to certain restraints as to their residence, mode of life and employment, and to certain compulsory services to which others of His Majesty's subjects are not liable . . .

Another type of restriction seems to have existed for different classes of free and non-free, in the form of sumptuary laws introduced in the mid-seventeenth century. Botha (1926: pp. 61–62) mentions restrictions laid on Europeans relating to the use of livery, the size of umbrellas, the wearing of silks and satins by ladies, and the degree of funeral pomp and ceremony —to be determined by the rank of the husband. De Kock (p. 220) refers to a *placaat* introduced in 1765 to curb the "exceedingly annoying practice" whereby "freed females" were actually surpassing the "standard of apparel" of respectable burghers' wives: thereafter they were to be prohibited from wearing "coloured silk dresses, crinolines, fine lace, trimmings on bonnets, hair that has been curled, also earrings, whether made of imitation or of precious stones".[25]

Free coloured persons could own property,[26] including slaves, and no restrictions on their right of bequeathal are mentioned. As for the right of testimony in the courts, which was so important an issue in Barbados, they possessed the same rights as did all freemen. How they fared in practice, in courts dominated by white burghers or Company officials, is a matter

25. Malays, whether slave or free, were not restricted from wearing Eastern dress throughout the eighteenth century (I. D. du Plessis, 1947: pp. 47–9). Slaves in general were apparently not allowed to wear shoes or stockings—Mentzel commented that, at the Cape, "the bare foot is the mark of the slave". (de Kock, p. 49).

26. Muslims were reportedly debarred from owning land without the express permission of the Governor up till the 1820s; but Clause 3 of Ordinance 50 (1828) laid at rest the doubts that had arisen as to "the competence of Hottentots and other persons of colour to purchase or possess land in this Colony" (MacMillan, pp. 211–212).

which requires further research. During the later period under British rule, little evidence is at present available to indicate that any special consideration was given to the general position of the free blacks of the West. More is known about the situation of the Khoisan, nominally free, but brought fully within the protection of the circuit courts only in 1811. Thereafter the eastern Boers were abruptly confronted with the unacceptable notion that their Hottentot servants had equal rights as free men and could hale them before the courts on charges of ill-treatment.[27] Equally unacceptable was the support given to servants and slaves with complaints by the "meddlesome missionaries" of the London Missionary Society. The Black Circuit of 1812, and the Slagter's Nek episode which followed it, were to pass into Afrikaner nationalist mythology as examples of the legitimate grievances of the frontier colonists against the new and alien system.[28]

Despite the many limitations on their civil status and rights, in custom more than in law, free blacks in the West, like the Bastards in the East, incurred the same civic responsibilities and duties as full burghers in respect of taxes, and, in the case of the men, some form of militia service. In the West, as we have noted, free blacks had their own Free Corps by the late eighteenth century (MacCrone, p. 133).[29] On the expanding frontiers the commando system began to evolve as early as the 1670s, for defence or retaliation against "wild" Khoisan cattle-raiders and later the Xhosa and other Bantu-speaking African peoples. Bastards formed their own units or served in Boer commandos, under the command of army or burgher officers. Hottentot servants also served in the commandos, and in 1793, when the Dutch government had to prepare to defend the Cape, they began to serve professionally in the armed forces, in a special Cape Corps or Regiment, under European officers.[30]

27. Cf. Barrow's description of the lament of the frontier farmer flogged and put in irons by the British military authorities for mistreating a non-Christian: "My God! is that a way to treat a Christian?" (MacCrone, p. 127, n. 3).

28. For this period and Boer reactions see Walker, pp. 156–157; Edwards, pp. 57–63; Marais, pp. 120–123, MacMillan pp. 90–91; S. Patterson, 1957: pp. 14–15; van Jaarsveld, 1961: passim.

29. Something like this apparently continued after Emancipation on a volunteer basis. Cf. Aldridge for a note on the Malay and Liberated African Burgher Force of the Cape District in 1846. The units of the Malay Company were commanded by British officers and each had its "priest".

30. The Hottentot corps was retained by the British authorities until 1870, successive governors having a high regard for their loyalty, endurance, discipline and general suitability for "Kaffir" warfare. Hottentot troops gave excellent service in successive Kaffir wars, and were also used against dissident Boers (e.g. at Slagter's Nek and in the 1840s).

The way to legal equality was opened up for Hottentots and "other free persons of colour" by Ordinance 50 of 1828, and for the slaves by the Emancipation Act of 1833 (although Apprenticeship ran its full term till 1838 in the Cape, unlike Barbados). Freedom of the press was gained for all in 1828, although the right of assembly could be refused until 1848. The colour-blind, property-based municipal franchise for males was brought in in the late 1830s, and in 1853 representative government was introduced, again on a property-based franchise, "such . . . as will enable the intelligent and industrious man of colour to share with his fellow colonists of European descent in the privilege of voting for the representatives of the people". (OHSA, p. 323; Marais, pp. 208–215). In both cases the "colour-blind" element was insisted on by London, and the Coloured People remained passive, if uneasy. From 1838 until the time of Union, no discriminating legislation was passed in the Cape, and the Coloured People were left to their own devices, to acquire sufficient economic and political power to transform theoretical equality into real equality. This they failed to do, entering the twentieth century as a backward, unorganized, resourceless, lower-class adjunct to the Cape whites, from most of whom they differed in nothing except their poverty and their colour.

Occupation and Economic Status

In the early decades of the VOC settlement at the Cape, there was a small minority of free black burghers. According to MacCrone (p. 70f.), they seem to have been originally skilled slaves of the Company brought from the East and emancipated as a reward for long and faithful service. Their names appeared more and more frequently in the burgher rolls from 1666 onwards and no official distinction seems to have been made between them and freemen of European origin. Later, "free blacks" began to appear in the documents, and MacCrone conjectures that this may have indicated a lower status than that of "burgher".

The VOC's policy was colour-blind at that time, and a despatch from the XVII in 1677 contained a suggestion that Company land at Hottentots Holland might be made over to freemen or to the Company's emancipated

---

As a result of the increasingly "strong prejudice that exists against the organization and arming of the coloured classes", the Cape Mounted Riflemen were disbanded in 1870 and in 1878 coloured people were legally relegated to the category of "levies" (cf. Marais, pp. 131–134; Patterson, 1953, pp. 45–46; Marks, p. 76). For the participation of freedmen in the Barbados militia, see Sio (1974) pp. 14–15; Handler (1974) pp. 110–116.

slaves on certain conditions. Not long after the arrival of Simon van der Stel as Governor, land was granted to a few black freemen in the Stellenbosch district. The best known of these was Antony van Angola, credited in the 1692 return with 1 female slave, 4,000 vines, 4 muskets, 154 sheep, 14 oxen and other goods and returns. Other black freemen were mentioned in some of the civil cases of the period, the reports indicating more free-and-easy social relations than were to develop later.

This was, however, a passing phase, probably reflecting VOC patterns further East. Not only were the designations "free black burgher" and "free black" sometimes applied to the same person in official documents but, as the importation of slaves increased, "the presence of a large number of black slaves within a community in which white slave-owners predominated was fatal to the prospects of a free black or coloured population, since they would only tend to fall, and could never hope to rise, in the social scale" (MacCrone, p. 73). The "free-and-easy" phase of course occurred at a time when there were 523 free adults of both sexes (plus 63 *knegte* or white indentured servants) and only 342 adult slaves. By 1710 the number had risen to 994 and 1,559 respectively, and by the middle of the eighteenth century, after the Council's decision in 1717 to rely on slave labour rather than to import free white artisans, there were 4,479 adult slaves to 2,296 adult freemen.

From then on the West became thoroughly dependent on slave domestic and field labour (as the East was to become dependent on Khoisan serf labour). Manual work became the province of the slave, the Hottentot, the mixed blood and later the Kaffir. In 1743, Baron von Imhoff commented sharply on the effects of slave-owning on the owners:

> Having imported slaves, every common or ordinary European becomes a gentleman and prefers to be served than to serve . . . the majority of the farmers in the Cape are not farmers in the real sense of the word . . . and many of them consider it a shame to work with their own hands.

Even in the early decades of the eighteenth century, slavery was becoming a permanent condition, the human status of the slave was declining as his property status increased, and, as Theal observed in 1882: "The view began to be held and asserted that slavery was the proper condition of the black race" (Chronicles, vol. ii, p. 465). Cape slavery (like Hottentot servitude) was of the small-scale, paternalistic, manorial or domestic type, not the large-scale, exploitative, plantation type. Few owners had more than a handful of slaves, and none had as many as one hundred (Hengherr,

1953: p. 17, n. 45, and p. 63 f.). Unlike Barbados,[31] slavery at the Cape was unenterprising, and unproductive of wealth. Slaves were a convenience and a habit, employed wastefully to underpin a modest comfort and social prestige. In such a society the situation of slaves and servants depended greatly on the whims of individual masters. It also ranged from the comfortable and permissive domestic slavery of Cape Town and the prosperous Western farms (where "even slavery wears a smile"—as Cowper Rose wrote in the 1820s) to the poverty, isolation and sometimes brutality of the more remote corn and cattle farms (Edwards 1942, pp. 12–20).

Escape from the slave-status by miscegenation or manumission became more difficult, and often led only as far as the largely Muslim or "Malay" group of free blacks, resident in Cape Town and engaged in urban occupations. The great majority of adult slaves manumitted were town slaves with urban or household skills (cf. de Kock, pp. 58–65). Thus the skills and aptitudes which had led to their attaining freedom were better suited to urban than to rural life (there were in any case no large plantations requiring freemen overseers and a variety of freemen artisans—as in some areas of the West Indies).

The occupations which the free blacks pursued included the trades by which they had earned their freedom, but there was a tendency to set up small independent businesses. By the 1820s, they constituted "a large proportion of the lower class of Tradesmen, Fishermen and Mechanics" of Cape Town (Marais, p. 162). Particular areas of trade were fruit and vegetable dealing and market-gardening. The Malays, both slave and free, were particularly active in fishing, building and cabinet-making, tailoring, shoe-making, coopering, confectionery-making and catering, gardening and coach-driving (I. D. du Plessis, 1947: pp. 43f). Their chances of self-manumission were said to be increased by the fact that their religion allowed them to work on Sunday, when they could earn on their own account. The free blacks, joined by the Prize Negroes and, after 1834, by the newly-emancipated skilled slaves, monopolized the skilled trades of Cape Town until their monopoly was gradually undermined by the arrival of British artisans later in the nineteenth century.

Few free blacks seem to have owned house property before 1828. This

---

31. Most contemporary commentators compared Cape slavery favourably with the plantation slavery of the West Indies (cf. de Kock, pp. 217–223; Marais, p. 162f). Dr. John Philip and Thomas Pringle were amongst those who differed (MacCrone, pp. 75–76; Edwards, 1942; p. 69).

was probably because the majority were Muslims and thus reportedly prohibited from buying land except with the permission of the Governor. Thereafter, some free blacks managed to accumulate property, mostly in Cape Town, according to data given in the almanacks of the 1830s and 1840s. It does not seem that the free coloured of the Western Cape bore comparison with the Barbados freedmen in terms of property ownership. On the other hand, 830 coloured persons owned or rented premises of sufficient value to enable them to qualify for the male, adult, property-based municipal franchise of Cape Town, where they constituted 40 per cent of the municipal voters' roll in 1840 (Hengherr, p. 84). Unlike the former freedmen of Barbados, however, they did not produce a leader of the calibre of Samuel Jackson Prescod, the first coloured man to sit in the Barbados House of Assembly after the electoral qualifications were equalized in 1840.

Religion and Education

The religious factor was more important in the Cape than in Barbados, in that relations between white and coloured were profoundly influenced by two opposed conceptions of Christianity; the unreformed exclusive Calvinism of the Boers and the evangelical inclusive humanitarianism of the missionaries and philanthropists who came in the wake of the British authorities. In the early 1800s these two conceptions—which Dr. Ben Marais (1952) calls the "conservative" and the "radical" principles (pp. 297–298)—met in a head-on conflict over the proper relations between master and slave or servant, a conflict which has not yet been resolved in South Africa.

In contrast to Barbados, therefore, where slavery was justified more on economic grounds, the Boers came increasingly to believe that the personal master-slave relationship was not only economically necessary and legally sanctioned but was actually divinely ordained. This conviction of their predestined superiority of race and faith was also applied by extension to the Hottentot servants who were more numerous than slaves in the East, and who were often characterized as *skepsels* or heathen creatures, somewhere between humans and beasts (MacCrone, 1937: p. 130, n.; Legassick, 1973: p. 8 and refs.) Amelioration and emancipation were thus seen not only as attacks on property rights, as in the West Indies, but as an intolerable interference with a divinely sanctioned relationship, in which the dichotomy between Christian and heathen had shifted to a dichotomy between white and non-white, free and unfree.[32]

This complex of religious beliefs and practices evolved as a result of isolation and challenge, out of the primitive seventeenth century Calvinism, with its emphasis on the Old Testament, predestination and the "elect", which the VOC brought to the Cape with the state church.[33]

In the early Cape, however, the factors of race and skin-colour played little part in relations between Europeans and non-Europeans, compared with religious differences. As MacCrone comments: "Men were, in the first place, Catholics or Protestants, Christians or non-Christians, Mohammedans or Kaffirs". A non-European, once he had been baptized, was accepted as a member of the Christian community and was thus entitled to his freedom, if he was a slave. The slave child of mixed parentage whose father was a European was officially regarded as belonging to the European community; as such, he was entitled, after instruction and baptism, to freedom in the right of the father. Marriage was only legal when both the parties had been baptized. Baptism conferred a legal as well as a social status and was a rite of extreme importance.

In contrast to Barbados, the Cape authorities recognized an obligation to instruct slaves and free Hottentots as well as whites in the doctrines of Christianity, and sick-comforters were enrolled for this purpose. In 1671, Commissioner Goske issued instructions that "the Company's slaves were to be forced to prayers; children, the progeny of Europeans and slaves of whom 12 were then at school, were to be taught, and particular care to be taken that they were not alienated, so as to remain in constant slavery, but that they might in due time enjoy the freedom to which in the right of the father, they were born."

This was followed up in 1685 by High Commissioner van Rheede, who urged that every endeavour should be made to bring the heathen slaves to Christianity. He noted that unwillingness to allow baptism of children of

32. This attitude was stated explicitly by Anna Steenkamp, sister of the Voortrekker leader, Piet Retief, in a letter giving the reasons for the Great Trek. She wrote of "the shameful and unjust proceedings with reference to the freedom of our slaves: and yet it is not their freedom that drove us to such lengths, as their being placed on an equal footing with Christians, contrary to the laws of God and the natural distinction of race and religion, so that it was intolerable for any decent Christian to bow down beneath such a yoke; wherefore we rather withdrew in order to preserve our doctrines in purity" (J. Bird, 1888, vol. i, p. 459).

33. No other denomination was tolerated until 1780, when the Lutherans received freedom of public worship. In the early period there were also some Roman Catholic slaves and freemen (cf. Valkhoff, 1972, pp. 85–98).

unbelieving slaves was linked with unwillingness to undertake to liberate them.

It had been the early custom for chaplains and ministers to baptize all children presented to them, whether European, of mixed origin or of slave and heathen origin. Gradually, however, the religious escape route to free status began to close, first for those of unmixed origin, then for those of mixed origins. The propriety of baptizing children of "heathen" parents came under debate early on, not only on religious grounds but because of the obligation to manumit mentioned above. As early as the 1660s two cases were noted of protests by visiting ministers against the baptism of the children of unbaptized slavewomen (de Kock, p. 110; MacCrone, p. 46).

Later, slave-owning opinion hardened, and in 1721 the ministers of the Cape, Drakenstein and Stellenbosch made a combined attack on the practice of baptizing children of heathen slaves. They also suggested that non-European children should be baptized at another time than that appointed for Europeans. The Council of Policy held by the established custom which had prevailed since the 1660s, but made some changes: thereafter no slaves were to be allowed to stand sponsors at the font, or *in loco parentis*. It was also noted that, "to the great annoyance and disrespect of the Europeans", the children of free blacks and slaves were generally better dressed at the ceremony than the European children; a sumptuary regulation was made to prevent this in the future (de Kock, p. 111).

As the number of slaves increased, conscious efforts to Christianize them died away. This was not only because of the lingering belief that conversion must lead to manumission but because slave-owners found it difficult enough to keep in touch with church and school on their own account. In 1770 the Council of India made an order—apparently designed to advance Christianity—that baptized slaves might not be sold and that Muslims might only sell their slaves to Christians. This inept measure led to a fall in the value of slaves: owners made sure that the Christianization of their slaves did not go beyond attendance at family prayers; and the slaves, like the free coloured, turned towards the missionaries of Islam.

In 1792, the baptism issue was raised again by the Church Council of Stellenbosch and this time local custom was acknowledged; the Church Council of Cape Town replied that neither the laws temporal nor the laws spiritual prohibited the retention of baptized persons in slavery. Two decades later, after the second British occupation of the Cape, Governor Cradock repealed the law of 1770, thus removing one of the colonists' main objections to the Christianization of slaves (de Kock, pp. 214–215), but not in practice stimulating a flow of converts.

The only missionary activity during most of the eighteenth century was the isolated and unsuccessful venture by the Moravian George Schmidt among the Hottentots at Genadendal, not far from Caledon. When the Moravians returned in 1792, they, like the later Berlin Society, the London Missionary Society and the Wesleyans, continued to concentrate their efforts upon the Hottentots and later the Bantu in the rural areas, not among slaves and free blacks in the West. The new interest in missionary work did, however, finally spread to Dutch Reformed Church circles.[34] In 1799, the South African Missionary Society was set up in Cape Town, stimulated by Dr. van der Kemp of the London Missionary Society. From the first, its work was to promote Christianity among slaves and servants in the West, but it ran into considerable opposition first from the Batavian Government and then from the British authorities, both of whom preferred to encourage missionary work beyond the confines of settled congregations (cf. J. S. Marais, p. 168; J. du Plessis, 1911: p. 91f.).

Other denominations entered the Cape with the British, the most energetic and effective among the coloured people being the Congregationalists of the London Missionary Society (cf. MacMillan, passim; J. du Plessis, Chs. XII–XVII), the most somnolent being the establishment church of the new rulers, the Church of England. Until 1834, the Anglican Church had no place of worship of its own in Cape Town, and until 1821 virtually nothing was done for non-whites excepting the baptism of a few freed slaves in Cape Town. Thereafter, the Rev. William Wright arrived as an emissary for the Society for the Propagation of the Gospel, and opened two schools in Cape Town and the vicinity for coloured children, free and slave (J. du Plessis, pp. 233–235).

The net result of the various efforts made to Christianize the slaves was not impressive, even after the slave reform programme began, with its injunctions of religious instruction for adults and education for children, (cf. J. S. Marais, pp. 168–169; Edwards, 1942, pp. 113–115 and Appendix

---

34. While the results in terms of converted slaves were modest, the fashionable evangelical preaching moderated, at least temporarily, the exclusive attitudes of some DRC slave-owners. By 1857, however, the prospect of a large free coloured membership (the DRC still has the largest share of coloured adherents) caused the synod to recognize the principle of separate worship as a practical measure. This in turn led to the setting up of a separate organization for coloured DRC members in 1881 (J. S. Marais, 1939, pp. 168–170; Ben Marais, 1952, pp. 290–292; Patterson, 1953, pp. 132–133; Hengherr, 1953, p. 83).

XII). In 1824, 2,200 slaves (out of a total of over 33,000) were regularly attending services in the 49 Christian churches of the Cape, but only a handful of baptisms and marriages were recorded.

Throughout the eighteenth century and for much of the pre-Emancipation period, there is little published material about free coloured Christians in the West. They would have been members of the Dutch Reformed Church, at least until the 1780s, but there could only have been a handful of them at most and they apparently faced increasing resistance from ministers and white burghers.[35]

From the early days of the settlement, however, there was a second, more attractive, religious focus for non-whites in the urban West. This was Islam, to which most Indonesian slaves, convicts and political exiles adhered, and it became the religion of their descendants, and of many more urban slaves and free blacks (J. S. Marais, pp. 161–162). The rapid spread of the Muslim faith in the eighteenth century caused sufficient concern for the VOC to take steps to discourage it.[36] For instance, in 1770 the Council of Batavia passed resolutions prohibiting Christians from selling their slaves to Muslims and forbidding any master to allow a slave to be circumcised by a Muslim priest. Islam nevertheless continued to grow in the Cape, helped by the British authorities, who allowed the Malays the right of public worship during their first occupation of the Cape (CHSA, I, p. 275).

By the 1820s the "Mohammedan congregation in Cape Town" was reported to include 846 male and 422 female slaves, with another 42 male and 16 female slaves in the country districts (the high male sex ratio suggests that there were still many first-generation slaves from the East Indies). The congregation also included the majority of the free blacks, about 2,000 in number,[37] and probably some of the Prize Negroes, about 2,000 of whom were landed in the Cape Peninsula between 1808 and 1816.[38]

35. Sparrman wrote that neither the half-castes nor any other illegitimate children were ever baptized, or indeed enquired after by the Christian ministers at the Cape, unless the father should present himself and insist upon such baptism. In one case, the adult son of a Christian man and a second or third generation "bastard negress" had been obliged to use influence and probably bribes to get admitted into the church by baptism so that he could marry. (Vol. III, pp. 184–185.)

36. For VOC reactions to Islam in the East cf. Boxer, 1973a, pp. 159–161.

37. A few Muslims (Cape Malays) were slave-owners. If their slaves became converts they were entitled to be considered as equals in the family and could not afterwards be sold.

38. For this group see Marais, pp. 161–162. They were taken from captured slave-ships and after a fourteen-year "apprenticeship" gained their freedom. There is little detailed information about their origins, except that they were presumably Africans. Prize Negroes continued to be landed till about 1840.

Of Islam at the Cape, Marais writes:

Mohammedanism did more to bridge the gulf between the slaves and the free-born than did the Christianity of most Christians in the Cape Colony . . . It welded all its adherents together into a compact community, the process being naturally hastened after the emancipation of the slaves. To the whole community the name of Malay was applied which belonged originally to the oriental section of it. The present-day [1930s] Malays are, therefore, a religious and not a racial group. (pp. 172–173.)

This Cape Malay élite of free blacks, freed blacks and skilled slaves in Cape Town is of special interest because it appears to have served as a haven or niche for many upwardly mobile Asians and non-Asians who were not light enough or otherwise equipped to pass into the burgher community.[39] Its specific sub-culture and self-segregating ethos were not, however, conducive to the establishment of an intermediate status group and potential bridge between slaves and white burghers, with values and norms orientated towards the latter, as happened for instance in Barbados. Moreover, because of, *inter alia*, the great ethnic diversity of the non-white and non-free population of the Cape, the Cape Malays were in no position to play a leadership role or provide a militant focus for general slave, still less Khoisan, discontent.[40]

In the nineteenth century and later, nevertheless, the Malay élite did produce a few potential leaders, although they were more orientated towards the British connexion and a liberal or radical multi-racialism than towards a "Malay" or "Coloured" identity.[41] On the whole, however, the Malays seem to have played a passive role, ensconced with reasonable security in their own economic and socio-cultural niche. Unfortunately, the special chroniclers of the Cape Malays have tended to present them favourably but patronizingly as a separate, exotic, conservative com-

39. I. D. du Plessis (1947: pp. 1–3) writing of the strength of the "Cape Malay strain" (mainly from Java, Sunda and Bali), mentions that other constituents have entered the group: Arab, Indian, Ceylonese, Chinese, Negro and European.

40. Cf. van Ryneveld (p. 6) on the "lesser apprehension of insurrection" because of the "variety of nations"; also Robert Ross, p. 6, contrasting the Cape situation with the massive revolts in Brazil by Muslims from the Western Sudan.

41. Instances were successive generations of the intertwined Abdurahman, Dollie and Gool families. In the third generation from self-manumission was Dr. Abdul Abdurahman (1872–1940), founder of the non-racial African Political (later People's) Organisation (A.P.O.) and the first Coloured councillor in Cape Town. Trained in medicine at Glasgow in 1893, Dr. Abdurahman married a Scotswoman. His daughter Zainunissa (Cissie) married Dr. A. H. Gool, and with a group of relatives they consisted a new and more radical group of Coloured political activists (some Communists) from the 1930s onwards (cf. J. S. Marais, pp. 275–280; Patterson, 1953: pp. 123, 159 *et al.*; Simons, 1969: pp. 116 f, 175–179, 486–490).

munity, given to colourful weddings, journeys to Mecca, Khalifah ceremonies and *amok*-running. In consequence, their position and importance
within the slave, free coloured and Cape Coloured groups has still to be
explored in historical and sociological terms.

At the Cape, as in Barbados during the period of slavery, the education[42]
of virtually all children, white, free coloured and slave, was bound up with
the church. In the early years, the VOC authorities in practice adopted a
more liberal policy than the British in the West Indies with regard to the
instruction of slaves. Not only were Company and private slaves instructed
in the Dutch language and religious doctrine[43]; mixed-race and co-
educational schools were also tolerated. The first mixed school opened in
1663, with eighteen Europeans, four boy slaves and one Hottentot. Girl
slaves were admitted to this school two years later.

Despite later efforts to segregate free and slave pupils, a report of 1779
showed that privately-owned slaves were admitted to all eight public
schools in Cape Town (82 out of a total school population of 696 boys and
girls). The Slave Lodge had as pupils 44 Company-owned and 40 privately-
owned slaves, but the Lodge slaves had by then earned such a bad name
that most burghers preferred not to expose their slaves to moral contagion.
By 1823, an estimated 1,551 slaves were attending the various schools in
Cape Town, 372 of them at a Muslim school (no figures are available for
free coloured). The British administration promulgated regulations in 1823
and 1826 making it compulsory for Christian slave-owners who lived near
a free school to send slave children between the ages of three and ten years
to school for at least three days a week. It seems, however, that these regulations were neither enforced nor obeyed; there were in any case only a
handful of such schools. Stellenbosch and Graaff-Reinet had special
schools for slaves. The others were mixed. Many farmers in the interior
hired private tutors (usually a somewhat motley crew); in some cases these
tutors also taught the slave and Hottentot children in the household.

In practice these educational initiatives did not amount to much more
than bare literacy and a smattering of knowledge for the vast majority of
free or slave children. Reading and the scriptures were acceptable, but
writing was not always encouraged for slaves and servants. In 1824, there
were only eight schools in the whole Colony which provided anything more

42. For early education in the Cape see Cruse, *passim*; Marais, pp. 172–173, 269 f;
Patterson, 1953: pp. 90–93; de Kock, pp. 100–106.
43. Since there was no rigid plantation structure, slave children may have had more free
time available for instruction than in Barbados (van Rensburg, p. 46).

than the most elementary education, and most of them were single-teacher schools. The minority of whites who wished for higher education for their children sent them to Holland. A number of visitors commented on the mental indolence and narrow horizons of white Capetonians (except for the young ladies' knowledge of French and English and skills upon the piano).

As for the farmers, they had a great respect for book-learning, but even in the settled West there was little need of literature other than the Bible or learning beyond the three Rs. In 1761 a German settler, J. N. van Dessin, bequeathed his library and a fund for its increase to the Colony; but an observer noted that he had been unable to bequeath the other thing needed— "a collection of readers". (Walker, p. 149)

The Boer pastoralists of the expanding East had drifted further away from the organized church and the book learning that went with it.[44] Many could read or recite the Scriptures and all knew their Psalms by heart. Some could write, still more could sign their names. There was little or no incentive to acquire further learning. As for their slaves and servants, any instruction was seen as inadvisable if not dangerous, and in any case not a matter for anyone other than the master to decide. Small wonder that these Eastern Boers did not welcome the arrival of the missionaries, with their interference with "proper relations" between masters and servants, their "institutions" and their subversive notions of education and training for the coloured races.

After Emancipation and the end of Apprenticeship in 1838 the number of mission schools and of coloured pupils attending them increased greatly (Hengherr, pp. 83–84), although for most the level of education was to remain pre-primary up to the time of Union. At the same time there was a rise in European hostility towards mixed schools and an increasing tendency in the English-speaking Cape administration towards educational segregation, despite the policy laid down in a memorandum of 1839 that "at all times every government seminary will be accessible to every individual in the community." By 1861, however, the Coloureds (and some poor whites) were confined to the inferior, often pre-primary mission schools, and the superior Cape government schools, which became entirely English-medium a few years later, had become virtually a European preserve, along

---

44. An additional impediment may have been the ever-growing disparity between the High Dutch of the Bible and written documents and the colloquial Dutch-Afrikaans, (sometimes interspersed with the Portuguese *lingua franca* or a Khoisan language) which they spoke every day among themselves or with the slaves, Hottentots and coloured servants in their households. (Valkhoff, 1966: pp. 234–235, pp. 203–204; 1972: p. 72.)

with the possibility of secondary education. The medium for instruction varied in mission schools, but educated English was the key to economic and social advancement after the 1820s, and by the 1850s had become the sole language of Parliament, the civil service, the law, commerce and social intercourse.

This educational segregation and the predominance of English were additional elements in the complex of customary impediments, political, economic, social and cultural, which worked to keep the Cape Coloured People down in much the same depressed, lower-class situation as they had been in at the time of Emancipation.

Some Concluding Observations

A number of points of contrast between the Western Cape and Barbados have been made in the account relating to the former area. Indications have also been given in the Cape section of spheres for which little or no information seems to be available. Here it remains only to make a few speculative comments on the issues raised in the introductory section.

Firstly, with regard to the idealistic and materialist approaches, the Barbados material, as interpreted, seems to emphasize the importance of the latter, but more enquiry is perhaps needed into the historical-traditional baggage and the socio-economic background of the British settlers and the ways in which their values and norms evolved over two centuries of slavery.[45] As for the Cape, it would seem that primitive Calvinism, as modified by nearly two centuries of increasing isolation and dispersion and the imported and increasingly ingrained habit of slave-owning, played a particularly important part in the ordering of attitudes and relationships among Western as well as Eastern farmers, and in fostering the development of a bi-racial, white/non-white society instead of the more flexible, pluralistic one imported from the Far East and partially preserved in Cape Town.

The very nature of the slave and servile system – small-scale, domestic and paternalistic (a paternalism which could be malevolent as well as benevolent)—seems to have produced in the masters a more tenacious and

45. Jordan (pp. 232–233 and 249) cites the Barbadian historian Richard Ligon's view (in 1657) that the slaves were "as near beasts as may be, setting their souls aside"; and late in the eighteenth century the ideas of the pro-slavery Jamaican planter Edwards Long on the Negro's lowly place in the Great Chain of Being, and his intimate connexion with the "oran-outang", were widely diffused through the Caribbean and the American colonies (ibid. pp. 484–485, 491).

emotional and a less pragmatic attachment to the master-servant relationship than prevailed in Barbados. As Dr. John Philip wrote in 1830 of the proposed "vagrancy" legislation: ". . . Arbitrary control, when indulged, becomes one of the strongest passions in the human mind, and the last species of authority which men are disposed to part with."

In the Cape one should also consider further the possible influence exerted on master-slave, master-servant and possibly patron-client relationships, by the varied values and mores imported and maintained by the different subordinate groups, since group identities were preserved far more than could happen in Barbados. It may be, for instance, that this ethnic and social pluralism, while providing a set of niches to ease the lot of many slaves and free coloureds, hampered the development of a more open, colour-related socio-economic, hierarchy with an intermediate mulatto class (despite early VOC hopes that such a class could be created). Since the majority of free blacks were geographically concentrated in Cape Town and socially and culturally self-segregated in their own Muslim community, it is difficult to determine to what extent they constituted an intermediate stratum even in the Western Cape, and thus to regard their position as any sort of measure of the character of slavery and race relations in the Cape. In this connection, as Hoetink points out for the contrasted cases of Surinam and Curaçao, ease of manumission and a prestigious status for freedmen were not necessarily associated with benign master-slave relations and good overall race relations—indeed the position of freedmen seemed to relate not to master-servant relations *per se* but to the overall social structure (1973: pp. 5–7, 39–40.)

If we turn to the demographic and economic aspects, we find that, while the ratio of whites to blacks in Barbados was relatively high as compared with most other West Indian societies, with Poor Whites used to perform certain intermediate roles, the ratio in the Cape was much higher, as a consequence of the non-plantation economy. Whites were, therefore, available to perform most of the limited number of intermediate non-manual economic roles, other than the skilled artisan work pre-empted by Eastern slaves and free blacks. There was in any case little need for such skilled work outside Cape Town and the settled Western farming areas. And while free blacks, Hottentots and Bastards performed an important military role for over two centuries, this does not seem to have effected a lasting improvement in their status.

The relatively even white/non-white ratio in the Cape did not favour the emergence of an intermediate coloured stratum, although it did not prevent miscegenation and even inter-marriage.[46] This was particularly the case in the early decades, when the white male-female ratio was so uneven, and before the bi-racial principle became dominant. This early "white escape hatch" for the children of the legally married, or later for those products of miscegenation who were sufficiently fair and acculturated to employ the "silent mechanism of passing", set a pattern for the future whereby the non-Muslim coloured group would be continually depleted by the loss of its potential élite. The bi-racial principle was thereby strengthened and the status of the intermediate group undermined.[47] The existence of a separate, cohesive Malay community did not really shake the bi-racial principle, since it occupied a niche and not an intermediate status in the hierarchy.

In Barbados, on the other hand, white society rejected both inter-marriage and "passing", and although it attempted from time to time to apply the bi-racial principle by reducing the freedman to slave status in law or custom, the freedman élite was able, sometimes with the assistance of white kin or well-wishers, to withstand these efforts and improve its own status and ultimately that of much wider groups of freedmen or emancipated slaves. This élite thus played, and continued to play, a pivotal role in the evolution of Barbados society, of a kind which the free blacks and coloureds of the Western Cape were not qualified to perform, even in the decades before South African society was enlarged and transformed by the incorporation of the Bantu-speaking peoples and the union with the former Boer Republics, founded by people who had trekked from the Cape to establish the principle of non-equality between whites and people of colour, both in church and in state.

46. Cf. Jordan, pp. 171–175 for a similar situation in the American colonies.
47. ibid.

Bibliography

General and Comparative

Boxer, C. R. (1973a). *The Dutch Seaborne Empire 1600–1800*, Pelican.
     (1973b). *The Portuguese Seaborne Empire 1415–1825*, Pelican.
Burn, W. L. (1937). *Emancipation and Apprenticeship in the British West Indies*, Jonathan Cape, London.
Burns, Sir Alan. (1954) *History of the British West Indies*, George Allen and Unwin, London.
Cohen, D. W. and Greene, J. P. (1972). *Neither Slave nor Free*, John Hopkins University Press, Baltimore and London.
Davis, David B. (1966). *The Problem of Slavery in Western Culture*, Cornell University Press, Ithaca.

Degler, Carl N. (1971). *Neither White Nor Black*, MacMillan, New York.

Elkins, Stanley M. (1959). *Slavery: A Problem in American Institutional and Life*, University of Chicago Press.

Equiano, O. (1789). *The Life of Olaudah Equiano*, reprint 2 vols (1969), Dawsons, London.

Fermor, Patrick Leigh (1950). *The Traveller's Tree: a Journey through the Modern West Indies*, Harper, New York.

Foner, L. and Genovese, E. D. (eds) (1969). *Slavery in the New World*, Prentice-Hall, New Jersey.

Freyre, Gilberto. (1946). *The Masters and the Slaves*, Knopf, New York.

Genovese, Eugene D. (1969). "Materialism and Idealism in the History of Negro Slavery". In Foner, L. and Genovese, (eds) *q.v.*

(1970). *The World the Slaveholders Made*, Allen Lane, London.

Goveia, E. V. (1965). *Slave Society in the British Leeward Islands at the End of the Eighteenth Century*, Yale University Press.

Harris, Marvin. (1964). *Patterns of Race in the Americas*, Walker and Co., New York.

Hoetink, H. (1967). *The Two Variants in Caribbean Race Relations*, Oxford University Press for Institute of Race Relations, London.

(1973). *Slavery and Race Relations in the Americas*, Harper and Row, London.

Hymes, D. (ed.) (1971). *Pidginization and Creolization of Languages*, Cambridge University Press.

Jordan, Winthrop D. (1968). *White Over Black, American Attitudes Towards the Negro 1550–1812*, University of North Carolina Press, Chapel Hill.

Lane, A. J. (ed.) (1971). *The Debate Over Slavery*, University of Illinois Press, Urbana, Chicago.

Lewis, Gordon. (1968). *The Growth of the Modern West Indies*, MacGibbon and Kee, London.

Lowenthal, David. (1972). *West Indian Societies*, Oxford University Press for Institute of Race Relations, London.

(1973). "Free Colored West Indians", *Studies in Eighteenth Century Culture, Vol. 3: Racism in the Eighteenth Century*. The Case Western Reserve University, Cleveland and London.

Patterson, Orlando. (1967). *The Sociology of Slavery*, MacGibbon and Kee, London.

Schapera, I. (1961). "Should Anthropologists be Historians?" *Journal of the Royal Anthropological Institute*, Vol. 92, Pt. 2, July–Dec. 1962.

Sewell, W. (1862), *The Ordeal of Free Labour in the West Indies*, Sampson Low, London.

2nd Ed. (1968). Frank Cass, London.

Sio, Arnold. (1965). "Interpretations of Slavery: The Slave Status in the Americas", *Comparative Studies in Society and History*, Vol. 7, No. 3.

(1967). "Society, Slavery and the Slave", *Social and Economic Studies* 16/3, September, pp. 330–344.

(1974). "The Status of the Freedman in the British West Indies: Jamaica and Barbados" (unpublished manuscript).

Sturge, J. and Harvey, T. (1838). *The West Indies in 1837*, London.

Tannenbaum, F. (1947). *Slave and Citizen: The Negro in the Americas*. New York.

Thome, J. A. and Kimball, J. H. (1838). *Emancipation in the West Indies*. New York.

Van Den Berghe, Pierre L. (1967). *Race and Racism*, John Wiley and Sons, London.
Wesley, Charles H. (1934). "The Emancipation of the Free Coloured Population in the British Empire", *Journal of Negro History XXIV*, pp. 137–170.
Wyndham, H. A. (1935). *The Atlantic and Slavery*, Oxford University Press, London.
(1937). *The Atlantic and Emancipation*, Oxford University Press, London.

Barbados

Bennett, J. H. (1958). *Bondsmen and Bishops*, University of California Press.
Collymore, F. A. (1965). *Barbadian Dialect*, Advocate Co. Ltd., Bridgetown, Barbados.
Dunn, Richard S. (1969). "The Barbados Census of 1680", *William and Mary Quarterly*, 3rd ser., Vol. *XXVI*, No. 1, January 1969 (pp. 3–30).
(1973). *Sugar and Slaves*, Jonathan Cape, London.
Handler, J. (1974). *The Unappropriated People*, Johns Hopkins University Press, Baltimore.
Handler, J. and Frisbie, C. (1972). "Aspects of Slave Life in Barbados: Music and its Cultural Context", *Caribbean Studies*, II, 4, pp. 5–46.
Handler, J. and Sio, A. A. (1972). "Barbados" In Cohen, D. W. and Greene, J. P. *Neither Slave or Free*, Johns Hopkins University Press, Baltimore.
Hoyos, F. A. (1972). *Builders of Barbados*, Macmillan, London.
Hutchison, Lionel. (1966/7). "Conrad Reeves: A Kind of Perfection", *New World* (Barbados Independence Issue), New World Group Ltd., Kingston, Jamaica.
Levy, Claude. (1959). "Barbados: The Last Years of Slavery 1823–33" *Journal of Negro History*, 44, pp. 308–345.
Lynch, Louis. (1964). *The Barbados Book*, André Deutsch, London.
Mack, W. Raymond. (1964). "Race, Class and Power in Barbados", In Bell, Wendell (ed.) *The Democratic Revolution in the West Indies*, Schenkman, Cambridge, Mass.
Molen, Patricia A. (1971). "Population and Social Patterns in Barbados in the Early Eighteenth Century", *William and Mary Quarterly.* XXVII.
Poyer, John. (1808). *The History of Barbados*, Frank Cass and Co. Ltd. (New Impression), London (1971).
Price, Edward T. (1957). "The Redlegs of Barbados", *Yearbook of the Association of Pacific Coast Geographers*, Vol. 10.
Schomburgk, Robert H. (1847). *The History of Barbados*, Frank Cass and Co. (New Impression), London, (1971).
Sio, Arnold A.—see Handler (1972).
Vaughan, H. A. (1966–7). "Samuel Jackson Prescod", *New World* (Barbados Independence Issue), New World Group Ltd., Kingston, Jamaica.
Waller, John A. (1820). *A Voyage to the West Indies*, London.
Watson, Karl. (1970). *The Redlegs of Barbados*, unpublished M.A. thesis, University of Florida.
Williams, Eric. (1970). *From Columbus to Castro, The History of the Caribbean 1492–1969*, André Deutsch, London.

Cape

Aldridge, B. (1972). "Cape Malays in Action", *Quarterly Bulletin of the South African Library*, XXVII 2, pp. 24–26.

Beyers, Coenraad. (1929). *Die Kaapse Patriotte 1779–1791*, Juta, Cape Town.
Bird, J. (1888). *Annals of Natal*. 2 vols, P. Davis and Sons Pietermaritzburg, S. Africa.
Birley, Robert (1965). *The Shaking Off of Burdens*. Seventh T. B. Davie Memorial Lecture, University of Cape Town.
Bond, John. (1956). *They Were South Africans*, Oxford University Press, London.
Botha, C. Graham. (1926). *Social Life in the Cape Colony in the Eighteenth Century*, Juta, Cape Town.
Colenbrander, H. T. (1964). (reprint) *De Afkomst der Boeren*, Cape Town. Originally published (1925) as *Koloniale Geschiedenis* (2 vols), The Hague.
Cruse, H. P. (1947). *Die Opheffing van die Kleurlingbevolkung 1652–1795*, C.S.V., Stellenbosch.
De Jong, Cornelius (1802–3). *Reizen naar die Kaap* (3 vols), Haarlem.
De Kiewiet, C. W. (1941). *A History of South Africa*, Clarendon, Oxford.
De Kock, V. (1950). *Those in Bondage*, George Allen and Unwin Ltd., London.
Du Plessis, I. D. (1947). *The Cape Malays*, Maskew Miller, Cape Town.
Du Plessis, I. D. and Lückhoff, C. A. (1953). *The Malay Quarter and Its People*, A. A. Balkema, Cape Town.
Du Plessis, J. (1911). *Christian Missions in South Africa*, Longmans Green, London.
Edwards, I. W. (1924). *The 1820 Settlers in South Africa*, Royal Empire Society, London.
(1942). *Towards Emancipation: A Study of South African Slavery*, Cardiff University Press.
Findlay, G. (1935). *Miscegenation*, Pretoria News and Printing Works, Pretoria.
Greenstein, Lewis J. (1973). "Slave and Citizen: The South African Case", *Race*, XV, 1.
Halford, S. J. (n.d., *circa* 1950). *The Griquas of Griqualand*, Juta and Co. Ltd. Cape Town.
Hengherr, E. (1953). *Emancipation and After: A Study of Cape Slavery and the Issues Arising From It, 1830–1843*, M.A. Thesis, University of Cape Town.
Hockly, H. E. (1957). *The Story of the British Settlers of 1820 in South Africa*, 2nd ed., Cape Town.
Hoge, J. (1939). "Miscegenation in South Africa in the Seventeenth and Eighteenth Centuries" (translated from German and reproduced by Valkhoff, 1972, *q.v.*).
Hooper, Mary Jane. (1964). *Slavery at the Cape, 1652–1834*: A Bibliography presented in partial fulfilment of the requirements for the Higher Certificate of Librarianship, University of Cape Town.
Hugo, A. M. (1970). *The Cape Vernacular* (Inaugural Lecture as Professor of Classics, University of Cape Town.)
Katzen, M. (1969). "White Settlers and the Origin of a New Society, 1652–1778", *Oxford History of South Africa*, Vol. I, Ch. V, Vol. II.
Legassick, M. (1972). "The Frontier Tradition in South African Historiography"; *The Societies of Southern Africa in the Nineteenth and Twentieth Centuries*, Vol. II, Institute of Commonwealth Studies, London.
Leibbrandt, H. C. V. (1905–6). *Memorials* (2 vols) and MSS in Cape Archives.
MacCrone, I. D. (1937). *Race Attitudes in South Africa*, Oxford University Press for the University of Witwatersrand, Johannesburg.
Macmillan, W. M. (1928). *The Cape Coloured Question*, Faber and Gwyer, London.
Marais, Ben. (1952). *Colour, Unsolved Problem of the West*, Howard B. Timmins, Cape Town.

Marais, J. S. (1939). *The Cape Coloured People—1652–1937*, Longmans Green, London.

Marks, S. (1972). "Khoisan Resistance to the Dutch in the Seventeenth and Eighteenth Centuries" *Journal of African History* XIII, 1, pp. 55–80.

Oxford History of South Africa (OHSA), (1969). See Wilson, Monica.

Patterson, Sheila. (1953). *Colour and Culture in South Africa*, Routledge and Kegan Paul, London.

(1957). *The Last Trek*, Routledge and Kegan Paul, London.

Ross, Robert. (1974). "Speculations on the Origins of South African Ideology" (unpublished essay—forthcoming).

Schapera, I. (1930). *The Khoisan Peoples of South Africa*, George Routledge, London.

Simons, H. J. and R. E. (1969). *Class and Colour in South Africa, 1850–1950*, Penguin, Harmondsworth.

Sparrman, A. A. (1786). *A Voyage to the Cape of Good Hope* (2 vols) Robinson, London.

Theal, G. M. (ed.) (1882). *Chronicles of the Cape Commanders*, Cape Town.

(1910). *History and Ethnography of Africa, South of the Zambesi, before 1795* (3 vols), London.

Thompson, G. (1827). *Travels and Adventures in Southern Africa* (2 vols) Van Riebeeck Society, Cape Town (1967).

Thompson, L.—See Wilson, M. (1969).

Valentyn, Francois. (1726). *Description of the Cape of Good Hope with the matters concerning it* (2 vols), Van Riebeeck Society, Cape Town (1971).

Valkhoff, Marius F. (1967). *Studies in Portuguese and Creole*, Witwatersrand University Press, Johannesburg.

(1972). *New Light on Afrikaans and Malayo-Portuguese*, Editions Peeters, Louvain.

Van Jaarsveld, F. A. (1961). *Awakening of Afrikaner Nationalism*, Human and Rousseau, Cape Town.

Van Rensburg, A. Janse. (1935). *Die Toestand van die Slawe aan die Kaap 1806–1834*, M.A. Thesis, University of Cape Town.

Van Ryneveld, W. S. (1797). *Memorandum on the importation of slaves into the colony* (original M.S. in Witwatersrand University Library).

Walker, E. A. (1947). *A History of South Africa*, Longmans Green, London.

Wilson, M. and Thompson, L. (eds). (1969). *Oxford History of South Africa*, Oxford University Press, London.

I I | A Shona Nheketerwa

G. Fortune

Nheketerwa

The poem which forms the nucleus of this contribution belongs to the *genre* of *nheketerwa* in Shona traditional poetry. *Nheketerwa* are critical in tone and corrective in function. They are uttered in situations in which the behaviour of a member of a family or clan calls for correction, and they provide an institutionalized outlet for grievances and complaints in an acceptable register.

Nheketerwa contrast sharply with *nhetembo*, the Shona clan praises. *Nhetembo* are poems which recognize the existence and due expression of normal relationships and the services which go with them. They are laudatory in tone and encouraging in function. They are also traditional and formulaic in content and diction, and leave very little room for innovation.

Nheketerwa depend upon the situation and the relationship which prompt them for their content, but this content, the burden of the criticism, is conveyed in rhythmic form. Our knowledge of the formal criteria of Shona traditional poetry and its social contexts is as yet very fragmentary. However, it does seem that different occasions and relationships calling for correction were marked by the choice of formally distinct verse, either sung, intoned or spoken. The sung complaints of daughters-in-law as they pound or grind are a very striking example of a simple repetitive form in which conflicts felt are given rhythmic expression. The *bembera* or public complaint uttered by a man who believes he is being bewitched is another. The songs sung at the *jakwara* (threshing bee), in which criticisms are freely aired, provide still other examples. In all cases we find that singers or speakers who wish to criticize and complain do so by withdrawing from the registers of straightforward speech in order to speak from within the privileged area of the *nheketerwa*. As long as the forms and conventions of the *nheketerwa* are observed, a speaker need not fear legal action.

The poem which is cited in this essay was inspired by a situation which will be described in some detail below. It was aimed explicitly at a certan person whom the speaker believed to be evading his responsibilities and thus to be endangering the life of his family and lineage. It was thus spoken more out of a sense of personal responsibility for a group than out of a sense of personal grievance. In common with other *nheketerwa*, however, it was corrective in function and critical in tone. The situation did not require allusive and indirect reference to its target. Rather it required explicit reference to him.

The Social Context

A certain man called Chikonochengwe (Male Leopard) had a daughter for whom he had received a good portion of the bride wealth from his son-in-law. The young wife died and Chikonochengwe had no other daughter to substitute for the dead girl. He badly wanted to keep the wealth and, to do so, went as far as to murder his bereaved son-in-law. He was the more tempted to do so since the son-in-law appeared to have no kinsmen who could claim the wealth after his death, no parents, no elder or younger brothers, not even a sister.

For three years the spirit of the murdered son-in-law lay dormant. But in the fourth it returned in the form of a *ngozi* (an avenging spirit) in order to put matters to rights. In quick succession Chikonochengwe lost a young daughter, his elder brother and a young weanling. The death of the latter was particularly distressing as it was caused by the action of a stampeding ox.

Chikonochengwe then went to have his case divined. The *n'anga* (diviner) needed to throw the *hakata* (divining pieces) only three times before he knew what was the trouble. He accused Chikonochengwe of coming to him with a complaint of which he knew the cause. Chikonochengwe agreed that he knew the cause. But he said that he had come for a charm which would nullify (*kutsipika*) the power of the avenging spirit. The diviner said that this was beyond his powers and referred Chikonochengwe to a specialist in these matters, one Chirapanebwe (He who heals with a stone).

Chirapanebwe gave Chikonochengwe a very hospitable reception, all the kinder for having discovered that they shared a *sahwira* relationship of ritual friendship, Chirapanebwe's grandfather having been buried by a member of the Hera clan to which Chikonochengwe belonged. There was no need for divination here. Chikonochengwe told Chirapanebwe plainly that he wanted him to neutralize the power of the avenging spirit of his son-in-law which had risen up against him. Chirapanebwe agreed that he could do so. He told Chikonochengwe to bring him a black goat without any spot upon it and he would treat it with a powerful magical substance (*mushonga*) at a token grave which they were to prepare.

It took Chikonochengwe several days to find a goat answering to Chirapanebwe's prescription. The purpose of his quest was not hidden from the people from whom he sought the goat. Behind his back they laughed at his folly in relying upon such a makeshift and vulnerable remedy. They knew that the only true remedy against the action of an avenging spirit was confession and the payment of compensation according to the exact requirements of the spirit, in order to redress the wrong done to the dead man and to his clan.

However, the goat was delivered to Chirapanebwe, the *mutsipiki* (neutralizing agent). It was ritually suffocated in a hole which had been dug for the purpose and filled with water. The head was cut off and, having been treated with a variety of substances, chief of which were the strong-smelling herbs *mbanda* and *zumbani*, was wrapped in the hide and buried in the token grave under a waterboom (*mukute*) which grew near a bubbling spring. The shade and the water would cool the spirit's anger and both mollify and reduce its inflamed condition to normal. Stones were also laid on the grave. In the meantime Chikonochengwe and his family were being treated with the *mbanda* herb, which *ngozi* are known to dislike, and with other evil-smelling medicines potent enough "even to rouse a pig from sleep". To such lengths was the family forced to go by Chikonochengwe's temporizing, due to the shame he feared that a full confession would involve.

After their treatment Chikonochengwe and his family returned home having been warned not to look back while on their way. The treatment was sufficient to keep further trouble away for a time, but it was only effective for as long as Chirapanebwe lived. After three years Chirapanebwe died, and, shortly afterwards, the *ngozi* struck again. Two weanlings died unexpectedly while their mothers were working in their fields, and two further adults. It was this situation which roused a certain old man at

Chikonochengwe's village to utter the *nheketerwa* which follows. Such a person, exercising such a role, could be called *Mafokonore* (He who reveals the secrets of the heart) or *Mavhazhure* (idem.) He was inspired by responsibility and concern to persuade the culprit to take the humbling but necessary step of confession and compensation to avoid further deaths in the family.

In the event Chikonochengwe agreed to reveal his guilt to his elders and ritual friends, and it was settled that he should pay a fine of eight goats. Since the murdered son-in-law was not known to possess any kin, the goats were driven into the wilderness, there to remain, without anyone to herd them, as the property of the spirit itself. The spirit never returned again and, when Chikonochengwe himself died, it was in a manner quite unconnected with the now pacified *ngozi*.

The Poem

Mushonga wengozi kuripa

  Iwe, Chikonochengwe!
  Chapinda musha wako chii chisingagadzirwe, chikapera?
  Chiona! Nhasi dzimba dzose misuo yapfigwa.
  Gona rawakachera rokupedzera mhuri igonai risina chipundutso?
5 Tenda mhosva, mudzimu igare pasi!
  Uri kupedzerei nguva nokutsvaga n'anga, iwe mhaka
    uchingunoiziva zvako?
  Mushonga wengozi kuripa.

  Chikonochengwe!
  Mhosva dzawakapara izhinji.
10 Ukasadzichenjerera, uchaguma wadziripa nesoro.
  Chiona! Nhasi paukama mofuratirana sembambo dzedenga.
  Chawakadya nhasi chava churu seri kwemusha wako.
  Nhunzi inogara pane karonda.
  Hapana anofira isiyake.
15 Garwe haridye chomupfupi nokureba.
  Charo chinoza neronga.
  Icho chako ichi chisi rudzii chisina musi?
  Kana dai hwaiva usavi,
  Hwaiva usavii husingatende munyu?

20 Chikonochengwe!
  Pamusha pako pamera gomarara remukute rauri kusakurira.

Kurumidza zvako kuridzura, zuva risati ratsvuka.

Chikonochengwe!
Akafa ndiye mupenyu.
25   Ari kunze agere pamabanzi.
Tsoka dzake dziri murufuse. Haana paanotsika.
Chakupa mbonje chati nhunzi dzikudye.
Chagugudzira chatsotsonya pfungwa nendangariro.
Irori ratova vende rinonamwa nevari kumhepo.
30   Vari kunze kwavari ratova zuru rakapinde nyoka.

Chikonochengwe!
Naka uno wakazvitorera rutsatsani.
Chiona! Nhasi wava kurara uchirezvana nematsiga emoto.
Chakabaya chakatyokera.
35   Ngwendere yakandirira mazai muruvanze rwako.
Mudzimba ndiwe uri kudzimba dungwe.
Kana dai rwuri rungano,
Runganoi rusina magumo?
Iyi ndiyo ngozi.
40   Chimbidza kuita chizangaziko!

Hezvino ndigere pano ndichikuombera.

The remedy against an avenging spirit is compensation

You, Chikonochengwe!
What is it that has invaded your homestead,
    that cannot be remedied and brought to an end?
See! Today death has closed the doorways of all the houses.
The charm you sought for yourself and which is destroying your
    family, what kind of a charm is it since it helps no one?
5   Confess your crime, so that the shades may rest!
Why are you consuming all your time in seeking diviners, while
    all the time you are conscious of your guilt?
The remedy against an avenging spirit is compensation.

Chikonochengwe!
The crimes you have committed are many.
10   If you do not take heed of them you will end by paying
    for them with your life.

See! You and your kinsmen are turning your backs on
    one another today like the rafters in the roof.
What you have consumed has today become a menacing
    graveyard behind your homestead.
A fly will settle where there is a sore.
No one dies for a crime which is not his very own.
15 The crocodile does not eat the food of a short man because it is long.
Its food comes along the furrow.
This time of your misfortune, of what kind is it that
    allows no normal day?
And if it were a dish of relish,
What sort of relish would it be which allowed no seasoning of salt?

20 Chikonochengwe!
At your homestead, a wild plum has sprouted a parasite which
    you are nurturing.
Hasten to pluck it out, before the day turns red.

Chikonochengwe!
He who is dead is the living one.
25 The one outside the grave is sitting upon thorns.
His feet are in the embers. He has no place to tread.
What gave you a bruise did so that flies might feed on you.
What knocked on your door has confused your thoughts and
    your judgement.
This matter is a crack which can only be sealed by those in the wind.
30 As for those in the world, it is no less than a hole entered by
    a snake.

Chikonochengwe!
This year you have fetched a chain of troubles for yourself.
See! You now spend your nights sleepless, blowing on the embers.
You have been pierced and the point has broken off inside.
35 The bird of vengeance has laid its eggs in your yard.
You are a hunter who hunts his own family.
If it were a story,
What sort of a story would it be which had no end?
It is the avenging spirit itself.
40 Make haste to make amends!

Here I sit supplicating you.

Literary Comment

The address which Mafokonore or Mavhazhure makes to Chikonochengwe falls into five sections, each commencing with the name *Chikonochengwe* to whom the whole passage is addressed. The stanzas are constituted by this rhythmic device of initial linking. The rhetorical process of convincing Chikonochengwe of his parlous state, and of moving him to remedy it, is also a rhythmic one. Stanzas 1, 3 and 5 appear to have *exhortation* as their dominant note, while stanzas 2 and 4 fall back on *argument*, no doubt with a view to strengthening the exhortation. A further pervasive device is the use of rhetorical questions to show the victim of the *ngozi* that his situation is not inevitable and that the remedy lies in his own hands. As is usual in Shona poetry, other devices, such as linking and parallelism, are used with local and restricted effect, limited to the couplet which they serve to define.

Stanza 1 (ll. 1–7) This stanza commences, as do all the others, with an urgent appeal for the attention of *Chikonochengwe*, the person addressed. His name suggests a hard-hearted man (*munhu ane mwoyo wakashiva*). I have suggested that the note of this stanza is exhortation and this is concentrated in the short urgent statements and commands in ll. 3, 5 and 7. These short lines alternate with longer questions in ll. 2, 4 and 6 which, being rhetorical, provide a good deal of support to the affirmative commands and exhortation by negatively clearing the ground. Thus in l. 2, *Chapinda musha wako chii chisingagadzirwe, chikapera?* (What kind of a threat to your home is it which cannot be remedied and come to an end?).

Rhetorical questions are equivalent to negative statements. "A negation carries more weight, it seems, if the reader (or hearer) is challenged to question the positive assertion, only to be overwhelmed by the realisation that none but a negative answer is possible." (Geoffrey N. Leech, *A Linguistic Guide to English Poetry*, Longmans, 1969: p. 184). Hence the above question is equivalent to the negative statement, "The threat to your home is not one which cannot be remedied and come to an end." Line 3 supports the effect of l. 2 with an urgent hyperbolic statement, *Chiona! Nhasi dzimba dzose misuo yapfigwa* (See! The doorways of *all the houses* are closed up today!). The next two questions are aimed at making Chikonochengwe look critically at his own deeds. The charm he obtained, which is harming his family and which has thus brought no good to anyone, can be no good charm (l. 4). The remedy he is seeking from the diviners (a desperate expedient and a substitute vainly employed for what he should do since he knows his own guilt) can be no true remedy (l. 6). These questions, as stated, lend strength to the urgent exhortations,

> Tenda mhosva, midzimu igare pasi!
> (Own up to your crime so that the spirits may rest! 1. 5) and

> Mushonga wengozi kuripa
> (The remedy against an avenging spirit is to make satisfaction, 1. 7)

There is no run-on from one line to another. The lines are uttered as written, in complete sentences. Their power and effectiveness is strengthened by the unity conveyed by the recurring alliterative concords. The dominant class affix of l. 2 is /chi-/ which conveys the disturbing overtones of the class 7 noun prefix used in secondary function, viz. those of evil, sickness, etc. The dominant affix of l. 4 is that of class 5 which emphasizes the word *gona*, already very prominent through being repeated in both subject and predicate. The dominant affix in l. 6 is that of class 9. It does not seem fanciful to sense a different "atmosphere" in each of these lines, conveyed by the recurrent class affix. The "atmosphere" is that of the meaning carried by the class affix as a primary or a secondary noun prefix. Its presence is more detectable in long lines than in short, and in those where there is a concentrated unity of meaning. This alliteration with its two aspects, those of sound and sense, of sound reinforcing sense, is clearly one of the important devices of Shona traditional poetry.

The first stanza is a powerful exhortation then, consisting of a rhythmic alternation of rhetorical questions and urgent injunctions. The force of the questions is strengthened by semantic alliteration, while the injunctions are suitably brief in order to convey a sense of urgency and concern. They reflect the seriousness of the situation. The tone is direct and the language is plain, though in l. 3 the metaphor *misuo yapfigwa* (the doorways are shut) is a metaphorical euphemism for death. The term *gona* (l. 4) is metaphorical as well and stands for the expedient to which Chikonochengwe has had recourse.

Stanza 2 (ll. 8–19) This stanza does not have an overall structure such as is observable in the first hortatory one. Its note is not so much an advance to exhortation as a withdrawal to argument. The aim of the argument is to convince the unfortunate Chikonochengwe of his guilt and certain retribution unless confession and compensation are made. The argument is pursued by metaphor and proverb rather than in the direct and plain speech of the first hortatory stanza. It is also aided by the use of linking and parallelism whose effect is to create couplets within the stanza in which

there is local concentration and heightened effect, all contributing, however, to the movement of the argument as a whole.

Thus ll. 9 and 10 are cross-linked by the presence of the affix of class 10
in *zhinji*, the final word of the utterance in l. 9, and in *Ukasadzichenjerera*,
the first word in the utterance of l. 10. As is normal with cross-linking, the
device serves to advance the thought and is thus useful in argument.
(Note that the syllogism, a classical instrument in logic, is cross-linked,

> e.g.   A is B
> but   B is C
> therefore A is C.)

In ll. 9–10, the class 10 affix is also widely present as an alliterative device
and it is the instrument for conveying the emphasis to be placed on *mhosva*
(crimes). But we have something further in these lines, a combination of
two alliterations in order to stress the link between the entities for which
they stand. The recurring affixes are those of the second person singular
and class 10 (referring to, and substituting for, *mhosva*). In the couplet as
quoted here the affix of second person singular is doubly underlined, that
of class 10 singly underlined.

> Mhosva dzawakapara izhinji
>
> Ukasadzichenjerera, uchaguma wadziripa nesoro

The interwoven series of these two alliterations, which, we must remember,
in contrast to those of English, are meaningful, serves to emphasize the
bond between the person the poet is addressing and his crimes, as well as
the further bond between him and retribution. The link between these two
bonds is poetically forged, as we have seen by the cross-linking. The
"crimes" of which the culprit is accused are murder, the deaths caused
among the innocent by the *ngozi* in its revenge, the infringement of the
ancestral laws which forbid murder and the neglect to make amends.

In ll. 11–12 the guilty person is addressed again in the second person
singular. The lines call on him to see the tension and division which his
crime has brought about within his family. For example, *Chiona!* (Just
see!). *Nhasi* . . . (Today . . .) is repeated in both lines 3 and 11. The
metaphors used are those of the rafters of a roof and the presence of an
anthill or termite mound behind the village. Members of the family,
though rigidly bound within the kinship structure, are turned from one
another like rafters which, though they converge to, or flow from, one
point, nevertheless present their backs to one another. Such is the position

among the living. The tension is due to the fear of the blows of the *ngozi*. Its presence looms ominously over the homestead like the termite mound which is also a symbol of the grave since so many of the family are buried there: Cp. the common oath,

> Naamai vangu varere pachuru!
> (By my mother who lies buried on the anthill!)

The deed of the culprit (*Chawakadya* (What you ate and made your own)) is now so divisive that it removes part of the family to their graves behind the homestead. This movement and the implication of the culprit is expressed by a further use of meaningful alliteration and repetition of the affixes concerned.

> Chawakadya nhasi chava churu seri kwemusha wako

We may see, I think, ll. 11–12 as semantically parallel, l. 11 concerned with estrangement in life and l. 12 with separation in death.

The next two couplets are composed of proverbs and so are metaphorical. They are concerned with guilt and punishment. Lines 13–14 are affirmative and negative in sequence and both state that punishment and guilt are inseparable. Lines 15–16 are negative and affirmative in sequence and state that death is not accidental. The crocodile can seize the property of a short man, not because it is long, but because it was channelled to it by destiny. Lines 13 and 14 are semantically parallel without the parallelism being reflected in the construction. The relation of *Nhunzi* (Fly) to *karonda* (sore) is similar to that of /-fir-/ (die for) to *yake* (his crime). Lines 15–16 are cross-linked by the presence of class 7 affix /ch-/ (thing) in *chomupfupi* and *charo*. Once again cross-linking advances the argument. Lines 17 and ll. 18–19 consist of two rhetorical questions which echo those of ll. 2 and 4. They are metaphorical in diction, but, like those of ll. 2 and 4, question the necessity of the present trouble. The effect of l. 17 is considerably heightened by the five-fold repetition of class 7 affix /chi-/, each one of which refers to the offending *chisi* (unlucky day) and queries its incessant necessity. Lines 18–19 are cross-linked by the repetition of *hwaiva usavi* (were to be relish), first participal and then principal, but repeated nevertheless. Once again cross-linking advances the argument beneath the rhetorical question. "Say if it were relish, what sort of relish would it be that could not be seasoned by salt?"

The metaphors are bold and point to a speaker who speaks with both knowledge and concern. Such a speaker could claim the title of *nyanduri* (master of words, master of poetry). He has the gift for saying what must be said, but in the way required by the occasion. He can correct without destroying, drawing on his considerable experience, skill in expression and proverbial lore in order to deal with any situation responsibly and elegantly. *Mwoyo womukuru ndimaorera* (The heart of an elder is a compost-heap), or *Mwoyo womukuru izarezare* (The heart of an elder is a rubbish-heap). It reconciles all sorts of things within itself in order to make them fruitful and life-giving. His concern and that of his art is the community. His presence is appreciated since he turns conversation into positive channels. As in the case of other gifts such as skill in hunting, the gift of speech comes unbidden and unlearned from a *rombe* or *shave* whose presence helps its *protégé* to speak in many ways.

Stanza 3 (ll. 20–22) The third stanza advances towards direct exhortation again. The metaphor of the parasite mistletoe, notorious for attracting the unwelcome attention of snakes and wild beasts, is used to symbolize the presence of the aggrieved spirit. Far from getting rid of it, the culprit is cultivating it by his silence and inaction. Here is paradox indeed. He is exhorted to pluck it out quickly before the sun turns red, before the day ends in blood.

A slight formal link unites these lines through the repetition of the class 5 affix in *kuridzura* (to pluck it out). They cohere through the working out of the metaphor centred on the *gomarara*, its presence and its desired absence. The contrast here is not one which is observed. It is advised in order to end the paradox in l. 21. The alliterative repetition of the class 16 and second singular affixes /pa-/ and /-ko ∼ -u-/ emphasizes the proximity of the pernicious growth, itself referred to alliteratively four times, viz.

> . . . gomarara remukute rauri kusakurira
> Kurumidza zvako kuridzura . . .

Stanza 4 (ll. 23–30) In the fourth stanza argument replaces exhortation and this is advanced, as in stanza 2, by means of linking and parallelism. The argument seeks to convince the culprit, by means of graphic metaphors, of the paradoxical situation, the unhappy and vulnerable position of the living and the need of recourse to the dead.

Lines 24 and 25 are front-linked and contrastive.

> He who is dead is the living one.
> He who is unburied is sitting on thorns.

Line 26 consists of two parallel parts.

> His feet are in the embers. He has no place to tread.

Perhaps we can detect two cases of contrived alliteration here, used to second and support the argument.

> viz. Ari kunze agere pamabanzi.
> Tsoka . . . paanotsika.

Lines 27 and 28 are two front-linked statements both internally parallel as well as parallel to one another. Thus the thought of each is mutually reinforced. The alliterative and significant repetition of /ch-/, class 7 affix, first as a relative subject prefix in the subject of each sentence and then as a principal subject prefix in the predicates is also reinforcing and echoes the more numerous but less metaphorical repetitions of l. 2. The second singular object prefix is also repeated in l. 27 to emphasize, literally, the position of the culprit as the object of the spirit's action.

> Chakupa mbonje chati nhunzi dzikudye.
> Chagugudzira chatsotsonya pfungwa nendangariro.

Lines 29–30 are cross-linked and contrastive in order to describe once again the identical paradoxical situation. The "gap in nature", lit. gap in a pot, can only be sealed by those who lie beyond. For those who stand this side of the grave, it is a hole in an antheap through which a deadly snake may come and go. The balance of this conflict is remarkable and could be expressed in the formula

> a b
> b a

But the cross-linked elements which are contrasted, viz. *vende: zuru* and *vari kumhepo: vari kunze*, are of course partly similar and partly different.

Stanza 5 (ll. 31–40) This stanza is one of metaphorical description of the situation and hence argument. It issues in direct exhortation. Hence it is a mixture of the two types. Lines 32 and 33 are merely paradoxical statements, parallel in thought. His own worst enemy, the culprit has sought a chain of troubles for himself. He is spending all night, sleepless, breathing on the burning faggots. Lines 34–35 are also parallel in thought. The point that pierced his skin has broken off inside his flesh. The *Ngwendere* (a euphemism for the *ngozi* and perhaps a term meaning the bird in the lightning) has laid in his own yard eggs which will hatch out as trouble. Yet ultimately the trouble lies in the culprit himself. *Mudzimba* is the one who is hunting his own family (*dungwe* (line of children)) whom he should be leading. There is possibly a pun on this word, cp. *mudzimba* (a hunter), *kudzimba* (to hurt). Lines 37–38 is another rhetorical question of the type already noted in ll. 17–19. "If all this were a tale, what sort of a tale would it be that had no end?"

At this place metaphorical argument yields to plain urgent speech and direct exhortation.

Finally the speaker adds actions to words by clapping as if in homage but really in supplication to the culprit. That this should be done by a senior to a junior is itself very sobering.

Acknowledgements

I am indebted to a paper by Mr. Aaron C. Hodza, Shona Language Assistant in the Department of African Languages, University of Rhodesia, for the poem cited in this article, and for the social background which formed its context.

It is interesting to compare the text of the poem cited by Mr. Hodza with that which appears in the final chapter of *Muchadura*, a novel written by E. Ribeiro on the theme of the *ngozi* (Mambo Press, Gwelo, 1967). The poems are remarkably similar in some of their lines. This is not surprising as both are drawn from the same oral, traditional source, in which recurrent situations are often treated, or referred to, in widely diffused formulae.

12 | Bird of the Storm

Hilda Kuper

Preface

Superficially it might appear inappropriate to contribute a short story to the *Festschrift* of a leading anthropologist, renowned for his scholarly and lucid presentation of facts. But I hope that Professor Schapera will accept this as a tribute to my appreciation of his wider intellectual interest, and his awareness that there is always an element of fiction in fact and of fact in fiction. To those readers who regard story-telling as a waste of time, I would suggest that "Bird of the Storm" be treated as a simple myth which will lend itself to dissection into oppositions, contradictions and transformations—"As flies to wanton boys". I trust Professor Schapera will read it purely as entertainment.

Uyapi (Whither Away) Shongwe awoke, yawned, swore and threw off her blanket. On the other side of the hut her husband still slept, breathing heavily, his neck resting on a wooden pillow so that his head drooped backwards. The woman knotted an old cloth over her shoulder, tied an extra print round her hips and crawled out through the small arched doorway.

After a brief wash, and a few large mouthfuls of cold porridge cooked the previous day, Uyapi left with her hoe over her shoulder to dig peanuts from her garden, which lay two miles away from her hut. Normally she would not have walked so far with a storm overhead merely to gather relish. But this was no ordinary day. Her husband had returned from gaol only the evening before. Three months he had spent there for "being in possession of hemp." Uyapi could not understand that law; why should the White men prohibit the smoke of her people? Then she smiled cheerfully as she thought of how he would enjoy his food at home, seasoned with nuts and shredded pumpkin leaf.

The huts scattered along the way were alive with the beat of grinding stone, the clack of tongues, the cry of babies. "We see you," people shouted in greeting. A few words here, a drink of soft porridge there, and at last she reached her fields. She rested for a minute, then set to work, bending with difficulty.

After a few strokes she felt battered, dropped the hoe and squatted with legs stretched straight in front of her. She looked down at herself, and spoke tenderly, aloud, "It is grown big now, it is already a person indeed. Mai. It scratches hard and bites me so. The Great One help me."

The pain past, she stood again, and the hoe clove the red earth. She picked out the exposed brown pods and had half filled her small tin vessel when it awoke again, acute and meaningful, insistent. As rapidly as her full body would allow, she stumbled homewards. On the narrow path, she met a youth who cried, "I see you, Shongwe." "You get away. Can't you see I'm dying?" He laughed, "What have you, Mother?" "Go and fetch a woman, you useless male. Run." He understood, and, still laughing, ran lithely to the nearest village panting on arrival, "Shongwe is dead at the crossroads with bearing."

Under the encouragement of a group of elderly women Uyapi exerted herself at the roadside. Heavy rain fell as the girl child was born. Two names at least were hers by right. Umqubelo (Saturday) and Inyoni Yelidulu (Bird of the Storm.)

Umqubelo grew very beautiful. Her body was clean and fine from the daily bathe in the river and the sporting in the little waterfall. So straight was her back that no drop of water spilt when she walked rapidly and rhythmically with her black clay pot on her small head. Many long hours she spent beating her head with the soapy leaves of the *incatsavane* plant till the hair clustered in tiny ringlets.

Her suitors were many. Some wrote her letters, according to pattern. They began, "Dear Umqubelo, I ask about your health. I, I am not well, and it is on your account. You trouble my health through disturbing my dreams." And all ended, "I who am yours . . . beg an answer soon." Umqubelo could neither read nor write, so she took her letters to the trader, who chuckled loudly as he read them, teased her and asked her to be his sweetheart.

At last she gave her love to Mona (Jealousy) Hlope, a young warrior in the King's regiment. His voice in the march songs was clear and deep, his feet in the dance raised great clouds of dust, his body was strong and proud and a string of glass beads glistened on the smooth darkness of his chest. His loins were girded with the skin of a fine gemsbok, tied over a gay spotted print. He could neither read nor write Latin letters, but he sent Umqubelo messages in beads, rich formulae of praise. Came the yellow which spoke, "You are beautiful as the yellow blossom which is as golden in its fullness as in its buds, its yellow petals do not wither on the ground." Then the red: "You. It is you. My blood runs like the feet of antelopes in irregular jaunt at the thought of you." And always at the end came the white: "My heart is white for love of you. Even after ten years of waiting it will be white."

One day she tied the little bead letters through the slit lobes of her ears Quickly the news spread. Mona proudly flaunted the horsehair engagement girdle she had plaited him. He bought her a cake of Velvet Skin soap, a pink comb, a mirror, and he promised her a fine blanket and a box for her clothes. She was his "singani."

A few months later, his father decided to *lobola* Umqubelo for his son. He had heard only good of the girl, and his wife was happy at the thought of a strong daughter-in-law to hoe, cook, gather faggots and draw water for her. Umqubelo's own mother was full of mournful advice, for was she not losing her precious child to strangers? Her father asked, indirectly, if the Hlope family really had enough cattle with which to give his daughter the honourable status of wifehood. In the presence of his future parents-in-law, Jealousy was humble, ashamed and as often as possible he avoided direct encounters, leaving his elder relatives to make the diplomatic overtures and arrangements for the marriage. He found it embarrassing, and besides it was unnecessary, to remain during the rapprochement of the two families, and in the middle of the negotiations he left to earn his tax money in the Johannesburg gold mines. He expected to find Umqubelo established in his mother's household by the time he returned.

II

Umqubelo's maternal uncle was childless and his wife fell ill, so he asked his sister, Umqubelo's mother, for the loan of one of her daughters. After a short discussion, Umqubelo was sent to lend temporary assistance. Her uncle's village was close to the Portuguese border, and her mother warned her against the wines sold openly to Africans in Portuguese territory. "My child, do not drink the beer of the white man. It takes away sense, and if you get drunk, the Portuguese police will beat the palms of your hands and the soles of your feet to purple pulp." But the girls told her it wasn't so bad for women. The little yellow men with the black eyes and rich unrestrained laughter were very sympathetic, nearer to the Swazi than the silent English or the poor Afrikaner.

Umqubelo found her new home exciting, but dirty and bad smelling. The women smeared their prints with fat of the castor-oil seed and seldom washed. Food, however, grew richly in the black soil: corn and millet, peanuts and jugo beans, little fat black and sweet red potatoes extravagantly curved and the *msobo* plant with its juicy berries and tender leaves. Umqubelo grew deliciously rounded, and wherever she went, men and women praised her openly. "She shines. See her tiny hands and feet. Her breasts are as firm and full as little clay pots of beer. When she walks her bottom goes nicely Qu Qu. Everything about her is beautiful." She became conscious of every feature and limb and she was happy.

One morning she slipped across the border with a few friends to buy clothes at Alfonso's. His was a good shop, cheap too. The shelves were laden with bottles of oil, packets of candles, sweets, odd groceries, a few pieces of gay silk and cloth, and an array of bottles filled with rich coloured liquids. The materials, the women admitted, were not as attractive nor as strong as those in the Jew's shop next door. But then he always hurried you, and didn't like you to finger things, and he had no wine with which to tease you. Alfonso was "more a person" and very popular. He smiled, suggested, was gracefully quick in his movements, and today and tomorrow meant as much to him as the sun, the moon, and the coquettish stars. He had been nicknamed "He for whom the girls are burning."

Umqubelo had heard many tales of this polite and dashing gentleman, and looked at him with eyes of limpid wonder. Noticing her loveliness, he treated her with special deference; when, after three quarters of an hour, she completed her six-penny purchase, he gave her a glass of *vinho tinto* "for friendship". The sparkling strong wine rushed faster than any cereal beer through her blood. She shivered with pleasure. Three times he filled her glass. Then she thanked him with the utterance of his name, according to the etiquette of her people, "Alfonso". The other girls looked on, whispered and giggled.

After that she slipped over the border on any pretext, alone or with her friends, with or without money. Alfonso always gave her a drink, a tender word, an occasional quick touch. Her uncle began to grow suspicious, and his wife questioned her closely. They spoke pointedly of girls from good families who had become *tingwadla* (prostitutes), had spoilt their chances of marriage and had eventually been sucked into the unfathomable slime of the port of Lourenco Marques.

III

Umqubelo listened quietly, and gave herself to Alfonso. Soon, their intimacy was beer-time gossip. Umqubelo felt no shame, nor did she wish to hide her love, although she was reticent in her speech. Mona's parents heard, and, without consulting their son, refused to accept her as a daughter-in-law. Later there came a message from the boy himself, ending in the black bead of refusal or rejection. Her parents called her home, but she ran to Alfonso, and—such is the law of Swaziland—once in Portuguese territory, they could not force her to return. She lived in a back room in his shop, and talked of him as her husband. Her relatives came to see them both, scolded and cried and swore, and even tried to take her back by force. Her mother wailed, "I thought I bore a child, and it was a wild animal, a night creature." She warned "Perhaps he has the white man's sickness." To this, Umqubelo replied, "Yes. He is with it." Her voice was without contempt, soft with the tolerance of a woman in love trained in the ideals of a polygamous society.

Three months later, Alfonso went to Johannesburg and met a white girl, daughter of an English prostitute and a Greek shopkeeper. She was fifteen, still fresh and golden haired; Alfonso felt he would not be ashamed to show her as his wife. The Greek owed him £85, and the girl was given in full settlement. She liked Alfonso and smiled dreamily through an elaborate wedding ceremony.

A friend of Alfonso's broke the news to Umqubelo, promptly asking her to look at him instead. She wept "I don't want you. Get off." She waited in her little back room for Alfonso to return, and he, anticipating this, left his young bride at the hotel before coming to his shop. When Umqubelo heard his footsteps on the wooden flooring, she trembled uncontrollably and as the door opened she met him with her radiant beauty warm in the height of desire. He greeted her with delight, and gave her a red silken shawl and a bottle of green perfume.

Later, holding her close to him on the bed which he had provided and of which she was extremely proud, he told her that he did not want her to live in the back room any longer, but to move to a hut in the home of his African salesman. "I will put in this bed, and I'll give you a red carpet like you see in the hotel," he promised. She agreed without resistance, asking only that he come to her.

But as the months went by she became moody and sullen. "I am black to you now," she would say sadly to Alfonso. He tried to soothe her with gifts of wine and cloth, and for a time she accepted everything with a brooding avarice. Then she fell pregnant and returned to happy life again, while Alfonso rejoiced and treated her with great tenderness. In the fourth moon, she miscarried. Tribal law forbade her from weeping for something that was not yet a person, simply a nameless thing. She lay on her bed all day, her eyes blank with unfathomable grief and not until the wife of the salesman finally protested at bringing food to her, did hunger drive her to take her turn again at the grindstone. After the period of pollution was past, Alfonso came to her again. She received him resentfully, "Have you made another child by the white one?" she asked bitterly, and hinted darkly "Every man can make a child." He realized he no longer possessed her entirely. She began to parade the streets of the Portuguese merchants, vaunting her beauty before the highest bidders. She inflicted disease over a wide area till the men grew wise, and the story went around that she had *likubalo*, a strange and terrible sickness given to a woman by a jealous husband or lover to guard her from being unfaithful. Alfonso was said to have bought this medicine and injected it into Umqubelo so that he alone could enjoy her with impunity.

After her second miscarriage, she lay on her bed screaming "They have bewitched me, father. They have bewitched me." It took her many weeks to regain her strength, yet her beauty remained untouched. Her mother came to see her, and implored her to return, but she cried "I don't know how, mother" and finally the old Uyapi went home alone, muttering "The Great One help us. The sufferings of women!"

One night Umqubelo fled from her hut, leaving no trace behind. Alfonso waited for her return, convinced that she would not leave him thus. He rented a little house for his wife, so that he was free to spend long hours alone in the now empty back room, in which he would start at every sweet loud laugh that resembled Umqubelo's. He took to drinking, but every night he went to his wife, seeking out no other women. One evening he brought home with him a doctor from Lourenco Marques who was holidaying at the Lamahasha hotel, and the two men sat on the dimly lit porch drinking wine and smoking. The conversation turned as usual to the women of the country, and the doctor said with the smile of a connoisseur "Never have I seen such wonderful creatures as *les femmes noires* of these parts. Of course some of them are hideous, grotesque. But others— *Nefeititi*." He gesticulated expressively. "Perfect. I remember . . ."

Alfonso's mind wandered as his guest launched into descriptions of beauties he had known, till suddenly Alfonso's attention was riveted by the name Umqubelo. "What's that?" he jerked out, wide awake and tense. "Umqubelo—the girl I'm telling you about. She had a much more suitable name too, I found out—Inyoni Yelidulu. Yes. Bird of the Storm. I'll never forget her." "Where is she?" Alfonso interrupted, not trying to hide the eagerness in his voice, but the doctor was absorbed in his own reminiscences and continued softly. "She was in a back room in the street of prostitutes near the dock when they called me to her. No one knew from where she came. Though she was riddled with disease she showed no flaw on face or flesh. It was extraordinary. She looked like a golden saint draped in an old red shawl. I tried to save her—but I don't think she wanted to live. We could trace none of her relations and she asked for no one. Only when she was dying she called in a wild bird voice, so sweet, so clear, the name of some fellow she must have adored. Let me see. It was an unusual name. It'll come to me later. Anyway that wasn't important to me." He paused, then continued engagingly "Then there was another . . ." In the semi-darkness he did not notice that Alfonso was weeping bitterly.

On his way home, the doctor suddenly stopped: "Mona. That was the name. Mona."

13 | Strangers

Meyer Fortes

> To be a stranger is naturally a very positive
> relation; it is a specific form of interaction
> (Simmel, 1950)

A few months after my first arrival among the Tallensi in 1934, I had the distressing experience of being robbed. We were at dinner when the discovery was made by one of our Tallensi servants. I immediately sent a message to the Chief, who soon arrived escorted by what seemed to be the entire population of Tongo. It was a moonless night and in the harsh light of the Tilley lamp he looked terrified. Even more terrified was the look on the faces of the Tendaanas who had accompanied the chief; for our house was beside one of their sacred earth-shrine groves, which made the robbery a sacrilege, offensive to the Earth and to them as well as an injury inflicted on me. An agitated exchange of speeches followed ending in one of the most dramatic scenes I ever witnessed among the Tallensi. In response to an angry exhortation by the chief, and amid a general hush, the Tendaanas one after another, at the top of their voices each delivered a long and impassioned harangue, invoking the Earth and the ancestors to expose and destroy the malefactor whosoever and wheresoever he might be. With my as yet inadequate knowledge of Talni I could follow these proceedings only in patches, so I turned to my interpreter, a semi-literate youth from a neighbouring Tallensi clan. What, I asked, had the chief been so angry about? He said, Anaaho explained, that it was bad enough that a white man had been robbed—it would surely get to the District Commissioner and the police and could bring endless trouble on himself. But what was worse was that this should have been done to his "stranger", his *saan*.

This was my introduction to a Tallensi notion about which I learnt a great deal as time went on. On a later occasion, for example, Anaaho, asked to translate an informant's remark, offered his own explanation of the situation. When I scolded him he protested that he knew the answer to my question quite as well as my informant; for said he "when I first came here I was a stranger but now I have got to know how they do things here". Again, a year or so after the robbery, I was one day talking confidentially with my friend and mentor Naabdiya. Suddenly he stopped and remarked, as if to account for our intimacy: "when you first came here you were a stranger, now you have become our kinsman (*mabii*)." Similarly, a newly married wife is described as a "stranger", (*saan*) in her husband's house. So, it is said, she must be treated with special consideration. Guinea fowls will be killed for her meals and she will be urged to be at ease and will be stopped from helping with the domestic chores that normally fall to a woman's lot. By degrees, as she becomes accustomed (*malem*) to her husband's family, and in particular to her mother-in-law, as she becomes incorporated in its economic and ritual activities, perhaps in some months, perhaps only after she has borne a child, and thus becomes a mother in her conjugal family, she stops being regarded as a *saan* and is accepted as a member of the family (*yidem*). Nevertheless, there is always a trace of feeling that a wife is never wholly free from stranger-hood. This is connected with the fact that a woman does not forfeit her status as sister and daughter in her paternal family and lineage when she marries. There is a reflection of this in the way her kinsfolk—above all either of her parents or her siblings—are received when they visit her. Choice meals should be offered to a husband's visiting affine, be he or she his wife's own parent or sibling or even a more distant lineage kinsman. The phrase for this can be translated "to receive them strangerly" (*die ba saan*), that is, hospitably.

I once heard this phrase used in an unusual context. It was at a ceremony for re-establishing a powerful domestic medicine shrine that had been neglected by its deceased owner's son, my friend Onmarra, for many years. Troubles had befallen the family and diviners had revealed the dead father's anger about this and his demand that the shrine be re-established. Noting the lavish provision of beer and of sacrificial animals for the ceremony, I asked for some explanation. "*U ka saan*, is he not a stranger?", came the answer; and, added Onmarra, was it not meet to welcome so important a stranger with generous offers of food and drink? Nor, it was made clear to me, was this merely a figure of speech. Medicines of this type, Onmarra insisted, as indeed I had often been told, go about, especially at night, when they are active in performing their tasks of defending the homestead and its occupants against evil trees or stones or other such mystical dangers. So they are a kind of person (*nit*, cf. Fortes, 1973) and, as they are also invested with peculiar mystical powers, to fail in hospitality to them is to run the risk of mystical retribution.

Here we come upon a notion that lies like a shadow behind the Tallensi concept of the stranger. To understand it we must realize that before the "coming of the white man"—say at the turn of the century—as old men relate, a solitary stranger of another tribe would not have been able to go about freely in any Tallensi settlement. He would have been seized and enslaved. To be safe, a person from outside must have either a kinsman or affine or at least a friend to vouch for him, initially at any rate, in the community he entered. There was one exception to this rule. Strangers who could enter a Tallensi community without such protection were the non-Tallensi clients of the External Boghar cult of the Hill Talis (cf. Fortes 1945, chapter VIII). They would have come, as I saw for myself in the nineteen thirties, escorted by a representative of the chapter of the cult to which they owed service who would have gone to fetch them carrying a *bogakyee*, a portable shrine of the cult, slung over his shoulder. This was an inviolable guarantee of safe passage, wherever he might go, though in fact he followed a traditional path that led in some cases for forty or fifty miles through settlements allied by clanship or cult connections to his own. To have attacked, let alone slain him, would have been outrageous sacrilege; it would also have provoked a war of reprisals. No such case had occurred in the living memory of any of the Talis elders of the Boghar cult known to me in the thirties.

A rarer exception was the occasional Mossi cloth trader who might manage to make his way to the house of the chief of Tongo, where, and partly by reason of the beliefs about the common Mamprussi origin of the Mossi and the Tallensi Namoos, he would be safe as the chief's "stranger". From there he could be escorted to a neighbouring Namoo community and so, by relays, out of Taleland.

Many cases conforming to all of these customary norms, came under my observation in the thirties, and in modified form even during my last spell of field work in Taleland in 1963. But there is a reservation to be noted and this concerns the notion in the background I have referred to. It is generally agreed that regardless of his provenance, a stranger may not be turned away from one's doorway. He must at least be offered a drink of water but should properly speaking be invited to share a family meal. This is in part a matter of elementary ethical propriety or more simply of plain human decency; to do otherwise is not only unbecoming, it carries the danger of *dulem*, unforeseeable mystical retribution (cf. Fortes 1949: p. 219). It is also some say a matter of magical prudence. For it is not impossible that a person presenting himself as an unknown stranger might in fact be a Being of the Wild or an evil tree or stone which has *ngalem* transformed itself into human shape to test and tempt one. To refuse hospitality in such a case lays one open to the mystical attack that might result in madness (cf. Fortes and Mayer, 1965). That is one reason why, in former days, anyone meeting with a solitary foreigner—stranger, would not himself seize and enslave him but would take him to the chief in the same way as he would take a lost sheep or cow to the Tendaana, to dispose of. Only chiefs have the ritual status to sell or give a human being into slavery. Then, when such a stranger is turned into a slave (*da'aber*) he ceases to be a stranger. He is at once placed under the ritual guardianship of his owner's lineage ancestors which transforms him into a quasi-adoptive son of the owner.

The myth of the origin of the Golib (Sowing) Festival illustrates the belief that hospitality to a stranger, regardless of his provenance or character, is a moral obligation conformity to which may be mystically rewarded whereas flouting it would be likely to meet with mystical retribution. Different versions of the story give the moral credit to different clans, usually the narrator's, but the central core is the same. A leper arrives at the house of the clan elder who is the main protagonist. The leper comes from the neighbouring tribal area and has travelled by stages from clan to clan in Taleland, following the route later to be taken by the sequence of the Golib ceremonies. He has been unmolested, for a leper would be useless as a slave: and in any case outside his own family there is revulsion and fear of contagion, which is well known to be a danger with leprosy. He has received food and drink wherever he went in accordance with the elementary rules of hospitality. But he has suffered one grievous insult. Whenever, with customary courtesy, he solicited members of his host's family to eat with him, the invitation was declined, sometimes spurned. This time, too his host offers him food and again the leper solicits his host to eat with him, after telling of the way he has previously been spurned. This time his host consents to share his dish of food, declaring that it is wrong to spurn a fellow human. When the leper arises to continue his journey his host, going beyond conventional hospitality, gives him a supply of water and millet flour to fall back on. But a storm blows up. The host, concerned for the leper, sends his sons after him. They find a small drum and the leper's staff which they take back to their father. Then a son dies, and in the divining session it emerges that the leper had been metamorphosed into the drum and the staff and that these were now the Destiny Shrines through which the spirit of the leper would bring benefits to his host. The drum became the sacred Golib drum and the staff the sacred dancing pole, and the ritual service ordained for them was the beginning of the Golib ceremony as it is now practiced. The further elaborations of the tale are not relevant here. The point of the leper story is clear to the Tallensi. As Naabdiya's comment on my change of status explains, the contrary of a stranger is a kinsman. It is for treating the leper, who is both a stranger by non-kinship and the prototype of incurable and therefore dehumanizing illness, as if he were a kinsman (by eating with him) that the man destined to found the Sowing Festival on which the very survival of all the Tallensi depends, is rewarded with his exalted status.

For the Tallensi, the status of the stranger who comes in from outside their society varies with time and circumstance. He may be regarded as a virtual enemy at the outset; but may at once or later be accepted as a welcome or at least tolerated guest. To be able to stay permanently, he must be given status in the host's domestic group and be thus brought into the community's kinship sphere or into the quasi-kinship sphere of adherence to a common ancestor cult. Affines represent a kind of middle term of privileged guesthood. At the person-to-person level there is a jural relationship with them which brings them into the domestic orbit of their son-in-law's family and so entitled to the respectful hospitality that mimics, but is palpably distinct from, the amity of kinsfolk. At the corporate level, their clan and their son-in-law's clan could, in former days, have been on opposite sides in war or in reprisal raids. It is relevant that in the ceremonies for making peace and reconciling enemy clans, it is women who are wives of one side and daughters of the other who are the main actors.

In the 1930s there were no foreigners resident among the Tallensi other than some members of my household. In 1963 there were a few Southern and Eastern Ghanaian school teachers and clerks as well as several non-local Northern administrative and police officers temporarily residing in Taleland. They lived in their own quarters or in rooms allocated to them, characteristically rent-free, in the houses of local people. Their Tallensi hosts spoke of them as strangers but found it awkward to deal with them as guests. They themselves were never fully at ease and made it quite clear that they regarded their period of service among the Tallensi as a trial and a temporary exile.

It is easy to recognize in broad outline, the pattern I have described as a variant of a very widespread institutional cluster. The Greeks, and other peoples of antiquity, naturally had a terminology for it. But before we glance at the customs of antiquity, I should like to turn briefly to some other West African data.

The status of the stranger has long been a cardinal issue in the Akan political and legal organization. The general term for stranger is *ohoho*, and there are many proverbs (cf. Rattray, 1916) which reflect the Akan attitudes to *ahoho*. "When a stranger has gone there is not wanting trouble (to clear up)" is a good example.[1] Equally significant is the maxim that a stranger does not break—i.e. is not subject to—customary laws,[2] that is, those binding on a citizen (*oman ni*) or a kinsman (*abusuani*). Lastly, there is the revealing saying that if you accept food from a stranger (he being your guest) you lost face gravely.[3]

Akan ideals of hospitality to strangers conform to the general pattern. Rattray remarked, forty-five years ago, that "food and drink were always available in a chief's palace for any man, woman or child who cared to claim it, including strangers" (1929: p. 114). Open house on so lavish a scale was not common in 1945, when I carried out field research in Ashanti, but chiefs and village headmen always insisted that it was a binding duty to give hospitality to "strangers" and they sometimes complained that lack of traditional revenue got them into debt through the exercise of this duty. On ceremonial occasions hospitality more on the scale implied by Rattray could be met with. My notebooks record many people of all ranks coming to pay their respects to a newly installed chief and staying to eat of the food generously displayed at his residence on the day of his installation; and in other places similar provision for all comers was made by chiefs on *adae* days (cf. Busia, 1951: p. 38).

As for the ordinary householder, a visitor could not depart without being compelled to take some food or at least some drink. Nineteenth century travellers in Ashanti like Dupuis, Bowditch and Hutton expatiate at length

1. Rattray gives a slightly different translation (1916: p. 142, No. 526) of this well known proverb. But my version, I believe, more accurately conveys its sense.
2. Ibid. No. 533.
3. Ibid. No. 534. Rattray translates this proverb: "when you accept the hospitality of a stranger, your dignity is small."

on the extravagant supplies of livestock and other food stuffs and the other munificent gifts sent to them by the King of Ashanti when they reached Kumasi, ostensibly in return for the gifts they brought, but also in fact, to show royal hospitality to them.

But this tells us nothing about the definition of a stranger in Akan communities; and the major interest of this question lies in the fact that strangers were and are essentially identified by political and kinship not cultural or residential criteria.

Fundamentally, according to Akan law and custom, the designation of "stranger" applies to any person who is a non-citizen in the local political community in which he is resident (cf. Fortes, 1969: pp. 143–145). This hinges on the rule, as is precisely exemplified in Ashanti, that primary citizenship, for the freeborn, arises strictly and solely by right of birth to a freeborn Ashanti mother who is a recognized member of a matrilineage that owes allegiance to the local chiefly "stool" and in consequence possesses all the rights and exercises all the duties of citizenship. It is a status independent of local domicile. Residence, even if it has been fixed for a whole lifetime, does not of itself confer citizenship. (Cf. Fortes, ibid., pp. 146–147, Kyerematen, 1971: pp. 20–21). Matrifiliation in a lineage-constituency of a chiefdom is the normal credential for citizenship; but entry by jural process was traditionally and still is possible in special cases. The essential step was and remains incorporation in a lineage-constituency of the chiefdom, in effect, that is adoption into such a lineage in a quasi-filial status. This was the usual way in which slaves, whether bought or acquired by capture in war, were formally incorporated. However, it was also possible for strangers of Akan origin to be incorporated by being accepted as an attached element in a local lineage of their home clan by extension of the rule of clan unity (cf. Fortes, 1969, op. cit., pp 158–160). In this way such outlying regions as Sefwi or Ahafo (cf. Dunn and Robertson, 1974) were populated in the nineteenth century by migrating Akan (largely Ashanti) groups of matrikinsmen who, on settling down, formed new political communities by the fusion of clan fragments from different areas.

Here we come upon a basic feature of the Akan notion of strangerhood. Two main categories of free strangers are recognized. Firstly, to any Akan speaking from the point of view of the community of which he is himself a citizen by birth, *ohoho* signifies an Akan who is a non-citizen of this community, whether he is temporarily visiting or is a long-term resident there. Such a stranger might belong by matrifilial citizenship to the next door village, one with which the host village has many ties of marriage and patrifiliation. He may even be connected by patrifiliation with the host village or chiefdom: or else he may have come from a village or town a hundred or more miles away and have no personal ties of kinship or marriage with the host village. There is a synonym for *ohoho* which expresses the essential idea. *Onanani*, as Christaller's gloss explains, is a stranger, *"nea ofi kurow bi so"*, i.e. someone who comes from some other place (Christaller, 1933: p. 32). He may well have the standing of a guest, either in a particular family or under the aegis of the chief or headman representing the community as a whole. If such an internal stranger is accepted by or allowed to take up long-term residence in the host community, he will live within the host community in the same way as his hosts, often not being distinguishable from them by an outsider. He may even accept some of the duties and responsibilities of citizenship, such as contributing to stool levies, road repairs or school building or other such communal activities by which all inhabitants of a place benefit. However, today, as in the pre-colonial period, only quasi-citizenship is thus gained. A quasi-citizen cannot, for example, succeed to an hereditary office in his chiefdom of residence even if it is vested in a local lineage of the clan to which he belongs (cf. Fortes 1969, op. cit., pp. 201–202). Nor does he thus acquire what has come to be, in modern terms, the most critical and most prized attribute of citizenship, namely, the right freely to take up for cultivation any portion of "stool" land (that is, the land that is vested in the office of the chief) provided it is not already occupied. As Kyerematen authoritatively comments "every citizen has the right to make use of any portion of land not previously occupied by someone else" (op. cit., p. 36), quoting cases decided in various courts. He also states that "the individual's right to land is determined by the fact that he belongs to a certain lineage" which establishes his citizenship indefeasibly. Hence "a subject [sc. a citizen] found guilty of committing a political offence against his chief is punished; but he does not thereby forfeit his farms or the right to use land" (ibid., p. 22).

Citizen rights to land became of critical importance as the cultivation of cocoa spread throughout Southern Ghana. From the outset, nearly a century ago (see Hammond *in* Wills, (ed.) 1962: pp. 182 ff.) right up to the present day, when new cocoa areas are still being opened up in North-West Ashanti and elsewhere in suitable rain-forest country, this fact has dominated the economic exploitation of cocoa. When citizens took up land to establish cocoa plantations they paid no purchase price or rent or tribute to either individuals or the community as represented by the chief and his council. When "strangers" came to seek cocoa land, they could do so only in return for some kind of payment in cash or produce. These payments, in some areas, took the form of what was regarded as outright purchase by those who acquired the land. Thus the earliest phase in the development of cocoa farming which occurred during the first quarter of the century, mainly in South-Eastern Akan areas of Akim and Akwapim, was substantially contributed to by migrant family and company groups, as Polly Hill has shown (1963); and these pioneers were all "strangers" in the areas they entered. They therefore had to "buy" the land they needed, both for their plantations and for the village community they established. They thus opened up great tracts of virgin forest which were far too extensive for the sparse population of native citizens of the area effectively to exploit. By the time of Dr. Hill's investigations, many of these stranger communities had been established for three or four generations and were more numerous in some chiefdoms than the native born citizens. But they were still strangers in the political sense and were still regarded and regarded themselves as citizens of their chiefdoms of origin.

These land sales later gave rise to many disputes and chronic litigation (cf. Kyerematen, *op. cit.*, Chapter 7; Hill, *op. cit.*, Chapter V). Only chiefs acting with the consent of their councils could "sell" these tracts of virgin forest land. Individual citizens had no control over unoccupied land and were (and are) indeed in theory prohibited for both legal and religious reasons from selling even parcels of land occupied by themselves. As, likewise, individual citizens had (and have) pre-existing rights in land, they could not purchase (or rent) any land in the possession of their own community. Thus the purchasers had by definition to be strangers; and since boundaries are very uncertain, disputes over sales became inevitable. These land sales, moreover, were in theory only admissible by customary law if the proceeds were to be applied to communal purposes but chiefs and councillors not infrequently appropriated large amounts to themselves and thus incurred deposition on the part of the citizen body.

Disputes arose also on account of opposed interpretations of what the sale of land really represented. The mere possession of the means to purchase land was not, in principle at least, sufficient to procure the land. A stranger had to be acceptable to the chief and his council as a politically reliable person of good moral character and respectable antecedents. The significance of this is that, what I have spoken of as the "sale" of land was not at the outset perceived as a commercial transaction by either party to it. Land was not sold at an agreed price per parcel based on estimates of economic productivity or market value. The amount of payment was first stipulated on the basis of the need and hopes of the sellers and was eventually agreed by bargaining and pleading in the same way as in certain marriage payments and court fines. Very often, moreover, a relatively small "down-payment" was enough to gain possession of the land. In short, the essence of the transaction, in principle, was to permit the stranger to acquire rights in the community's resources that are parallel to those of a citizen but are based on a politico-jural contract as opposed to the kinship orientated and ascribed status of the latter. From the "sellers" point of view it could be argued that the land was only loaned to the "buyer", not alienated, whereas the buyer claimed full and free possession of it. No wonder long drawn out and fierce litigation often ensued. (Cf. Kyerematen, op. cit., passim).

This contrast is strikingly apparent in the political and economic structure of the Ahafo region of Ashanti, recently subjected to a virtuoso examination by Dunn and Robertson (1974). Ahafo is still a region of small communities[4] grouped in a congeries of relatively autonomous minor chiefdoms many of which have client-like attachments to captaincies and chiefdoms associated with the kingship at the capital of Kumasi. Exploited meagerly and primarily for its forest product and game before the advent of cocoa, Ahafo has, since about 1920, been an area of immigration for farmers seeking cocoa land. Thus today "more than two-thirds of the present inhabitants were born outside Ahafo, mainly in neighbouring Ashanti and are therefore categorized as "strangers" (Dunn and Robertson, p. 11). "The interests of the Ahafos [i.e. those who are citizens by birth] and the strangers are to some extent opposed" our authors tell us, the former fearing "that the local wealth is being drained away to other parts of Ghana", the latter being "on their guard against economic and political exploitation by the natives". The strangers and natives tend to live separately and the strangers tend to keep out of local politics and to concern themselves rather with the politics of their home communities. "This is indicative" the authors comment "of the Akan idea of citizenship . . ." It is to be noted that the strangers here in question are all Ashanti like their Ahafo host community. But the distinction is constantly emphasized by Ahafo citizens. "In spite of his pro-Ashanti orientation" the authors say of one Ahafo chief, he explained that "when the people of Kumasi come here they are called strangers. But if an Ahafo meets an Ahafo man here they are not strangers" (p. 31).

4. The largest Ahafo town, Mim, has only 8,000 inhabitants.

Hence the problems of accommodating them in these communities and of finding a place for them as time passed in the local traditional political structure (as opposed to national party politics in which they had as much of a place as the native citizens) have been in the forefront of Ahafo political life for 50 years. Thus "sharp conflicts" occurred in 1957–1958 which "involved complex issues of local citizenship and its duties in which the liability of stranger-farmers to pay both cocoa tribute (because they did not belong to the community) and special levies voted by a majority . . . to promote the development of the community (because they grew their crops within its jurisdiction) was forcefully denounced as discriminatory" (Ibid. pp. 54–55). Signs of such conflicts were apparent in 1945, when I paid a visit to Ahafo. A big issue was the complaints of some local chief that the cocoa tribute still comprised mainly small, traditionally fixed annual payments, not economic rents related to the size of the crops and their market price. It is above all to such stranger farmers that the maxim applies that strangers do not observe local laws. What is meant is not the civil laws relating to, for instance, debt or property or marriage, but the religious laws concerning local divinities or taboos, to which citizens must conform or the ritual obligations of chiefs and elders, to the performance of which citizens must contribute in money or in kind. It applies also, to obligations such as contributing to stool levies, which have taken the place of the traditional military duties of citizens.

So much for the first category of *ahoho*, the internal strangers. There is a second category that has been recognized in Akan society from the earliest time. Its material expression is the institution of the *Zongo*, the "foreign" quarter that is found in every Akan town and in many villages. Typically, nowadays, the Zongo is located on the outskirts of the town or village, and it is not without symbolic significance that this is often in the vicinity of the town garbage dump, the latrines, the cemetery and the fringes of the bush. The inhabitants of the Zongos are always non-Akan "strangers". In rural areas a large number are unskilled or semi-skilled labourers working on the farms or the roads for the local authority in one or other menial capacity. Others are petty traders or domestic servants. Though it is esti-mated that, in Ahafo for example, nearly 16 per cent of the inhabitants are Zongo-strangers, only a handful of them have been able to establish cocoa farms for themselves. In the larger towns of Ghana the Zongos have been in existence for many generations and the inhabitants have a wider range of occupations, with unskilled labour at one end of the scale and specialized branches of commerce and services (such as the cattle trade, butchering, and the export of kola nuts) at the other.

The distinguishing feature of these strangers is that they differ in language, culture and traditional forms of social organization and provenance from the Akan peoples. They include Hausa and Yoruba immigrants from Nigeria as well as numerous Mossi and other tribal elements from the Francophone hinterland of Ghana. But the majority of them are Ghanaians from the northern half of the country (cf. Fortes, 1971; Hart, 1971). The general Akan attitude about these strangers was well exemplified by the measures taken in 1969–1970 to expel those of non-Ghanaian provenance or parentage from Ghana. They are felt to be outsiders, aliens, in a way that does not apply to the Akan strangers. It is indicative of these attitudes that intermarriage—that is, legally validated unions between men and women as opposed to transient cohabitations—is very rare between Akan host groups and Zongo strangers, whereas it is not uncommon in the case of Akan strangers. Thus, Zongo strangers, who are debarred from absorption into the host community by political or jural arrangements, are equally debarred from absorption at the domestic level by the very common route of intermarriage (cf. Goody's observations on this, 1973) as is the case for instance with strangers among the Mossi of the Upper Volta (cf. Skinner, 1973).

It is noteworthy that Zongo strangers have played a part in the political and economic life of Akan societies from a time long before the colonial period opened up the country to immigration on a large scale. Thus Bowdich makes frequent reference to the "Moors" whom he met in Kumasi and from whom he obtained most of the geographical information about the interior of the Western Sudan recorded in his book. As Bowdich depicts them, the "Moors" were all Moslems, mostly traders, some coming from what is now northern Ghana, others coming from farther north and east, perhaps from as far north as the "Moorish" countries bordering on the Mediterranean. However, the significant point is that the Kumasi Moors apparently all lived together on "one street" (Bowdich, p. 129) as a relatively closed Moslem community. Moreover, there is no evidence that aside from trade and what might best be described as necessary diplomatic relations with the Ashanti court, they had any personal or social relations with their hosts. It is noteworthy, for example, that they made no converts to Islam among the leading personalities of the Ashanti kingdom. There are two other items of relevance in Bowdich's report. One concerns the reference to "Dunkoes". As Bowdich notes, the Ashanti called all the slaves they brought to the coast by this term—correctly *odonko*; and as these slaves always came from the non-Ashanti hinterland, the term came

to be applied to all "foreigners" from the interior. This led to the speculation that there was a country in the interior of Africa called "Dunko".
Bowdich correctly concludes that this is a mistake, that the term was
"merely an epithet, synonymous with the barbarian of the Greeks and
Romans, which they apply to all the people of the interior but themselves,
and implies an 'ignorant fellow' " (p. 188).

More important is the reference to an interior town or country called
Inta in the geographical information Bowdich collected (e.g. p. 171). For
Otani, plural *Ntafo*, is the common Akan term for the people from the
north who have traditionally formed and still form the largest part of the
Zongo-strangers.

Ntafo are primarily people from the interior, that is the savannah zone
north of the Volta; but the term has been extended to include all foreigners
who reside in the zongos, by contrast with *ahoho* who are primarily Akan
strangers and guests.

The contrast is brilliantly examined in a short study of the political history of Atebubu Town by Dr. Kwame Arhin (1973). This town of about
4,200 inhabitants was, traditionally, a stopping place on the main trading
route between Ashanti and the north. It is the traditional capital of a
small Brong chiefdom. The Brong are an Akan people, following the
same principles of matrilineal descent in their family and social organization, the same patterns of chiefship and of eldership and the same rules of
citizenship as other Akan groups.

At the present time, Arhin explains, Atebubu consists of two quite
distinct divisions. On one side are the Brong, who are the traditional rulers
of the town and the traditional owners of the land on which it is built. On
the other, spatially as well as culturally and socially distinct, are the *Ntafo*
in the Zongo. Though the Ntafo comprise people of some eight or ten
different northern tribes, they all, in contrast to the Brong, have patrilineal
descent and family systems. Characteristically, the majority of the Brong
continue to practise their traditional religion, based on worship of the
ancestors and of a wide range of divinities and other spiritual agencies, but
about a third of them have become Christians. By contrast, not one Zongo
stranger has been converted to Christianity in over forty years of missionary activity. The Zongo strangers are overwhelmingly Moslem and no
Brong have been converted to Islam though the two communities have
been living side by side for about a century. Formal gifts are exchanged
between them at the times of their respective communal rituals but neither
group participates in the rituals of the other. Nor has intermarriage in the

legal sense ever been permitted between members of the two groups, though sexual liaisons between individual Brong and Ntafo seem to occur. To complicate the cleavage, it appears that the Zongo is at the present time more populous and also wealthier than the Brong division. Indeed, the whole economy of Atebubu as, primarily, a market town, is dependent on the commercial activities of the leading people in the Zongo and on the supply of labour provided by the Ntafo. Just fifty years ago, conscious of their economic superiority, the Zongo attempted a coup to seize the political control of the town. They failed, and today the Zongo is again politically subordinate to the Brong. They occupy their own "stranger" ward in the community and though they pay local government dues and taxes and thus contribute to the maintenance of local public services and amenities and, likewise, take part in national politics on an equal footing with the Brong, they are still essentially non-citizens in the chiefdom. "The two groups" Arhin concludes, "tolerate but do not accept each other". The cultural divide, reinforced as it is by language, religious, and basic structural differences, remains unbridgeable (cf. Schildkrout 1970).

Here we have a striking example of the contrast between what I have called the internal stranger, who comes from the same cultural and political community in the widest sense as the host group, and the external, foreign or alien stranger who may be left to live in peace segregated from the host group but is not permitted to become assimilated into the host group even in a client or other dependent status.

This is a picture that can be paralleled from many contemporary local communities in Ghana. To give only one more example: Tamale is the administrative headquarters of the Northern Region of Ghana. In the 1930s it was still primarily a Dagomba community with a sprinkling of southern teachers and civil servants, European government officers and professional employees, and a Zongo of Hausa and other, mainly Muslim traders, Mallams (i.e. teachers of the Koran) and artisans from elsewhere in the interior. Today it is a large, sprawling cosmopolitan town. Inquiring there about the status of "strangers" I was given one revealing definition of the stranger who is not a guest: he is someone who pays rent for his dwelling by contrast with a native who has his dwelling "free". The parallel with the Akan stranger farmer in Ahafo is patent.

Nor, I might add, are these ideas and practices confined to Ghanaian societies. To give but one of a number of possible examples from elsewhere in West Africa, among the Yoruba of Nigeria, Lloyd writes (1963: pp. 86–92), a person who is residing in a community other than the one he belongs to by birth, is designated by the term *alejo*, stranger. "A stranger in a kingdom" he comments, "is a man who recognizes no allegiance to its Oba or chiefs (though he must obey its laws), the implication being that he still gives his allegiance to the Oba and chiefs of his home town". Similarly, anyone not born into it is a stranger to a descent group, even if he belongs to another descent group in the same community; and at this level, just as at the level of the kingdom, a stranger must have the permission of the head of the community before he is allowed to take up residence in it. He may be allotted land to farm but is not deemed to own it outright unless and until he has been incorporated in the land owning group. Since, in the traditional political system, citizenship depended on membership of a descent group, a stranger had to be absorbed into such a group, usually by marriage, in order to be allowed to reside permanently. Even then it would take several generations before his descendants were regarded as full citizens of the kingdom and community.

An exact parallel to the Zongo in a Ghanaian town is the type of Hausa trading enclave in a Yoruba town described and analyzed by Cohen (1969). The enclave is, to all intents, a closed Moslem community within the Yoruba town, avoiding intermarriage with its Yoruba neighbours and having more social relations with other Hausa groups elsewhere in Nigeria than with its fellow-townsmen. The members of this miniature "state within a state" pay their municipal dues and take part in national politics but are not regarded as citizens of the Yoruba town in the traditional sense.

I said, earlier, that the Greeks had a word for the stranger. In a delightful paper on the theme of the stranger (1963) Julian Pitt-Rivers begins by noting that the whole of the *Odyssey* "may be viewed as a study of the laws of hospitality"—which we might rephrase as the reciprocal of the laws of strangerhood. He points out that the Greeks distinguished between *Xenoi*, strangers who were Greeks, and *Barbaroi*, foreigners who spoke another language, which is reminiscent of the Akan distinction between *ahoho* and *ntafo*. Pitt-Rivers ranges far more widely, both ethnographically and in his theoretical analysis, than I have attempted to, but some of his conclusions are obviously applicable to the African data. Thus he remarks that "in contrast to a member of the community whose status is identifiable by reference to its norms and is recognized by everyone, the stranger is incorporated only through a personal bond with an established member; he has . . . no jural relationship with anyone else . . ." One way of incorporating the stranger, he suggests, is to change him into a guest and this is normally accomplished by offering the stranger food and drink in accordance with

the principle that commensality creates the kind of bonds that are ritually
—I would say also morally—compelling, substituting as it were for bonds
of kinship or of common citizenship. This, too, parallels West African
beliefs and practices.

Reading the *Odyssey*, one cannot fail to realize the force of the law of
hospitality in Homer's Greece which made it "morally incumbent on gods
and men alike" (Jones, 1956: pp. 28–30) never to turn a stranger away. The
reception of Odysseus, rising naked and battered from behind the bushes
where he has sought shelter, by Nausicaa in Book VI and his sojourn
among the Phaeacians is one of the more dramatic examples of this.

But the Greeks, like West Africans, also had the problem of how to
accommodate themselves to and absorb free strangers into their city states.
Under Pericles, citizenship in Athens was limited to individuals both of
whose parents were citizens. To Aristotle "himself an alien resident in
Athens, citizenship meant participation in legislative and judicial functions
and so was clearly the outcome of state grants rather than of birth. But
while basing citizenship on law rather than parentage, he agreed that the
wholesale admittance of foreigners as citizens . . . might be so revolutionary a change in the constitution as to alter the identity of the status"
(Jones, ibid., pp. 52–53).

In other words, it was a problem of replacing citizenship by right of
filiation to citizen parents with citizenship achievable by compliance with
laws permitting the equivalent of naturalization in the modern state. It
recurred repeatedly in the history of the Greek city states, as Jones shows
(op. cit., passim). It is a problem that has become significant in Ghana
only since the establishment of the modern national state.[5] Formerly, and
at the level of the traditionally autonomous tribal divisions, there was no
road to citizenship in any local political community by other than filiative
or adoptive filiative membership of a constituent segment of the community. A free stranger could never become a full citizen of his host community; for one reason because he never ceased being a citizen of his natal
community and no one could be a citizen in two separate communities.
A slave, captive or refugee, being by definition kinless, could be absorbed

5. Reviewing the subject, Bennion, who was Technical Adviser to the Government of
Ghana on the preparation of legislation, soon after the establishment of the state, comments authoritatively (1962, Chapter 4) "Although the wording of the Acts of 1957 and
1961 (which laid down the laws of citizenship) is relatively simple, it conceals a mass of
complexity. In many cases it is a formidable task to ascertain conclusively whether or not
a person is a citizen of Ghana", as many people of foreign extraction found when they were
expelled in 1969.

by some form of adoption for males, or marriage for females, into a constituent segment of the host community. This did not confer citizenship on the adoptee, but it did give him a status that was quite distinct from that of a stranger. He had what I am inclined to call vicarious citizenship: he could exercise all the economic and legal—but not the political and religious—rights and perform the corresponding duties of a citizen but only as his master's or sponsor's deputy. He could, for instance, amass wealth, marry and have children, but could have no heirs of his own body. His wealth and offspring belonged to his master or sponsor and reverted to the latter when he died. He never, in other words, achieved jural majority; and lacking authentic descent connection with his master's or sponsor's lineage, he could never hold political office in the community, eligibility for which is the ultimate test of citizenship status. And this ultimate bar will persist for his descendants, though they will in time acquire all the outward attributes of full citizens as members of attached lineages (e.g. among the Tallensi, c.f. Fortes, 1945) or the equivalent in Akan lineages and clans (cf. Fortes, 1969, ch. X).

In Akan communities in general and in Ashanti in particular there was and remains the paradox of an ostensible contradiction between citizenship at the national level and citizenship at the local level. The Kumasi people who are regarded as strangers by the Ahafo host communities in which they have cocoa farms are not only of the same cultural and social provenance as their hosts but are, like them, citizens of the Ashanti Union, subjects of the King. The distinction remains and is enforceable at the level of the local chiefdom because no one can have direct citizenship in the kingdom, at the national level. It is only by virtue of primary citizenship in a local chiefdom that he can have citizenship at the national level. As Ashanti put it, an Ashanti "serves" the king "through" his lineage head and local chief (Cf. Fortes, 1969, p. 145 ff). It was and is as much the impossibility of their having such primary citizenship as their cultural and social incompatibility that defines Zongo strangers as unassimilable aliens, not just stranger-guests, in Akan communities.

There are echoes of the Ashanti situation in European and American societies. The "strangers" who loom so conspicuously in the Welsh village described by Frankenberg (1957) are fellow citizens of the villagers at the national, and often also at the municipal level, but not native villagers by birth or upbringing. Accommodation to them takes the form of permitting them to share in the social and recreational life of the village, if their assimilation by kinship or marriage does not occur, and whereas resident strangers remain marginal to the community throughout, absent native villagers are counted as members of the village even if they seldom return. Like Akan *ahoho* in Akan communities, these strangers are both inside and outside the village community—inside as residents outside as non-native marginals, permanent guests as it were. Thus ambiguously situated they have no choice but to stay neutral when factional differences emerge in village affairs; and this makes them peculiarly eligible to be called upon to serve as impartial arbitrators or referees, catalysts of co-operation in such situations. The stranger has—or is believed to have—the "objective of one who is not tied down in his action by habit, piety and precedent", which Simmel (1950: p. 405) underlines. An even closer parallel to the Ghanaian situation—in this case more particularly that of the Tallensi—is reported from Northern Ireland. Writing of the Protestant village of "Aughnaboy" Leyton (1966) says that its kinship system "can be summarized as a bilateral one with a strong agnatic bias". And he continues "Aughnaboy" individuals divide their universe into two fundamental categories, "friends" (kin) and "strangers" (non-kin)—the latter, as his analysis shows merging into "connexions" (affines).

A stranger is so defined in relation to the host community; and the notion has everywhere a wide range of connotations, as every good dictionary of a language, ancient or modern, shows (see, e.g. O.E.D. s.v. *stranger* and Liddell and Scott *Greek English Lexicon*, s.v. *Xenos*). What has principally interested me here has been the politico-jural aspects of the status of stranger. It is, as Finley comments in his discussion of guest-friendship and strangerhood in the *Odyssey* (1967: pp. 115–117) by reason of his "rightlessness, his lack of kin to safeguard or avenge him . . . against ill-doing" that the stranger is at first met with fear and distrust. The encounter of Odysseus with Nausicaa, which I referred to earlier, illustrates this. She has to reassure her maidens that in spite of his appearance he is a man not a wild beast, a hapless wanderer not an enemy. This opens the way for him to be received in accordance with the religiously sanctioned laws of hospitality that apply to all humans. But it is interesting to observe that, after his installation as a guest, the stranger is required to identify himself by genealogy and citizenship as a normal person, equipped with normal kinship and human rights (*Odyssey*, Bk. VII, p. 236 ff.). Much the same procedure, in a more prosaic variant, of course, is followed in the corresponding situations in the West African societies I have considered. In these societies, too, the moral obligations of hospitality, sanctioned by religious beliefs, are sufficient to ensure the temporary presence and eventual safe onward passage of transient strangers. But, as we have seen, specific and more precisely legal and political rules come into play with strangers who want to settle.

And if the Greek notion of *xenia* affords us a classical model of the moral evaluation of strangerhood, it is interesting, in passing, to compare the Hebrew and Roman concepts. The Hebrews distinguished between two classes of stranger the *ger* and the *nochri* (cf. Pedersen, 1926: p. 40; p. 356; p. 391; Robertson-Smith, 1927 edn., p. 75; Max Weber, 1952 translation, Ch. II). The *ger* is the "stranger within thy gates" of Deut. 5. whom the Israelite is exhorted not to wrong or oppress but to love and deal with under the same religious and secular laws as an Israelite, remembering that "you were strangers in the land of Egypt" (Deut. 10. 19; Exod. 22:21; Lev. 24:22). He is a free person, therefore able to gain wealth and rank like an Israelite of the host community, as Pedersen explains. He is a resident alien, a denizen as the mediaeval lawyers put it, and therefore able and likely eventually to join the community by being permitted to adopt the distinctive Israelitish religious beliefs and practices, notably circumcision and the observance of the Sabbath.

The status of the *ger* especially as it developed over time in the history of Israel is, of course, much more complicated than I can here indicate. But the essential point is that, regardless of his provenance, he was considered to be a potential recruit to the host community, subject to its laws and religious observances from the outset, and permitted in due course to be absorbed into it in accordance with the rules of the theocratic political order of Israel. What this amounts to is, in effect, that he is made into a quasi-kinsman by ritual and legal prescription.

The *nochri* was a foreigner in the strictest sense. His status is well set out in Deut. 15; 1–4. In contrast to a neighbour and brother whose debts must be annulled by his creditor in the seventh year, a *nochri's* debts may be exacted, though he must not be harried and starved. For, as Pedersen emphasizes (p. 357) he is entitled to the rights of hospitality denial of which is sinful. He is, as other commentators have noted, a transient stranger, typically thought of as a passing trader, even if he stays for some time. Unlike the *ger* he is not subject to any of the political or religious obligations that are binding on the normal citizen, and have to be respected by the *ger*.

Though the correspondence is not exact, the Hebrew concept of the *ger* is reminiscent of the Tallensi *saan* and the Akan *ahoho* who succeeds in finding a way into the host community by attachment to a lineage or by

S.A.S.A.—9*

marriage, and the *nochri* can similarly be compared to the Zongo stranger. Incorporation into the host community still fundamentally depends, in the Hebrew case, on some form of kinship fiction.

For an example of a system in which the dominant principle is citizenship by law rather than by birth we must turn to Rome. There is no doubt that the normal morality of hospitality (the English word is etymologically derived from the Latin *hospes*, which Lewis and Short gloss as (a) host, (b) visitor or guest and (c) stranger as opposed to native) prevailed in classical Roman civilization, no less than elsewhere in the civilizations of antiquity. The stranger, *hospes* or *hostis* could count on hospitality which—perhaps by way of the kind of tests described by Pitt-Rivers—converted him into an honoured guest. But one need only compare the way Odysseus is received in Phaeacia with the way in which Aeneas and his armed companions are received by Pallas and Evander when they reach Arcadia, in *Aeneid* VIII, not as suppliants or beggars but as kinsfolk returning to help reconquer their ancestral land, to realize how different were the Greek and the Roman ideals. Roman hospitality gives the impression of being almost a legal right exacted or earned by the stranger-guest, not a moral obligation of the host as in the Odyssey. The difference is clear when we compare the lengthy struggle to establish citizenship by law in Aristotle's Athens with the elaborate provisions for conferring legal citizenship in Rome. By the time of Gaius (middle of the second century A.D.) we are told (de Zulueta, 1953, Pt. II, p. 24) "the status of citizenship is taken for granted" as the basis of the Law of Persons. Legally proper manumission conferred citizenship—civitas—on slaves; indeed even from earlier times slaves and Latins were "the sources from which the class of *cives* is constantly recruited" (Buckland, 1921: p. 61)

Citizenship, *civitas*, embraced three major groups, *Cives*, *Latini* and *Peregrini* and it was primarily among the *cives*, notably in the Senatorial Order, that the status was acquired by agnatic descent (Buckland, op. cit., pp. 87–88). Complex as the class structure was in the empire, "access to citizenship" says Buckland (ibid., p. 95) "was made very easy by legislation". Cicero's proud "Civis Romanus sum" could have been uttered by many free subjects of Rome of foreign birth and origin. In the Roman system citizenship by law rather than by birth predominated.

And this brings me to my main reason for choosing this topic for a tribute to Isaac Schapera. Ever since the publication of *African Political Systems* (which as I have noted in the Introduction was inspired by a suggestion I received from Schapera) I have been impressed by a major contrast between Tswana political structure, as depicted by Schapera, and the West African systems with which I am familiar. From Schapera's account of the Ngwato system in *African Political Systems* (p. 56–82) we learn that the "tribe" in 1936 included a large number of "foreign" groups who were subjects of the chief but had kept "sufficient corporate life to be regarded as separate communities . . ." and were able to maintain their separate identities by being placed in separate wards under their own hereditary leaders. "This grouping into wards, common to all the Tswana" Schapera notes, "explains the facility with which immigrants or conquered peoples were absorbed into the tribe" (p. 58). In his later publications this general statement is further elaborated and exemplified. There is a detailed discussion of the nature, procedures for acquisition and circumstances of loss of citizenship in the *Handbook of Tswana Law and Customs* (Ch. VI). We are told that a distinction is made between a tribe's own members and "visitors or other aliens". The latter, known as *baditshaba* can be incorporated in accordance with the rule that "membership of a tribe . . . is defined not in terms of birth, but of allegiance to the Chief" (p. 118). Hence "people not born into a tribe" can become "the subjects of its chief either by conquest or by placing themselves voluntarily under his rule", and the political framework for this is the ward system. Once placed in a ward the foreign group or individual acquires full citizenship status though in a subordinate position to the original tribesmen. Citizenship by law is therefore possible though it is normatively secondary to citizenship by birth. It is made possible because local organization is the basis of the internal administrative and judicial structure of what is a highly centralized city state system. The Tswana solve the problem by assimilating the stranger, in ways reminiscent of the Romans. By contrast, among the Tallensi and the Akan, different as their political systems are, the rule that citizenship accrues fundamentally by right of descent is more reminiscent of Greek and Hebrew ideas.

It hardly needs adding that the Tswana norms of hospitality to strangers as guests conform to the general ideals we find in most societies. Visitors must be given food and gifts to take back with them; selfish hosts are despised and generous hosts praised and respected; and at ceremonies connected with births, marriages, initiation and similar passage situations lavish provision of choice foods and drinks is made for the guests with special portions of meat and beer being reserved for those who come uninvited (ibid., p. 227). But it is the fate of the stranger who, even if he is of the same cultural provenance as his host, is defined as a non-citizen, that has concerned me primarily in this essay; and the conclusion that presents itself is that the likelihood of incorporation in the host community is determined by the balance struck between kinship and law, as the basis of citizenship. The decisive factor is the degree to which citizenship is defined as a direct relationship to the supreme political authority, whether centralized or diffuse, in precisely politico-jural terms, not as an indirect relationship pre-supposing a kinship or other intermediate credential of membership. The same inference is drawn by Cohen and Middleton in their review of the data presented by the contributors to their symposium on the incorporation processes found in the context of modern political development in Africa (Cohen and Middleton, eds, 1970, "Introduction").

My main point is that this contrast is well exemplified in the different procedures and rules followed by the Tswana on the one hand and the Tallensi and Akan on the other in handling the problem of how to fit the stranger who wishes to become a resident into the social structure. It is a problem that confronts tribal societies all over the world and is of course of daily concern in our own society at the present time. The stranger, however he is identified and defined, is the prototypical "other", the alien outside the fence of custom, belief and rule that marks the limits of the moral community to its members. If he is merely a passer-by he is readily accommodated to by the ephemeral hospitality enjoined by religious and ethical rules in most societies. This holds even if, as in such a small and marginal hunting and collecting community as the Trio of the equatorial rain forest of Surinam, the stranger is initially regarded as a sorcerer (Riviére, 1969). As Pitt-Rivers rightly observes, such hospitality can be understood as a means of defending the host community against the ambivalent hostility initially aroused within the community by the fact of strangerhood. But when the stranger wants to become a resident there is the problem of endowing him with rights where before he has only had moral privileges, the kind of rights to which Bloch alludes when he remarks that a stranger waits to be offered food in contrast to a kinsman who "has a right to his kinsmen's food and may *demand* food"(Bloch, 1971: p. 101). So he must be turned into either a kinsman or a citizen.

The passage from the status of stranger to that of guest, then to that of friend and, with luck, eventually to that of the quasi-kinship of the accredited sojourner, is familiar to anthropologists from their own experience. The reminiscence with which I began this essay may not be typical but most beginnings in field research are bound to meet with the apprehension if not suspicion that is the common initial response to strangers. This happens even in relatively sophisticated, newspaper-reading, economically and socially complex communities, as Frankenberg found. "When I arrived in the island" Firth records (1936: p. 8) "my motives were of course suspect, and though outwardly very friendly and hospitable, the people were really greatly disturbed". We have all had similar experiences. "I was a *ger*" says Evans-Pritchard, using the Hebrew word, of his stay among the Nuer, "what they call a *rul*, an alien sojourner, among them for only a year". (1956: p. ix). It is a step forward when the stranger-enquirer is accepted as a guest, permitted some degree of participation in the community's life. This is a probationary period, as in the Mediterranean cases referred to by Pitt-Rivers. Only after demonstrating disinterested respect for the customs and values of his hosts and after showing his good faith and trustworthiness in other ways, does the way open up for the anthropologist's admission to the friendship and possibly even quasi-kinship that will give him the freedom of the community. In effect he thus becomes, if he is lucky, an honorary citizen of the community and it is this that will enable him to complete his task. Schapera's magnificent corpus of Tswana studies, ranging from linguistic texts and collections of praise chants to political, kinship, economic and ritual monographs, could not have been brought together by anyone who had failed to be accepted first as a guest and finally as an honorary citizen.

Acknowledgement

I am indebted to the Leverhulme Trust for a grant which provided secretarial and research assistance drawn upon in the preparation of the present paper.

Bibliography

Arhin, Kwame. (1973). "Strangers and Hosts, A Study in the Political Organisation and History of Atebubu Town". *Transactions Historical Society of Ghana*, Vol. 12, pp. 63–82.

Bennion, F. A. R. (1962). *The Constitutional Law of Ghana*. Butterworths, London.

Bloch, Maurice. (1971). *Placing the Dead*. Seminar Press, London and New York.

Bowdich, T. E. (1819). *Mission from Cape Coast Castle to Ashantee*. (3rd edn 1966, W. E. F. Ward (ed.).) J. Murray, London: Frank Cass. Reprint of 1819 edn.

Buckland, W. W. (1921). *A Textbook of Roman Law from Augustus to Justinian*. Cambridge University Press, Cambridge.

Busia, K. A. (1951). *The Position of the Chief in the Modern Political System of Ashanti*. Oxford University Press, London.

Christaller, J. G. (1933 edn). *Dictionary of the Asante and Fante Language*. Basel Evangelical Missionary Society, Basel.

Cohen, Abner. (1969). *Custom and Politics in Urban Africa*. A study of Hausa Migrants in Yoruba Towns. Routledge and Kegan Paul, London.

Cohen, Ronald and Middleton John (eds). (1970). "Introduction" *From Tribe to Nation in Africa*, pp. 1–34. Chandler Publishing Company, Scranton, Pennsylvania.

Dunn, John and Robertson, A. F. (1973). *Dependence and Opportunity: Political Change in Ahafo*. Cambridge University Press, London.

Evans-Pritchard, E. E. (1956). *Nuer Religion*. The Clarendon Press, Oxford.

Finley, M. I. (1972 edn). *The World of Odysseus*. Penguin Books, London.

Firth, Raymond. (1936). *We, The Tikopia: A Sociology Study of Kinship in Primitive Polynesai*. Allen and Unwin, London.

Fortes, Meyer. (1945). *The Dynamics of Clanship among the Tallensi*. Oxford University Press, London.

(1949). *The Web of Kinship among the Tallensi*. Oxford University Press, London.

(1969). *Kinship and the Social Order*. Aldine Press, Chicago; Routledge and Kegan Paul, London.

(1971). "Some Aspects of Migration and Mobility in Ghana". *Journal of Asian and African Studies*, VI. 1, 1–20.

(1973). "On the Concept of the Person among the Tallensi", In *La Notion de Personne*, Germaine Dieterlen (ed.), Colloques Internationaux du Centre National de la Recherche Scientifique, No. 544, Paris.

Fortes, Meyer and Evans-Pritchard, E. E. (eds). (1940). *African Political Systems*. Oxford University Press, London.

Frankenberg, Ronald. (1957). *Village on the Border*. Cohen and West, London.

Goody, Jack. (1970). "Marriage Policy and Incorporation in Northern Ghana", In Cohen, Ronald and Middleton, John (eds) 1970 *From Tribe to Nation* cit. supra., pp. 114–149.

Hammond, P. S. (1962). "Cocoa: A. Agronomy", In Wills, J. Brain, 1962, *Agriculture and Land Use in Ghana*, Chapter 18. Oxford University Press, London, for Ghana Ministry of Food and Agriculture.

Hart, J. Keith. (1971). "Migration and Tribal Identity among the Frafras of Ghana", *Journal of African and Asian Studies*, Vol. VI, 1. pp. 21–36.

Hill, Polly. (1963). *The Migrant Cocoa Farmers of Southern Ghana*. Cambridge University Press, Cambridge.

Jones, J. Walter. (1956). *The Law and Legal Theory of the Greeks*. The Clarendon Press, Oxford.

Kyerematen, A. A. Y. (1971). *Inter-State Boundary Litigation in Ashanti*. Vol. 4, African Social Research Documents, Afrika Studie Centrum, Leiden.

Leyton, Elliott. (1966). "Conscious models and dispute regulations in an Ulster village", *Man*, N:S:, Vol. 1, 4, pp. 534–542.

Lloyd, P. C. (1962). *Yoruba Land Law*. Oxford University Press, London and Nigerian Institute of Social and Economic Research.

Pedersen, John. (1926). *Israel: Its Life and Culture, I–II*. Oxford University Press, London. Poul Branner, Copenhagen.

Pitt-Rivers, Julian. (1968). "The Stranger, the Guest and the Hostile Host", In *Contributions to Mediterranean Sociology* pp. 13–30 Peristiany, J. G. (ed.) Mouton and Co., The Hague.

Rattray, R. S. (1916). *Ashanti Proverbs*. Clarendon Press, Oxford.

(1929). *Ashanti Law and Constitution*. Clarendon Press, Oxford.

Riviere, Peter. (1969). *Marriage Among the Trio*. Clarendon Press, Oxford.

Schapera, I. (1938). (Second edn. 1955) *Handbook of Tswana Law and Custom*. Oxford University Press, London.

(1940). "The Political Organization of the Ngwato of Bechuanaland Protectorate", In Fortes, M. and Evans-Pritchard, E. E. (eds), *African Political Systems*. Oxford University Press, London.

Schildkrout, Enid. (1970). "Strangers and Local Government in Kumasi", *J. Mod. African St.*, 8, 2, 251–69.

Simmel, Georg. (1950). *The Sociology of Georg Simmel*. (Translated by K. H. Wolff.) The Free Press, Glencoe, Illinois.

Skinner, Elliott, P. (1970). "Processes of Political Incorporation in Mossi Society", In Cohen, Ronald and Middleton, John (eds), *From Tribe to Nation in Africa, cit. supra*.

Smith, W. Robertson. (1927). *The Religion of the Semites*. (3rd edn). Introduction etc. by Cook, Stanley A. A. and C. Black, London.

Weber, Max. (1952). *Ancient Judaism*. (Translated by H. H. Gerth and Don Martindale). The Free Press, Glencoe, Illinois.

Zulueta, F. de. (1953). *The Institutes of Gaius* Part II. Commentary. Clarendon Press, Oxford.

Index